THE FEELING OF TEACHING

USING EMOTIONS AND RELATIONSHIPS TO TRANSFORM THE CLASSROOM

Elizabeth D. Burris PhD, MSW, LCSW

Cover art "Lifelines" © Terry Wise
Cover design: Brad Wells and Mary Velgos

Library of Congress number available upon request.

ISBN: 978-1-6192761-9-2

RESPONSES TO THE FEELING OF TEACHING

"This truly should be a must-read for all educators in the field, and especially a required text for teacher education programs."

"Thank you for writing this book. It is THE BEST professional development tool I have been exposed to in my twenty years of teaching. I have been silently suffering (not so silently at times) through the emotional work of being everything to everyone and not having a secure sense of self in the classroom. This book is chock-full of nuggets of wisdom and validation. I will continue to refer to it on a regular basis and look forward to a day in my professional career when I can have supervised support to reinforce the concepts presented in this book."

"[This] book amazed me. Not only did I learn a lot from it in general terms, but it gave me some very strong specific ideas that I can totally use in my own teaching; and also the discussions about button-pushing, what it means and how to deal with it . . . will change my life."

"I am just loving [this book]: so readable, truly substantial, and what a resource . . . it is for educators at large, parents, teachers, coaches, counselors, really anyone who interacts with kids on a regular basis."

"There is a treasure trove of information for receptive educators. It's amazingly accessible work."

"I think it is a really important book for teachers. I think it should be integrated into every student teaching program in the country."

"This was a sheer pleasure to read. The concepts are exciting, and the writing is powerful. I enjoyed every bit of it and learned a lot — and I'm neither a teacher nor a psychologist!"

Dedicated
to an inspirational teacher and a beloved friend
Steven Dennis Bodner
(1975-2011)

TABLE OF CONTENTS

Acknowledgments   7

Introduction   9

1. Pushing Buttons: Enactments in the
Classroom   29

2. Insults and Compliments: Teachers as
Developmental Partners   93

3. Boundary Crossings: Being a "Great Enough"
Teacher   151

4. Power Struggles: The Third in the Classroom   205

5. Know Yourself: Rigorous Reflection and
Supervision   261

Conclusion: Putting It All Together: Seeing Structure   311

For More Information   323

Appendix: Defenses   325

Glossary of Terms   335

References   341

ACKNOWLEDGMENTS

I have many people to thank:

For partial reading of one of the many drafts of the book, I thank Ali Benjamin, Paul Gitterman, Enroue Halfkenny, Brian McKibbon, Mary Jane Panke, Sarah Jey Whitehead, and several anonymous reviewers.

For reading the manuscript at least once (and, in some cases, twice) all the way through, I thank Jen Bernard, Deb Burns, Eileen Clawson, Ronadh Cox, Jen Hyatt, Joe Johnson, Carrol Moran, Gail Newman, Janneke van de Stadt, Brad Wells, Orli Zuchovitsky, and the brave teachers in my study groups and support groups.

For support, advice, and inspiration, I thank Amy Antongiovanni, Eileen Boté, Stewart Burns, Sue and John Burris, Thom Burris, Cathy Crosky, Mary DeBey, Stephanie Dunson, Susan Engel, Richard Q. Ford, Nel Noddings, Carol Meyer, Nora Padykula, Peter Smagorinsky, and the scores of student teachers and master teachers I have worked with over the course of my career.

For help creating the cover of this book, I thank Terry Wise, Brad Wells, Mary Velgos, and Mars Vilaubi.

I wish to give credit to Joe Johnson for coming up with the idea of designating yellow, blue, and black belt moves; to Dan Coleman for the name "Moments that Matter"; to Harold Schrager for introducing me to (my own) "negative grandiosity"; and to Mary DeBey for her suggestion that teachers might choose to teach at certain academic levels for their own developmental reasons.

I thank my psychotherapeutic clients for teaching me so much about the power of relationship, and I thank my many supervisors – among them John Miner, Karen Theiling, and Margi Wood – for showing me the power of psychodynamically oriented supervision.

I thank my husband, Brad Wells, for his patience, his clearheaded and intelligent feedback, and his excitement about this project. I am blessed to have him as my partner in life.

And I thank the greatest teachers I could ever ask for, Mae Burris-Wells and Wilder Burris-Wells, whose love, trust, and relentless accuracy remind me every day that the difficult work of being "good enough," or "great enough," is the most important and precious work I can do.

Finally, while I have received extremely useful feedback from many different sources, any errors in this book are all mine.

INTRODUCTION

A DAY IN THE LIFE

Karen Madison pulled out of the school parking lot after a long day at work. Twenty-five minutes later she pulled into her driveway — and realized she could not remember a single moment of her drive home. Where had her mind gone?

It had stayed at school. All the way home Karen had been thinking about the events of the day. She had certainly reviewed the happy moments: when Maurice had been able to stop talking to his neighbor after just one warning, when Cindy was able to finish her in-class assignment before the end of the period, when Tasha had told her what a great teacher she was.

The bulk of the drive, however, was devoted to reviewing distressing moments. Why, for example, had Karen felt so irritated when the students began packing up their books before the bell had rung for lunch? She had actually continued the lesson after the bell, forcing the students to be late for their precious meal.

Later one of her colleagues had given Karen a menacing look when they passed in the hall. What was that all about? What had Karen done wrong?

And should Karen have spoken so harshly to Rochelle because she had forgotten her homework yet again? When Karen had asked Rochelle where her work was, Rochelle had sat silently. Feeling a rush of frustration and anger, Karen had said, "I'm sick of this! When are you going to do your homework?!" Maybe Karen had hurt Rochelle's feelings; maybe Rochelle would complain to her parents, who could be calling the school administration at this very moment. . . .

Sound familiar? Such musings often plague teachers at the end of a school day. And "plague" is an apt term, for many of the events that take place in classrooms are both persistently bothersome and seemingly incurable.

What impact did Karen's irritation at lunchtime have on her students? Was her colleague actually angry at her? Had Karen in fact hurt her student's feelings? Should Karen feel bad about what she had done today? What should she have done differently? Being immersed in her worries and lacking perspective, Karen's only option was to obsess about these questions until they faded away or were replaced by new ones. And the complexity of every school day guarantees that new worries and questions will always arise.

This "plague" causes a great deal of personal suffering. Worse, the suffering it causes tends to be private. Karen might vent to her partner or her best teacher buddy, but venting is not the same as exploring and understanding. If Karen really wanted to answer her questions thoughtfully, where would she do it? The emphasis in school is not on emotions and relationships but on teaching and learning. And the two realms — relational and academic — have nothing to do with each other.

In this book I beg to differ. Contrary to many formulations of the educational enterprise, emotions and relationships have everything to do with teaching and learning. Because teachers and students are human beings, they drag their latest fights; their stresses from the night before; their anger, insecurity, and anxiety as well as their characteristic methods of dealing with all of these into the classroom. Every day. Every moment of every day.

And because teachers and students are human beings, these psychological elements affect what teachers and students are able to perceive, how they interpret what they perceive, and what they can or will do about it. In short, the feeling of teaching, the intimate, personal experience of emotions and relationships, forms the core of what happens in every classroom.

Three premises underlie this book:

Teaching and learning are inseparable from emotions and relationships.

Teachers need to understand how relationships work and what emotions mean if they are to optimize their students' learning.

Teachers need support in understanding (and, in some cases, surviving) classroom emotions and relationships.

Premise #1:
Teaching and learning are inseparable from emotions and relationships.

Let us return to Karen Madison's story. We know that Karen arrived home from school feeling plagued. If she were to return to school the next day feeling stressed and confused about her colleague's "menacing" look or her students' disrespect or the possibility that some parents had called the school to complain about her, it is fair to assume that her teaching would be negatively affected.

She might be a little more impatient with and intolerant of her students, for example. She might punish them for irritating her. She might have difficulty concentrating on her lesson plan and skip steps or flub a presentation. In short, her emotions (anxiety, fear, self-doubt) and her relationships (with herself, her colleague, the administration, parents, and her students) could have a significant impact on her teaching.

The same is true for students. Students, like teachers, bring emotions such as anxiety, fear, shame, and self-doubt into the classroom. And those emotions affect the relationships students are able to have in class: what students can take in from their teacher, how (or if) they can organize information internally, how easily they can cooperate with others in the room.

If, for example, one or more of Karen's students came to school feeling stressed because they did not complete their homework assignment or were humiliated by a friend or had not eaten breakfast or had intervened in a fight at home, these students' ability to learn would be weakened. They might have difficulty concentrating; they might constantly distract themselves and others; they might act out to relieve some of their internal pressure. That is, the students' learning would be profoundly influenced by their emotions and their relationships with friends, family members, classmates, and, of course, their teacher. *Teaching and learning are inseparable from emotions and relationships.*

11

Premise #2:
Teachers need to understand how relationships work and what emotions mean if they are to optimize their students' learning.

It is not enough that negative emotions and charged relationships would affect Karen's teaching and her students' learning. On top of their individual suffering, Karen and her anxious students would be on an emotional collision course; that is, their individual emotional states could intermingle and lead to problematic interactions that would make their experiences of teaching and learning that much more distressing and difficult.

What do I mean by "problematic interactions"? In this book I focus on four different types: *pushed buttons, compliments and insults, boundary crossings,* and *power struggles.*

PUSHED BUTTONS

All of the worries Karen Madison thought about on her drive home are examples of *pushed buttons,* or extremely irritating interactions that trigger immediate strong emotions.

For example, as soon as she saw her students packing up their backpacks, something inside Karen snapped. She felt outraged and disrespected. The same went for Rochelle's aggravating failure to do her homework and her refusal to even talk about it. The colleague's "menacing look" also pushed a button. This one was less dramatic than the others, but Karen's anxiety was definitely activated by her belief that her colleague was upset with her.

As anyone who has had a button pushed knows, the outrage and anxiety that accompany these experiences can take some time to fade away. And the negative feelings often lead to regrettable reactions that escalate the problem rather than solve it.

Chapter one explores the phenomenon of pushed buttons. It explains why different people develop different buttons and why other people seem to be experts at pushing them. It gives several examples of pushed buttons in classrooms, among them,

- when a teacher argues with a student;

12

- when a teacher loses patience with a student;
- when a teacher stereotypes a student.

Importantly — and this is a crucial perspective that permeates the book — chapter one describes how the button possessor and the button pusher work together to create distress. And it goes into detail about what a teacher can learn about herself from her buttons, what she can learn about her button-pushing students, and what she can do with that information not just to de-escalate the interaction but to actually turn it into a learning opportunity.

COMPLIMENTS AND INSULTS

Fortunately for Karen she had one compliment to think about on her drive home. According to Tasha, she was a great teacher! In fact, she was one of the best teachers in the school, and why couldn't all of her students recognize that? If they did, they certainly wouldn't pack up their backpacks before she finished her lesson! This insulting act felt to Karen like a stinging slap. Her knee-jerk reaction to feeling hit in this way was to take revenge, to punish the students for their thoughtlessness by keeping them in class well into their lunch time.

It had felt good to get back at her students in the moment, but after the fact Karen felt terrible. She worried that her students thought she was boring and, worse, mean. Sure, Tasha had complimented her, but maybe Tasha was just buttering her up. How did her students *really* feel about her?

Chapter two considers the phenomena of compliments and insults and the temptation to take both of them personally. It shows how teachers can succeed in *not* taking insults or compliments personally and why such self-restraint is necessary for students' learning. Insisting that teachers are developmental partners to their students, chapter two explores how teachers can be *used* as

- twins;
- statues on a pedestal;
- mirrors;

and why such use is essential in all classrooms.

BOUNDARY CROSSINGS

And what about that menacing look? Karen couldn't make sense of it. Just thinking about the possibility that her colleague was angry at her — and for what?!? — made Karen anxious.

Karen didn't know it, but she was crossing a boundary with this worry. She was stepping out of her realm of responsibility and into her colleague's. The truth was that Karen had no idea what her colleague was feeling or what the "menacing" look meant, but she grabbed at an interpretation anyway. By assuming her colleague was upset with her, Karen took on blame and responsibility without knowing why or if it was even appropriate. And rather than feel concern for or curiosity about her colleague, Karen felt guilt and anxiety, which focused her attention on herself and effectively erased her colleague.

That's quite a lot for a passing moment in the hallway!

Chapter three addresses the many ways in which teachers and students cross each other's boundaries, causing distress and misunderstanding and handicapping learning. It looks at instances of

- disrespect;
- enabling;
- revenge.

Chapter three considers how teachers can be "great enough" by setting and enforcing reasonable limits and by establishing and maintaining healthy boundaries in the classroom. And it discusses the inevitability of pushback and the work teachers can do to survive it and strengthen the classroom environment as a result.

POWER STRUGGLES

Power struggles come in many forms. The easiest ones to see are those in which a teacher and a student are actively scrabbling for dominance. But power struggles can also involve passivity, as in the case of Rochelle. Her silence, her refusal to engage with her teacher about her homework, initiated a power struggle that was just as maddening for Karen as outright defiance would have been.

Of course, Karen might have been wrong about Rochelle's silence. Perhaps Rochelle was just tired; perhaps she was afraid of Karen and didn't know what to say in the face of her teacher's obvious agitation. While these interpretations (and more) were possible, what was important for Karen was her *feeling* that Rochelle was resisting her. This feeling, one of the many feelings of teaching, must be Karen's starting point for making sense of her interaction with Rochelle.

And the bottom line for both Rochelle and her teacher was that their communication had broken down. Rochelle, through her silence, had withdrawn, and Karen, through her anger and frustration, had taken over. Power struggle or not, the effect — domination by one person, disappearance of another — was the same.

Chapter four explores power struggles of all types, including

- bullying;
- distracting;
- refusing to learn.

Chapter four looks closely at where power struggles originate — specifically, at forced compliance, resistance, and conflict — and offers means to defuse them, making way for open-minded communication and, ultimately, lasting learning.

Experiences of pushed buttons, compliments and insults, boundary crossings, and power struggles depend on relationships, on human interaction, and inevitably involve emotions. Such experiences make up every teacher's day in every classroom. The default response to these experiences too often resembles Karen Madison's: fruitless worrying that generates bad feelings and no positive action and, sometimes, deeper entrenchment in negative behaviors. What teachers need to know is that disturbing interactions at school carry valuable information, or emotional and relational data, that teachers can use to transform their classrooms.

Put another way, as my second premise does, *teachers need to understand how relationships work and what emotions mean if they are to optimize their students' learning.*

Premise #3:
Teachers need support in understanding (and, in some cases, surviving)
classroom emotions and relationships.

Teaching is a difficult job. It demands the impossible: to force students to know and do what other people think they should even when those students might not want to or might not be able to. It involves pressure from administrators, parents, and state and federal governments. It requires teachers to manage large groups of sometimes undisciplined and aggravating people. It carries with it huge responsibility. In short, teaching is emotionally taxing.

And teachers generally bear this tax alone. Sure, some vent in the teachers' lounge or at home or to their friends. But venting, while usually relieving, is not truly productive. Despite the momentary outlet, teachers must return to the classroom, often with simmering, unresolved emotions that threaten to erupt at the slightest provocation.

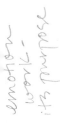

Instead of merely venting their emotions, teachers need to *understand* their emotions, to work through them and use them to plan better, more attuned responses to their students. In this book such work is called *emotion work*. Emotion work is different from venting in that it recognizes the value of all emotions, even the most negative, and examines them for accurate information about how teaching and learning are going in the classroom.

Emotion work requires certain skills:

- Self-awareness
- Describing
- Looking for good reasons
- Guessing
- Listening
- Self-disclosing
- Planning

These skills appear throughout the book. They are defined in chapter one and applied abundantly in all five chapters. While teachers will likely have a good idea of how the skills work by the time they have completed the book, those who need practice will find concrete guidance in chapter five.

Emotion work is not easy. It requires maturity, curiosity, fairness, and detachment. It leads to personal change that can feel uncomfortable in the moment and risky over time. It is the best way to make use of emotional and relational data and to transform the classroom, but sticking with it demands commitment, discipline, stark honesty, faith, and a good sprinkling of compassion for oneself and others.

And emotion work requires strong support. Because every single teacher has blind spots — emotions she doesn't feel, responses she doesn't perceive, and relational patterns she doesn't pick up on — every teacher needs help seeing what goes on in her classroom. And because emotional and relational data can be tricky to interpret, every teacher needs help decoding what she sees.

In sum, teachers need support in understanding their classroom experiences and developing the skills of emotion work. They need support in actually seeing interactions and figuring out what to do about each unique instance. And perhaps most important of all, they need to be seen, heard, and cared for just as their students do.

Like any other caretaking profession, then, teachers need nonevaluative, nonjudgmental, supportive supervision; that is, they need regular opportunities to vent productively: to share their emotions in all their shocking fullness and to work through those emotions with the help of respectful and accepting others. They deserve a place where they can reveal the truth about their work — that teaching is emotionally taxing — and use that truth to attune their teaching and facilitate desired learning. They need supervision that comes without judgment, without sanctions, and with abundant empathy.

This last premise, that *teachers need support in understanding (and, in some cases, surviving) classroom emotions and relationships*, is discussed and illustrated in chapter five. Because the notion of nonevaluative, nonjudgmental, supportive supervision may not be familiar to all teachers, I offer a rationale for it in hopes that teachers will begin to seek such support in their own schools and districts.

Of course, this book is a first step in supporting teachers through emotion work. If readers leave this book convinced, first, that they need to be alert to and informed about the emotional and relational data that surrounds them in their classrooms and, second, that they have a right to nonjudgmental, empathic supervisory support in making sense of these data, then the book will have done its job.

17

ORIGINS OF THE BOOK

Unlikely as the focus of this book might be in an era that glorifies standardization and test scores, it seems senseless, not to mention downright self-defeating, to deny the power of emotions and relationships in the classroom. This stance is confirmed by experience and theory.

Experience

My experience has spanned more than three decades of working as a teacher, a teacher educator, and, most recently, a psychotherapist.

As a teacher I was struck by my own emotions about my teaching, the worry and self-doubt that could nag me after even the most successful lessons. Why did this student irritate me so? Why did I dread this particular class? How should I have responded to that student's smart-aleck comment? It was stunning how worried and uncertain I could feel at the end of a day!

As a teacher educator I watched student teachers act out insecurity, anger, and fear, often in their placements, often in my classroom, often at me. Well before I trained as a therapist, I felt as though I played the therapist's role with my student teachers, listening to their worries, bolstering their confidence, supporting them in entering what I called their discomfort zones. Working in a teacher preparation program felt, to me, like jumping into a swamp of emotion.

My interest in teacher emotions took root in a doctoral program, when I wrote a dissertation on spontaneity in the classroom. Simply put, my hypothesis was that teachers' emotions drove their spontaneous acts of teaching. Observing and interviewing master teachers confirmed this suspicion and hinted at the richness of their emotional lives in the classroom. For the next decade and a half, I paid attention to my own and my students' emotions, experimenting with the ways such attention could inform and enhance teaching and learning.

These musings eventually led me to the realization, during a long walk one autumn day, that I wanted to be what I called a "teacher therapist." I wanted to be able to help teachers make sense of the emotions they felt that had such a major impact on their actions in the classroom. During my master's program in social work (MSW), in which I trained to be a psychotherapist, I was able to translate "teacher therapist" into "teacher supervisor." The two are quite different, I discovered. While the one delves deeply into past experiences, the other — the supervisor — focuses on the here and now, illuminating blind spots, looking for patterns, and coming up with plans for future action.

I organized and ran my first teacher support groups, groups that offered this type of nonevaluative, deeply supportive supervision to teachers, during my MSW program and wrote a thesis about the experience. This book is a direct result of that experience and that thesis.

Theory
Though I have been a teacher, a supervisor of student teachers, a designer of instruction and academic programs, and a director of academic degree programs, it was not until I undertook clinical training that my emotional experiences in education began to make sense to me.

They made sense because of psychoanalytic theory, theory that attempts to unravel and demystify the workings of relationships and the meanings of emotions. Sigmund Freud is the first name that usually comes to mind when one hears "psychoanalytic theory," and his ideas are extremely important.

But there are many different schools of psychoanalytic thought. The ones that have influenced me the most are associated with other names: D. W. Winnicott, Melanie Klein, Anna Freud, Heinz Kohut, Carl Rogers. These men and women have codified their understanding of human relations in ways that are extremely helpful. Not only have their ideas clarified for me teaching experiences that were doggedly bewildering, but they have actually framed my relational life — my actions and understandings as a parent, a spouse, a friend, a sister and daughter, and, of course, as a psychotherapist. This book presents my personal take on these theories in the very pragmatic context of everyday teaching life.

I have also been deeply influenced by complexity theory, an overarching theory that explains human behavior as nonlinear, coconstructed, and self-organizing. Principles of complexity fill this book, though I do not identify them as such. They appear whenever I talk about how classroom or family "systems" work, how people "fit together," how "reality" is "cocreated" or "coconstructed," how teaching and learning are "nonlinear," how shared experience "emerges," how no person can control another, how systemic change depends on personal change. While I fell in love with complexity theory when I was a doctoral student, I was glad to discover that psychoanalytic theory dovetails beautifully with it. The concepts I explore in this book represent this fusion.

WHAT ARE THE CONCEPTS?

Every chapter in this book has a practical focus and a conceptual one.

- Chapter one, which is about pushed buttons, introduces a concept that is fundamental to understanding any relationship: the concept of *psychic structure* and the ways people fit together to create *enactments*.
- Chapter two is about handling insults and compliments; the overarching concept is that teachers are *developmental partners* and, as such, are *used* by their students in ways that can be maddening but also developmentally necessary.
- Chapter three focuses on teachers' and students' *boundary crossings*, or invasions into each other's emotional or cognitive territory. The concept discussed in this chapter is that of the *great-enough* teacher, the teacher who knows how to establish and respect *limits* and *boundaries*.
- Chapter four addresses power struggles through the lens of *the Third*, or the "third reality" that can emerge out of healthy interactions where creativity and lasting learning can take place.
- Chapter five suggests ways to develop each of the skills of *emotion work*. It also discusses the value of *nonevaluative teacher supervision* and illustrates what such supervision can look like.
- The conclusion pulls together the basic ideas from the previous chapters into a worldview called *seeing structure* that can help teachers imagine generally how it might feel to bring the perspective from this book into their classrooms.

The concepts explored in this book can help a person understand any relationship. But their relevance to teaching in particular became clear to me through the teacher support groups I ran over the past five years. The stories the teacher participants told made sense to me when I thought about them through these conceptual lenses: psychic structure, being used, setting limits and respecting boundaries, and making way for the Third. Though the practical application of these concepts matters, understanding *why* the practices work is essential to constructing a personal lens that makes seeing structure automatic.

Theory is important. Being able to fall back on a framework that helps make sense of confusing and confounding experience can be both illuminating and relieving. But I recognize that not everyone finds formal theories agreeable. And I know that teaching is a fundamentally embodied act. So I have attempted in this book to present my understanding of psychoanalytic and complexity theories and concepts in nontheoretical terms. When I cannot avoid such terms, I have defined and illustrated them very concretely both in the body of the text and in a glossary at the end of the book. As an author, I am still a teacher. I hope this comes through as clearly as I intend it to.

ORGANIZATION OF THE BOOK

As I just mentioned, every chapter in this book has a dual focus. Each chapter addresses a practical problem and introduces a conceptual lens, or frame, through which to consider the problem. The chapter layout is on the next page.

Neat as these divisions look, there is actually a fair amount of overlap across the chapters. For example, insults and compliments, boundary crossings, and power struggles can all be considered instances of pushed buttons. Power struggles can involve boundary crossings, as can insults and compliments.

The point, fortunately, is not to categorize every teacher experience accurately. The point is to offer teachers a variety of ways to look at their experiences so as to hit upon an interpretation that resonates, or makes sense, given the particulars of their emotions, relationships, and classroom circumstances. The conclusion chapter is offered, then, as an attempt to summarize the approach or stance or attitude that this book recommends teachers take if they want to make sense of emotional and relational data.

Chapter	Practical problem	Conceptual frame
One	Pushed buttons	Psychic structure and enactments
Two	Insults and compliments	Being used as a developmental partner
Three	Boundary crossings	Being a "great-enough" teacher
Four	Power struggles	The Third
Five	Knowing yourself	Rigorous reflection and nonevaluative supervision
Conclusion	Putting it all together	Seeing structure

Stories

This book is filled with stories. They are all based on actual experiences of actual teachers. They come from my own experiences of teaching, from stories teachers have told me, and, in some cases, from stories students have told me. A couple are based on stories from books or articles I have read. Of course, I have altered elements of the stories to protect their sources and, in some cases, to help them resonate more broadly. But they are real. And they are brief.

Names

I have deliberately given the characters in these stories names that suggest a variety of racial and ethnic backgrounds to emphasize the diversity of real classrooms. At the same time I have focused on specific types of interaction that overlook the possible influences on the characters' behaviors of all kinds of identities (racial, ethnic, religious, gender, class, etc.) and biases. Some stories directly address the impact of prejudice on school interactions, but most do not. Though they are taken from real life, the stories are used in this book for narrowly illustrative purposes. They do not — cannot — represent the totality of all possible influences on teacher and student behavior.

Inclusiveness

Where there are students, there are caregivers, a great variety of caregivers: heterosexual couples, same-sex couples, single parents, aunties, grandmothers, foster parents, neighbors, nannies, babysitters, guardians, social workers. All of these caregivers can have profound influences on children and must be honored. But to name them repeatedly would get clunky. For the most part I use the word "parents" to refer to primary caretakers throughout the book. Sometimes I include other words, such as "parent" (singular) or "guardian," but for ease of reference I do not always use inclusive terminology. It is nonetheless intended.

Thought Experiments

Each story in this book describes a problematic interaction and is then analyzed. For every story I ask the question, "What could the teacher have done differently?" and offer an exploration of what, how, and why.

Generally speaking, my explorations are fictional. More accurately, they are thought experiments, considerations of what the teacher in each story *could* have done had she known about the concept the story is meant to illustrate. The processes I trace are necessarily influenced by my own approach to teaching and are not meant to represent the *only way* to respond to each story. These explorations, anchored as they are in theory, are intended to inspire teachers to experiment for themselves. My analyses and interpretations are meant only as guides and provocations.

Spotlight on the Teacher

Note that the story about Karen Madison and the discussions of it center on a teacher. That is because this book deliberately spotlights teachers. In a classroom system, where the emotional and relational landscape is so complex, teachers occupy a crucial position. They are the targets of much acting out. And being only human, they are just as likely to act out as their

23

students are. If teachers can become aware of obstructive enactments, learn from them, and shift their own behaviors in response to their understanding, students will follow suit.

This axiom bears repeating: If a teacher desires to change her students, a good way to accomplish this, an effective starting point, is to change herself. Despite popular conceptions of teaching and learning, no teacher can actually control what a student does, thinks, or learns. Rather, she can control her own actions and take note of the impact these changes have on the other people in the classroom. Because teacher and students are connected through their emotions and relationships, it is very likely that positive changes in the teacher will have a positive ripple effect on her students.

This book focuses on teachers, then, because teachers hold a great deal of unexplored power: the power to change themselves and, as a natural consequence, to encourage desirable change in their students.

TEMPTATIONS

There are a few temptations that readers of a book that indulges in psychological analysis must resist.

Judge Not

The first temptation is to judge the teachers in the stories. As I reinforce throughout the book, the point of doing emotion work is not to blame, compare, valuate, or condemn. It is to *understand* and, based on that understanding, to make changes that will improve teaching and learning. Readers who are tempted to judge or blame the teachers in this book might also be inclined to judge or blame themselves for similar actions, and that just increases personal suffering. So reading this book with a conscious intention to suspend judgment is a good way to practice self-awareness and cultivate the empathy that every teacher deserves.

A second temptation is to judge the students in the stories. Once again, blaming and judging cloud the fundamental fact of any problematic event, which is that teacher and student cocreate their interactions and are, therefore, both responsible. The reader who enforces a no-blame stance on herself as she moves through this book will develop some of the muscles that are crucial to the emotion

24

work I advocate, muscles she can use to good advantage in her own classroom.

Another temptation might be to lean toward diagnosing students, or pigeonholing them as psychologically deficient in one way or another. This temptation is also counterproductive. It goes without saying that even the most mentally ill person is, in fact, a person, not a diagnosis. And all people, regardless of their symptoms or behaviors, deserve the type of openhearted regard that is advocated in this book.

At the same time it befits teachers to be aware of mental illness. Teachers, administrators, parents, and students can suffer from any number of afflictions. Some of these afflictions are chemically based, while others stem from life-changing and often deftly hidden experiences of trauma. While teachers are in no position to diagnose, they are in a position to notice symptoms, to wonder caringly about the possible sources of those symptoms, and to seek help — from parents, administrators, supervisors, school counselors, social workers, and psychotherapists — for students and others who may be overwhelmed, frightened, or severely agitated by their experiences, feelings, and actions.

Another temptation is to blame parents for the way their children have turned out. Surely, parents play a central role in their children's psychological development. And some parents are better equipped than others to foster healthy growth. But parents, like students and like teachers, have had their own formative experiences and have constructed themselves in relation to them. Blaming someone for adapting to her home environment and repeating the relational patterns she learned there is like blaming a plant for contorting as it grows toward a sliver of light. We become who we need to be to survive. The ideal stance is not to blame but to wonder, to empathize, and to figure out how to ally with parents rather than to oppose them in the shared project of helping their children.

In general, it is tempting to make judgments based on one's definition of "normal." While a teacher's attention might be drawn to a behavior because it strikes her as "abnormal," it is important to remember that "normal" cuts a wide swath. More to the point, once a student is on a teacher's radar, all emotional and relational data are "normal" insofar as they carry vital information about *that particular student* at *this particular time*. Responding to that student, whatever his position on the normal–extranormal continuum, is always customized, never formulaic. Responses must be based on the particular information the student offers about what he might need from the people around him and the sense teachers and others can make of this information.

Teachers Are Not Therapists

Yet another temptation, and, frankly, danger, is for teachers to see themselves as therapists. In fact, teachers are not therapists. They have neither the permission nor the training to engage in the intimate and delicate work that psychotherapists do.

And teachers are not their students' parents. They do not carry parental authority, and they are not members of their students' family cultures. Fortunately for teachers, their connections with their students are less visceral or umbilical than parents' connections tend to be, and their responsibilities to students are generally well defined and limited.

But teachers, like parents, are developmental partners. As such, they are doomed to be tested and tried just as parents are. While it is inappropriate for teachers to probe into students' family lives or psychological backgrounds or to compete with parents for influence in students' lives, it is appropriate for teachers to use emotional and relational data to make sense of and respond to their students' educational and developmental needs.

To do this, teachers need emotional muscles. They need to practice the skills of emotion work so they can gain crucial understanding of classroom interactions. Parents use emotional muscles. And many therapists use them, too. But the fact that parents, therapists, and teachers often use the same skills and muscles does not make them equivalent. Each role has different purposes and contexts, and the boundaries between them must be protected as sacrosanct.

Teachers Are Learners

Some teachers might be familiar with the ideas and practices in this book; others might not. Because the perspective taken in this book is not generally applied in teacher education programs or in schools, my assumption is that much of this book will be new to most teacher-readers. A final temptation for these teachers, then, might be to lose patience with themselves as they encounter knotty concepts or interpretations or solutions they could not have come up with themselves.

To these teachers I say: Please relax and enjoy the stories. You can't know how to do something you don't know how to do. Think of reading this book as a chance to experience what your students experience in your classroom. Practicing empathy for yourself as you survive learning will only help you feel empathy for the difficult learning processes students undergo every day.

And if you want to practice thinking about emotions and relationships in the classroom and applying the concepts from this book to actual experiences, visit the Teaching through Emotions website at *teachingthroughemotions.com*. There you can post your own stories and comment on other people's teaching stories. This practice will help you refine your ability to do emotion work and see structure.

CONTEXTS

It is important to underline that, just as a teacher's or student's or parent's behaviors stem from personal, historical contexts, so does every classroom have an institutional and cultural context. I do not directly address these various contexts for the stories in this book; I leave it to the readers to import the stories into the contexts in which they themselves work.

But I want to acknowledge that the environment in which teachers function is crucial in many ways. The condition of the school building; the attitude of the administration, staff, teaching faculty, and parents; the emotional and teaching supports available; the nature of the surrounding community; and state and federal policies all influence the emotions and relationships teachers (and students) must wrestle with.

What this book ultimately advocates for is a transformation of every educational environment, no matter what the actual contextual elements are, into one that helps teachers bear the relational responsibilities they inherently carry as instructors of and caregivers for children. I cannot offer a template for what such an environment should look like, but I can, and vigorously do, point to the need.

Here is the bottom line: Teachers have strong emotions about their teaching and their students. They engage in charged, high-stakes relationships at school. These emotions and relationships have direct and powerful impacts on the teaching they do and on the learning their students do. And most teachers have absolutely no formal training or support in managing these feelings and relationships or in utilizing the valuable information they contain to improve classroom performance.

Indeed, while these heavy responsibilities are inherent in the job, few if any teachers enter the profession thinking explicitly about or preparing deliberately for them. It is my fervent belief that teachers need to do this thinking and preparation. And they need to do it throughout their careers in safe, nonevaluative, supportive settings.

What would it have been like for Karen Madison to think about her students through the lenses of pushed buttons, compliments and insults, boundaries, and power struggles? What if she had driven from school to a supervision session in which she could talk over and think about her worrisome experiences with someone who appreciated her and had no interest in judging her? This book offers a vision of that achievable reality.

CHAPTER ONE

PUSHING BUTTONS: ENACTMENTS IN THE CLASSROOM

Thanks to circuitry and electricity, pushing buttons can be a very positive act. Push one button and you can communicate instantly with someone living on the other side of the world from you. Push another button and your room can be filled with music. Push yet another button and your car starts without any noise at all.

But there are some buttons that just shouldn't be pushed. These buttons touch off strong negative emotions that can be surprisingly difficult to control. Just a hint of arrogance can make some people tense and impatient. Conversing with someone who is needy and helpless can make other people want to run away. People who squeeze the toothpaste tube in the middle, who never say, "Thank you," who become melodramatic at the drop of a hat — all are potential button pushers.

These personal buttons cannot be seen. But when they are pushed, they might as well be "ON/OFF" switches. Somehow, a circuit is completed and electricity flows. Voices rise, tempers flare, and people who just moments ago were calm and reasonable become irritated and inflexible. This patterned exchange of energy, when it happens in a classroom, can instantly shut learning down.

But what *is* a "button"? Where are these buttons located? Why is one behavior or experience a button for one person and not for another? The answers have to do with *psychic structures* and *enactments*, the ways people "plug into" each other to complete a circuit and allow relational electricity to flow. Understanding how buttons get pushed can help teachers step back from aggravating interactions and think about different responses that might better accomplish instructional and interpersonal goals. This understanding requires a *psychodynamic perspective* on classrooms, or a view

29

of relationships as collaborative, since it actually takes two to push a button.

CHAPTER QUESTIONS
- *What is a "button"?*
- *Where are these buttons located?*
- *Why is one behavior or experience a button for one person and not for another?*

FITTING TOGETHER

Human beings are living organisms with physical structures that determine how they perceive and act in the world. Because we humans have opposable thumbs, we can grasp and manipulate objects in ways that cheetahs and elephants simply cannot. Walking upright on two legs gives us access to views that moles will never have (even if they had better eyesight). Although scientists claim that the world at the atomic level is mostly space, human beings both see and interact with a world in which matter is absolutely solid. In other words, our bodies allow us to "fit" with, or plug into, the environment around us, depending on our specific biological capabilities.

The ways we match, or fit with, our environment are determined by our physical structures, but those structures are moldable: They flex and change over time. Whereas beginners cannot imagine being able to, say, draw an accurate portrait or play a piano concerto or run a marathon, practicing the fit over and over again — that is, training ourselves — results in physical changes that make such feats easier to do.

These changes offer evidence of the remarkable plasticity of our physical structures. So while our actions in the world are limited by our structures, our ability to change ensures that the range of experience we are capable of having is virtually limitless.

Flexible as our structures are, human behavior does tend to organize around patterns. Playing the piano is not a random activity; it requires a set of moves that become more automatic as time goes on. This is another important property of living systems: that actions repeated over time can become ingrained, as involuntary as reflex reactions. While practice may not actually make perfect, it can indeed make an action automatic.

Clustering our responses to the world in this way makes good sense, as it frees up energy and attention for other activities that we can do simultaneously — say, singing while playing the piano or planning a lesson while driving a car. As any right-handed person who has tried writing with her left hand knows, though, changing patterned behaviors can be quite uncomfortable. The more automatic a behavior becomes, the more difficult it is to change.

KEEP IN MIND
When people repeat behaviors over and over again, the behaviors become ingrained into automatic patterns. Changing these behavioral patterns can be difficult and uncomfortable but well worth it when the changes improve relationships and learning.

PSYCHIC STRUCTURE
So there are certain properties that distinguish physical structures:

- Physical structures determine people's perception of and ability to interact in the world.
- Physical structures are plastic, meaning they can flex and change.
- Physical structures can be trained to execute patterned actions that are reinforced through repetition over time.

What is true for our physical structures is true for our psychic structures as well. Psychic structures are to human relationships what biological structures are to the material world. Just as my biological structure allows me to fit with objects in the physical world, my psychic structure allows me to plug into other people in the relational world.

That is, psychic structures are the structures, or models, or tacit sets of beliefs and behaviors that determine the ways people perceive and behave in, or plug into, relationships.

DEFINITION
Psychic structures *are the ways people plug into each other, or fit together, to make relationships work (for better or for worse).*

31

Attachment Styles

Attachment theory illuminates the notion of psychic structure beautifully. Proposed by John Bowlby and elaborated by Mary Ainsworth and many others, attachment theory claims that human beings construct, with the help of primary caregivers, distinct patterns of behaviors and attitudes (what the researchers call "Internal Working Models") that guide their interactions throughout their lives. The purpose of these models is, at first, developmental. They reflect a young child's growing understanding of how to maintain the human connections, or attachments, that will allow him to survive. With time the Internal Working Models coalesce into automatic coping mechanisms that reflect and perpetuate the child's expectations of the world even when the particular coping skills might be inappropriate.

Based on experiments she called the "Strange Situation," in which young (white) children were exposed to strangers during their mothers' brief absence from a room, Ainsworth hypothesized three different "attachment styles": secure attachment, insecure attachment of the anxious-ambivalent type, and insecure attachment of the avoidant type.

- *Secure attachment* was demonstrated by children who (1) protested the mother's leaving, (2) were able to revert to playing comfortably during her absence, and (3) touched base with her upon her return, then continued playing. Securely attached children could accept comfort from the stranger in the room but obviously preferred their mother's.
- *Insecure attachment* of the *anxious-ambivalent* type was evident when children (1) protested the mother's leaving, (2) were unable to settle into comfortable play during her absence, and (3) expressed anger upon her return and, while seeking comfort from her, resisted when it was offered. These children made little use of the stranger's efforts to comfort them.
- Children with *insecure attachment* of the *avoidant* type (1) expressed no emotion when the mother departed, (2) played with little or no affect, and (3) ignored the mother when she returned. They also ignored the stranger in the room.

[Note that Ainsworth (1978) focused her research on mothers and their young children but emphasized that primary caregivers can be male or female, related or not.]

A fourth type of insecure attachment has been added to Ainsworth's model: *disorganized attachment*. Disorganized attachment behavior reveals a child's complete confusion as to how to respond to separation and reunion with a caregiver: The child is inconsolable and incoherent, sometimes freezes, and sometimes engages in self-harming and other contradictory behaviors.

Ainsworth correlated these attachment styles to parenting styles. Mothers of securely attached children tended to be attuned to the children; that is, they were alert to the children's needs, could even anticipate them, and they appropriately and consistently responded to the children. Mothers of anxiously-ambivalently attached children responded inconsistently to their children's needs. Sometimes the mothers responded appropriately; sometimes they ignored the children's needs. Mothers of avoidant children rarely responded to the children's needs, encouraging independence instead. And mothers of disorganized children tended to be misattuned and therefore threateningly inconsistent: overly stimulating and intrusive one moment and neglectful or withdrawn another.

From the perspective of survival (which is the perspective Bowlby took), or the chances an infant has of ensuring the care he needs to stay alive, all of these attachment styles are adaptive. The securely attached infant knows how to activate his mother's caregiving behaviors by crying and seeking proximity but is also busy strengthening his ability to be independent by exploring and experimenting in the world around him. The anxious-ambivalent child intensifies his bids for attention from his mother in hopes of overriding the neglectful response and triggering her caregiving response. The avoidant child chooses not to activate caregiving at all, since he has learned it will not be forthcoming anyway. Disorganized children have little or no idea how to guarantee their survival and might even endanger themselves in their desperate reactions.

We can see the growth of psychic structures in the attachment styles of young children. To put it concretely, each attachment style manifests in a "prong" that children seek to plug into a particular type of "outlet." Securely attached children, whose prongs seek reliable adults to plug into in times of stress, might become disoriented in the absence of such an outlet. Anxious-ambivalent children, who feel threatened when they are "unplugged," might become distraught at the first sign of loss in hopes of encouraging an outlet to appear. Avoidant children, whose prongs are generally retracted, might resist attempts by adults to connect. And disorganized children's prongs are often unrecognizable and confusing, reflecting their own bewildering, inconsistent experiences of plugging in.

What might prongs and outlets, or psychic structures, look like in the real world? Imagine a child who has internalized an anxious-ambivalent attachment style (where she fears abandonment and makes escalated bids for caregiving). Imagine this child in a stressful situation with an attachment figure — say, a teacher.

SELF-FULFILLING DEPRIVATION

Mr. Jackson has just handed out a unit test. This is the second time he has had to administer this test in his tenth grade science class, as the students did poorly on it the first time and required intensive review over the past week. Everyone in the room can feel his tension as they bend to their work.

Not one minute into the test, Mr. Jackson notices one of his students, Ingrid, straining to look at a neighbor's paper. He redirects her quietly but curtly. Two minutes later Ingrid's eyes are wandering again. After several rounds of redirecting her, Mr. Jackson barks, "Ingrid! Enough! Get out!"

What was going on with Ingrid? How might her attachment style, her psychic structure, have helped her to plug into her teacher and push his buttons?

First, it is likely that Ingrid was conscious of her teacher's tension and potential disapproval. Unconsciously, given her insecure attachment style, she probably associated disapproval from an attachment figure with withdrawal and neglect, which we can guess had been frightening and confusing for her all of her life. To prevent the loss of connection and these unnerving emotions, she unconsciously sought safety in correct test answers (which would, ultimately, ensure her teacher's approval). As a young child she might have stayed connected by repeatedly asking her teacher for help; as an adolescent, she turned not to her teacher but to her peers, seeking answers to the test questions from their papers.

Unfortunately, the very strategy she employed to make her safe helped to create the situation she both expected and dreaded. Her almost compulsive attempts to get answers from others (her prongs) drew repeated corrections from Mr. Jackson (his outlet). Eventually, he became so irritated with her that he not only sent her out of the classroom but verbally humiliated her in front of her peers.

In a roundabout way Ingrid helped to re-create the very circumstances that had shaped her attachment style in the first place: She was rejected and reviled by her caregiver and shamed for her needs. Objectively speaking, this was a negative outcome. Subjectively speaking, from the standpoint of attachment style and psychic structure, Ingrid succeeded in turning a stressful situation into a familiar, if educationally ineffectual, one. Much as she unconsciously craved something different, Mr. Jackson's impatient response to her was one she knew how to handle. A connection was, in the end, made. Ingrid could not have felt good about it, but she had a lot of practice in surviving the terrible emotions that seeking connection brought up in her.

KEEP IN MIND
Even the most dysfunctional behavioral patterns serve an important purpose. At the very least, they invite responses from other people that are familiar. And familiar responses, damaging or distressing as they may be, can be validating.

And what about Mr. Jackson's attachment style? Do adults even have attachment styles? Ainsworth's work shows that attachment styles, and hence psychic structures, are built from birth and depend on the relationship a child has with her primary caregiver(s). Over time attachment styles can grow stronger if the caregiving remains consistent. And they can change dramatically: Trauma can transform a securely attached child into an insecurely attached one; shifts in caretaking behaviors can change an insecurely attached child to a securely attached one. Research has shown, though, that attachment styles carry through to adulthood.

FOOD FOR THOUGHT

Adult attachment patterns basically correspond to children's attachment styles. **Securely attached adults** *are comfortable with both intimacy and independence and can balance the two.* **Preoccupied adults** *crave closeness and fear separation, which they can perceive as abandonment.* **Dismissive-avoidant adults** *are uncomfortable with closeness, preferring independence and self-sufficiency. And* **fearful-avoidant adults** *both crave and fear intimacy, finding closeness confusing and threatening. The prongs and outlets that form from attachment styles have an influence on such significant life elements as one's sense of self, one's choices of and interactions with romantic partners, one's perceptions of the world, and one's defenses against anxiety.*

[Credit for the influences of attachment styles to P. R. Pietromonaco & L. Feldman Barrett (2000), The Internal Working Models concept: What do we really know about the self in relation to others? *Review of General Psychology, 4,* 155–175.]

Mr. Jackson's response to Ingrid's bids for care might, indeed, reveal his personal attachment style. It is possible that Ingrid's repeated approaches to him triggered his need for distance in potentially intimate relationships, implying that he might have a dismissive-avoidant attachment style. It is also possible that, completely independent of his attachment style, Mr. Jackson simply felt revulsion for and impatience with Ingrid's behavior. What can be said with certainty is that, for whatever reason, Ingrid's prong fit neatly into Mr. Jackson's outlet and completed a circuit that manifested in Mr. Jackson's banishment of Ingrid from his classroom.

Put another way, Mr. Jackson and Ingrid unconsciously engaged in an *enactment* with each other. And unpleasant as

36

that enactment might have been, it contained a lot of useful information.

Enactments

Enactments are the behaviors and interactions that are driven by people's psychic structures. They are the evidence, the traces, of how people are constructed, where their prongs and outlets are, how they are able to fit with or plug into other people (and objects and ideas) to let energy flow.

Enactments are happening all the time; when they are friendly, we do not even notice them, as when we interact pleasantly and efficiently with a competent salesperson at a store. It is the jagged or alarming or irritating enactments — experiences of getting our "buttons pushed" — that we notice. This is where the psychodynamic perspective can be not just interesting but quite useful.

What is the *psychodynamic perspective*? It is a stance that scans for prongs and outlets and seeks to understand the purposes of their snug fits. To think psychodynamically is to ask questions such as the following:

- How am I or someone else fitting with other people in this situation?
- What am I or another person getting out of these interactions; how do we benefit from the ways we behave?
- Why might a particular behavior or attitude feel validating or familiar to me or another person?

In short, the psychodynamic perspective looks for the *good reasons* behind every action and emotion. And "good" does not mean "approved" or "condoned" but rather "understandable," "logical." For the objective of taking the psychodynamic perspective is not to judge, not to weigh in with criticism or advice. The objective is to understand. If a person can understand why she and others do what they do, that person can come up with alternative approaches that might encourage everyone to behave better.

So the psychodynamic perspective involves seeing enactments: looking for prongs and outlets and the good reasons people are plugging into each other the way they are. Let's use this perspective to help reframe a teacher's experiences with a difficult student.

Enactments *are the ways people act when they are plugged into each other. A prong fits into an outlet and energy flows: That's an enactment. In this book the focus is on instances when students or teachers act in disruptive or destructive ways, usually under conditions of stress. So while enactments can sometimes be positive, the use of the term in this book points to negative experiences.*

The **psychodynamic perspective** *is a stance that looks for prongs and outlets in oneself and in others and seeks to understand the reasons and purposes for the relational fits.*

FOOD FOR THOUGHT

QUESTION: How do you know when you're caught up in an enactment?

ANSWER: When you feel as though your buttons have been pushed. Here are some possible clues:

- *You are suddenly experiencing very strong emotions, and you're not sure why.*
- *A person is treating you as if you were someone else.*

If either or both of these clues are true, try detaching from your own responses and observing the situation with curiosity and self-awareness. Emotion work (see below) will help you figure out what might be going on.

CLASH OF THE TITANS

Ms. McNamara readily admits that her fourth-grade student, Jeannie, "pushes her buttons." Jeannie is needy and manipulative, maneuvering among her friends in ways that exclude and hurt. She is dishonest, telling blatant lies that are indefensible and pouting and hiding when she is confronted. She disobeys Ms. McNamara's instructions and yells at her teacher when limits are enforced. And she is relentless: In a given day Ms. McNamara can tangle with Jeannie up to ten times.

For example, one morning the students were working independently at their desks while Ms. McNamara circulated quietly among them. Jeannie's hand shot up at about the same time that another student's did, and Ms. McNamara moved to help the other student. Jeannie called out, insisting that she had raised her hand first. To avoid a fuss (and feeling vaguely guilty, as Ms. McNamara preferred the other student), Ms. McNamara switched to helping Jeannie. But the damage was done. Jeannie pouted for the rest of the lesson.

Later, on the way to art class, Jeannie screamed in the hall. Ms. McNamara told her firmly that she had to walk silently at the end of the line. In no time, Jeannie reappeared at the head of the line. "Jeannie, this is not the back of the line," Ms. McNamara said. "YES, IT IS!" Jeannie shouted. "NO, IT IS NOT!" Ms. McNamara shouted back and, taking her arm, jerked her to the end of the line.

When Ms. McNamara picked up the class after art, Jeannie asked if she could lead the class back to their room. Ms. McNamara consented, despite Jeannie's abominable behavior on the way to art class, and Jeannie hugged her tightly. But Jeannie was bossy in the hall, moving students around, sending some to the end of the line, and speaking loudly as they passed other classrooms.

When Ms. McNamara chastised her, Jeannie whiningly denied any wrongdoing. Ms. McNamara lost her patience. "Do NOT speak to me in that voice!" she snapped at Jeannie. "And I am TIRED of your lying! I'm tired of being taken advantage of, too. YOU get to the back of the line, and I don't want to hear another word out of you!"

Jeannie started to cry, and her friends gathered around, trying to comfort her. This made Ms. McNamara even angrier, as the last thing she felt Jeannie deserved at this point was comfort; rather, what Jeannie needed was to suffer some consequences for her behavior. Ms. McNamara heard Jeannie telling her friends, "I HATE her!" and had to admit that she felt the same way about Jeannie.

Where are the prongs and outlets in this story? How do Jeannie and Ms. McNamara fit together?

For one thing, Jeannie seems to need a great deal of attention. She seeks it from Ms. McNamara positively, by hugging and raising her hand, and negatively, by pouting and screaming and whining. These methods seem to work with Ms. McNamara: When she feels guilty and wants to avoid a scene, she helps Jeannie; when she feels angry, she punishes Jeannie. In both cases Jeannie and Ms. McNamara are plugged in.

But Jeannie is insatiable and inconsistent. She cannot seem to get *enough* attention, and she alternates between positive and negative tactics. In this way she keeps Ms. McNamara on her toes: Her teacher is grateful and relieved when Jeannie is affectionate and shocked and furious when she acts out. In all cases Jeannie's prongs — her positive and negative bids for attention — fit into Ms. McNamara's outlets, which impel her to attend to Jeannie in hopes of satisfying her endless need but also, importantly, to gain some emotional relief for herself.

At first glance it may be difficult to perceive Ms. McNamara's outlets. Jeannie is undeniably maddening, after all! But Ms. McNamara's responses reflect her own structure. It appears that Jeannie's distress makes Ms. McNamara nervous, and Ms. McNamara's preferred response to her anxiety is to take control: to fix the offending problem (Jeannie). The fact that Jeannie is *always* anxious, *always* acting out, *always* forcing Ms. McNamara to fail at fixing her makes it impossible for Ms. McNamara to like her. Sometimes she even hates her student! And that, of course, just makes things worse.

What are some possible good reasons for this fit? Jeannie's incessant attention getting, her inconsistent expressions of affection, her chronic acting out point to the possibility that Jeannie (like Ingrid) is insecurely attached. This hypothesis suggests a "good" reason for Jeannie's infuriating behavior: She might crave connection at the same time that she deeply distrusts it because she can never be sure her needs will be met. This ambivalence impels her to behave in ways that ensure *failed* connection, which (like Ingrid's behavior) reminds Jeannie of the environment and relationships she has grown up with.

Reframing Ms. McNamara's experiences with Jeannie in terms of structure (prongs and outlets) and good reasons — that is, in terms of enactments — sets the stage for the next step: changing the relationship.

Positive Change

The bad news for Ms. McNamara is that Jeannie cannot grow and learn from the responses Ms. McNamara is offering her. Because of the ways Ms. McNamara responds to Jeannie's behaviors — with guilt, resentment, frustration, and anger — she simply reinforces Jeannie's psychic structure and her expectations of charged, confused connection. The good news is that, by continuously pushing her teacher's buttons, Jeannie is giving Ms. McNamara lots of chances to break the cycle and relate in ways that will foster new learning.

What, then, could Ms. McNamara do differently? What alternative behaviors could she try that would encourage an entirely different fit with Jeannie, one that might allow Jeannie to grow and learn? The simple answer is that Ms. McNamara could experiment. She could plan a change in herself based on the hypothesis she has formed about the types of connection she and Jeannie enact; she could try that plan out; and she could see what happens.

FOOD FOR THOUGHT

Experiments that are informed by a psychodynamic perspective may not work the first time. They may not work at all. Or they may hit the mark instantly. One outcome is ensured: They will flush out more emotional and relational data that can be used to refine the experiments until desirable change is achieved.

But the simple answer is actually quite complex. In order to plan a change that might have a positive impact on Jeannie, Ms. McNamara would have to do some *emotion work*, work that would help her see her own and Jeannie's structures and craft what she saw into some sort of understanding. The plan she could then come up with would vary depending on the depth of emotion work she was capable of and her personal comfort with different types of intervention.

Emotion Work

Emotion work is the foundation of the psychodynamic perspective. It is the work one does to see and understand how relationships function and to plan experiments that will foster desired changes in the classroom. Specifically, emotion work involves

- practicing awareness (of self and others);
- describing;
- looking for good reasons for observed behaviors;
- making guesses;
- self-disclosing;
- listening;
- making a plan.

Practicing awareness. Practicing awareness requires discipline. It means noticing what is going on internally and externally and detaching sufficiently from all of it in order to observe as accurately as possible. Practicing awareness requires an ongoing commitment, as the skill improves with experience. It is a crucial first step in making positive relational changes in the classroom.

Questions teachers can ask themselves when they practice awareness are

- What am I seeing?
- What am I feeling?

DEFINITION

Detachment *is crucial to every aspect of emotion work. When a person detaches in emotion work, she pulls back from her experience just far enough to observe it. She lets herself feel but also turns her attention to her feelings and thinks about them. In this way she is able to work with emotional and cognitive information, a very powerful combination.*

Describing. Describing is best done with detachment. It involves stating as objectively as possible what is happening, stripping out biases, and seeking, as a detective might, "just the facts, ma'am."

A question that can help with describing is

- What are the facts of the matter?

42

Looking for good reasons. Looking for good reasons for enactments is a central aspect of the psychodynamic perspective. It requires a curious, nonjudgmental stance that sees attitudes and behaviors as valuable data. It also requires knowledge of the psychological forces that are at work in every relationship, forces this book describes.

Questions teachers can ask as they look for good reasons are

- Where is the fit?
- How is this fit working for everyone who is involved?

Making guesses. Once a teacher has posited possible reasons for a behavior, she can take some action. Making guesses involves sharing one's hypotheses with a student or a class. Making guesses out loud can help students feel seen and understood. Even when the guesses are wrong, sharing them can help a teacher gather more information about students' experiences.

Questions teachers can ask to help with making guesses are

- What's my hypothesis?
- When and how can I share my guess with my student?

Self-disclosing. Self-disclosing is when a teacher shares information about her own experience. This step can be very helpful if it provides information students can readily use. It is not helpful if the information is inappropriate, irrelevant, or overly burdensome. Self-disclosing should be undertaken only after careful thought.

FOOD FOR THOUGHT

Self-disclosing, when it reveals important and relevant truths, can be powerful. But it can also be perilous. Teachers must use self-disclosure sparingly and strategically, always keeping an eye on the impact it will have on the students.

One pitfall of self-disclosure is offering TMI: Too Much Information. Students do not need to know all the details of a teacher's experience. In fact, students need not to know much about their teachers. This ignorance, which can be shockingly shattered when, say, a student sees a teacher at the movie theater, is developmentally useful. As is discussed in more detail in the next chapter, students need to use their teachers as models of who they themselves want to be or, as Jeannie exemplifies, as targets for informative enactments. Constraining students' imaginations and range of behaviors with TMI, then, limits a teacher's usefulness.

It can also alter the roles teacher and student play in relation to each other. Depending on what a teacher reveals and how she reveals it, students can feel compelled to fix the teacher or take on a problem for her. This can happen automatically, without any conscious intent on the teacher's or the student's part. But it amounts to a role reversal in which the student becomes the teacher's caretaker. Obviously, such a role reversal is unacceptable. Teachers must be clear that the purpose of self-disclosure is to relieve students. It must never further burden the students.

And sharing feelings is not always recommended. Again, teachers must carefully avoid TMI. Fortunately, self-disclosure that reveals understanding of a situation can come in many forms, including **humor** *("Whoa! I really bombed that one!"),* **description** *("I am being really confusing right now, aren't I?"), and* **changing course** *("Let's leave this for now and try something new"). When thinking about self-disclosing, then, teachers need to exercise self-restraint, always keeping in mind the potential impacts their revelations might have on the people their sharing is meant to help.*

When considering self-disclosing, teachers can ask themselves
- Is there anything about my experience students might need to know?
- Why do I want to share this information?
- What impact do I hope it will have?
- Am I sharing this information for my sake or for the students' sake?
- How might this self-disclosure backfire?

Listening. When students share information about their experiences, teachers can gain a lot by listening receptively, by taking in what the students have to say. Sometimes listening

44

means feeding back what one has heard; often it means falling silent so as to give students time to think and muster the courage to talk.

Questions teachers can ask to help guide their listening are

- What are students telling me with their words? their body language?
- What are they *not* telling me?

Making a plan. This is the step where teachers make deliberate use of the information they have gathered and the understanding they have gained. Plans are experiments, never surefire solutions. The basic purposes of making plans are (1) to change oneself, how one feels and what one says and does; (2) to facilitate desirable changes in students; and (3) to collect more data about what changes might be most effective.

Questions teachers can ask themselves to help with making plans are

- How or what can I change? What effects do I think this change might have?
- What can I look for to see if this change has worked?

DEFINITION

Emotion work *is the work one does to see and understand how relationships function and to plan experiments that will foster desired changes in the classroom. It involves practicing awareness, describing, looking for good reasons, making guesses, self-disclosing, listening, and making a plan.*

HANDY TIP

Detailed discussions of each of the skills of emotion work appear in chapter five.

It is important to emphasize that the ways any individual teacher uses emotion work and the interventions emotion work leads to can vary depending on who the teacher is and what she is comfortable doing. The interventions also vary according to each teacher's level of competence in each skill.

Fortunately, the more a teacher practices the skills of emotion work, the more active and effective her interventions can be. But even the smallest changes in attitude or behavior — privately transforming anger into compassion, for example — can have a palpable impact on a student and a classroom. Emotion work can certainly be difficult or trying, and it can lead to unfamiliar and therefore uncomfortable new behaviors. It is also remarkably illuminating and relieving. Quite simply, emotion work inspires informed personal change based on understanding.

Making the Moves

In order to underline the value of all types of intervention influenced by emotion work, discussions of future teacher stories will include three different categories of moves teachers can make:

- yellow belt
- blue belt
- black belt

Yellow belt moves are those teachers make internally and, therefore, privately (unless the teacher makes them with someone else's help). While yellow belt moves require rigorous emotion work, they are easier to control, as they happen within the teacher. These moves involve the basic risks of self-discovery, of dwelling in uncomfortable emotions, of taking responsibility for one's actions, of seeing clearly. They are foundational moves, the moves all the others build on.

Blue belt moves are those that involve interactions with individual students. These, then, are public moves, but they are one-on-one. They require the ability to think on one's feet, to improvise effectively. They are the next step a teacher can take after having made her yellow belt moves.

Black belt moves are those that involve interactions with groups of students and with elements of the school system: parents, administrators, colleagues. These moves tend to feel the most risky because they can engage power structures and can be quite public. A teacher might never make a black belt move in her entire career; others might feel comfortable working at this level from the get-go. Black belt moves are only as valuable as a particular teacher deems them to be.

46

Throughout this book, for every story told, I suggest moves teachers can make that fall into each of these categories. But the moves are recommendations only. The goals of all emotion work are, first, understanding, and, second, classroom change. How a teacher accomplishes these two basic goals must reflect her own particular personality and sense of comfort and appropriateness in her particular classroom with her particular students. The best moves, however they might be labeled, are those that work.

In addition to yellow, blue, and black belt moves, there is a very basic move, a white belt move, that teachers should make before all else: the cognitive move of considering whether a student's acting out signals an inability to do what is being asked of him. When students lack the skills or knowledge they need to perform in school, they will often misbehave. Addressing the possibility of a learning disability or a need for patient remediation is, of course, a teacher's first, white belt, move.

Ms. McNamara's Emotion Work

We are now ready to imagine the emotion work Ms. McNamara might have done and the plan she could have come up with for changing herself and, hence, the ways she and Jeannie plugged into each other.

YELLOW BELT MOVES

To *practice awareness*, Ms. McNamara would have to take some time to notice her own emotions about Jeannie and to wonder about Jeannie's emotions. She might easily identify such feelings as anger, frustration, disappointment, confusion, and hatred arising for both her and Jeannie at different times during each school day. She might also note that she and Jeannie (and hence the entire class) lived in a perpetual state of tension because of their ongoing enactments. What was at the bottom of these feelings and interactions? What were they telling Ms. McNamara about herself and Jeannie and the relationship they were plugged into?

Focusing on any one enactment by *describing* it and wondering about the *reasons for it* or focusing on an emotion by feeling it fully would help Ms. McNamara answer these important questions. She might notice, for example, that she was generally uncomfortable when she or anyone else was unhappy or needy. When she perceived a negative emotion or a need (a prong), her automatic response (her outlet) was to try to fix whatever was causing the emotional discomfort. When her attempts to satisfy others' needs failed, she flared.

Ms. McNamara could wonder about the *good reasons* behind her impulse to stamp out unhappiness and satisfy all needs. "Why are negative emotions and unmet needs so hard for me?" she might ask herself. "What do they mean to me? What would happen if I let Jeannie feel upset and needy? How would I feel if I refused to rush in and fix her?"

This thought experiment might raise in Ms. McNamara the specter of chaos and the strong, opposing impulse to control. If she did not plug into Jeannie by trying to change her into a happy, fully satisfied child, all hell might break loose. The fear of losing control is a familiar one for teachers, and Ms. McNamara might have to explore what "control" and "losing control" looked and felt like for her as well as what they meant. Did "losing control" mean she was a failure? Did "being in control" mean she was a success? A competent person? Blameless?

Ms. McNamara could also wonder about the sources of Jeannie's emotions and behaviors. Why was Jeannie acting out? What situations tended to activate her? What did she do when she was activated? Ms. McNamara might notice that Jeannie herself had a strong desire to control. Jeannie's inflexibility during morning independent work suggested that Jeannie wanted very much to control her teacher's attention. Constant connection to Ms. McNamara, in other words, seemed to be very important to Jeannie. The illusion that Jeannie was in complete control of this connection also seemed important to her.

The outright disobedience on the way to art class could offer Ms. McNamara a different angle on the "good" reasons for Jeannie's behavior. At times, it appeared, Jeannie did not even trust her teacher's authority. This was when Jeannie took control of the rules of behavior for the entire class, moving and bossing her peers around. She even controlled the definition of reality by perversely deciding where the "end of the line" was. From these reflections Ms. McNamara could gain a strong sense of the anxiety Jeannie might feel on a constant basis: anxiety that she would lose connection with a vital authority figure coupled with fear that the authority figure could not keep the world and, hence, their connection under control.

Interestingly, these possibilities for Jeannie might illuminate Ms. McNamara's own feelings about connection, control, and their absence. For example, Ms. McNamara might notice a certain attraction to the chaos Jeannie introduced into her classroom. After all, Jeannie gave Ms. McNamara endless opportunities to exert her competence and to "clean up" Jeannie's messes. Any exploration of these feelings in herself and the possibly familiar situations that triggered them could, in turn, sharpen Ms. McNamara's insights into Jeannie.

This internal "yellow belt" work could make a big difference in Ms. McNamara's dealings with Jeannie. Mere understanding could shift Ms. McNamara's attitude in class, allowing her to view Jeannie not as a time bomb but as a child who needed structure and consistency from the adults in her life. Even if Ms. McNamara made no curricular changes, even if the only shift she brought to Jeannie was tolerance and empathy, Jeannie would notice. As the outlet changed, so would Jeannie's prongs. The enactments might not stop altogether, but Jeannie's behaviors would undoubtedly shift, and Ms. McNamara could continue to gather information about Jeannie and herself and to fine-tune her own behaviors.

This is a point worth underlining. In the psychodynamic world, where people fit together, a shift on one side of a relationship forces a shift on the other side. Putting it simplistically, if a horizontal outlet suddenly becomes vertical, the prong is going to have to change its orientation or no connection will be made. Assuming Jeannie wanted to stay connected to Ms. McNamara, a change in Ms. McNamara's attitude or behaviors toward Jeannie would prompt Jeannie to shift to make the fit work.

In relationships where people fit together, changes in one person's attitude or behavior invite corresponding changes in the other person's attitude or behavior. The changes are not necessarily predictable, though. One response could be to protest the changes by escalating negative behaviors. Another response could be to disconnect entirely. But in relationships where ongoing connection is the goal, changes in one person can have a very positive influence on the other person and on the relationship overall.

BLUE BELT MOVES

But Ms. McNamara could take her emotion work further. Having looked for and found some good reasons for Jeannie's maddening behavior in class, Ms. McNamara could explore her newfound understanding with Jeannie.

In a private meeting Ms. McNamara could try out some *guesses* with her student. She could share her perception of Jeannie's need to be close to her but also to push her away. "That must be very confusing — to want my attention but to get it in ways that make me angry at you," Ms. McNamara might say. She could wonder with Jeannie about what makes Jeannie feel safe in the classroom.

Ms. McNamara could explore her hypothesis about chaos and control. Without accusing Jeannie of having a "control issue" and without directly revealing her own, Ms. McNamara could say to Jeannie, "It can be pretty scary when it feels as though no one is in charge. I know I hated that when I was a kid." They could share examples of when children might feel out of control, thus approaching the heart of the matter without revealing too much about themselves.

Ms. McNamara could *self-disclose*. "Hoooeee!" she might say. "I sure can get mad at you, Jeannie. I really don't like it when I do, and I want you to know that I am taking full responsibility for my reactions and working on changing them." Note that this disclosure does two things: It confirms what Jeannie already knows — that Ms. McNamara gets angry — and asserts that Ms. McNamara is committed to managing her own feelings and, therefore, to keeping Jeannie safe.

Making guesses and *self-disclosing*, if they are results of genuine care, can encourage truth telling on a student's part.

Ms. McNamara could *listen* to Jeannie's responses and learn something about Jeannie's experience in the classroom, her perceptions of her own needs, and her expectations of Ms. McNamara. Listening would require honest curiosity on Ms. McNamara's part, a conscious commitment to closing her own mouth, quieting her own reactions, and taking in Jeannie's words and feelings, even playing them back to her — "You say you believe I hate you" — without judgment or immediate discussion.

Based on all this work, Ms. McNamara could come up with a *plan* for her dealings with Jeannie. Given the very good reasons for her own and Jeannie's behaviors, and given the serious and ongoing nature of her aversion to Jeannie, Ms. McNamara's plan would best be both *relational* and *structural*.

Relational Changes

On the relational level Ms. McNamara could *plan* what to say and do when Jeannie began pushing her buttons, plans she could share with Jeannie ahead of time. Here are some possibilities:

- "Jeannie," Ms. McNamara could say, "you need my attention right now, yet I am unable to give you as much as you would like. Let's agree to have lunch together today so I can give you my full attention"; OR
- "Jeannie, I see that you are agitated right now. Why don't you draw a picture that shows how you're feeling or write a letter to me that we can read together later"; OR
- "Jeannie, I am way too angry at this moment to talk with you. Since I can't take a time out right now, you must. If you can go sit in the rocking chair quietly while I get the class started on this next activity, I'll be able to calm down enough to come talk with you so we can work this out. If you can't sit quietly, you know what the consequence is"; OR
- "Jeannie, now's the time to go visit the school counselor."

Structural Changes

The basic "white belt move" Ms. McNamara could make is recommending that Jeannie get tested to determine if she would be eligible for any accommodations. Ruling out the (very reasonable) possibility that Jeannie had disabilities that frustrated her terribly would be very important, as the question of Jeannie's, or any student's, cognitive abilities and needs is an essential one.

BLACK BELT MOVES

Other structural supports would involve Jeannie's caregivers — a single parent, two parents, her guardians — and Ms. McNamara's school administration. Jeannie could be given the option of visiting a psychodynamically oriented school adjustment counselor when she felt out of control in class. Ms. McNamara and Jeannie's caregivers could discuss their responses to certain behaviors of Jeannie's and agree on consistent ways of handling those behaviors. They could come up with ways to communicate about their progress so they could keep learning from Jeannie and each other.

Jeannie and Ms. McNamara (and Jeannie's caregivers, if appropriate and feasible) could come up with a specific code of rules, consequences, and, importantly, rewards for Jeannie in the classroom that Ms. McNamara would enforce consistently. Such a code could work wonders: It could partly relieve Ms. McNamara of the unpleasant roles of judge and sentencer that activated both her and Jeannie, thus clearing the way for a more effective alliance between teacher and student. Being partners could make their experiences in the classroom much more fulfilling and productive.

Of course, talking, listening, and having plans does not guarantee that Ms. McNamara would start liking Jeannie or would never lose her temper again. But behaving differently based on understanding of herself and her student could improve the chances that a difficult and counterproductive classroom relationship would change.

FOOD FOR THOUGHT

*Teachers spend a lot of time with their students. Such daily exposure can make **relational changes** in the classroom both necessary and powerful.*

But obviously, students are members of many different systems. The school system is just one of them. The family system, of course, is another. And as attachment theory implies, the family system can easily trump any efforts teachers make at relational change. That is why **structural changes**, *or plans that involve parents or guardians (and administrators and, in appropriate cases, other teachers), are so important.*

Although calling on others, especially caregivers, to help with students' maladaptive classroom behaviors can feel risky, teachers must consider the value of teaming up with parent figures to increase the chances of a student's success. Any collaboration a teacher can enjoy with parents, guardians, and administrators can help. Of course, collaboration means relationship, and relationship can mean more enactments. Doing emotion work on relationships with other adults — as many of the stories in the rest of this chapter and book show — can be just as effective as doing it with students.

Emotional and Relational Data

Pushed buttons are extremely useful sources of information. Teachers can gain much by simply observing their students' behaviors. But still greater illumination results when teachers observe themselves; that is, when they practice *self*-awareness. This first step of the emotion work teachers can do to understand enactments, or pushed buttons, is the most important, the one out of which all the other steps necessarily fall.

Self-awareness is important because it draws teachers' attention to their emotions. And paying attention to their emotions gives teachers access to extremely valuable information:

- Information about themselves
- Information about their students' preferred relational styles
- Information about their students' emotions

In other words, self-awareness gives teachers access to emotional and relational data that are crucial to understanding the ways students are or are not learning in their classrooms.

Information about Themselves

Since it takes two to push a button, gathering information about the potential role one is playing in an enactment can be enormously valuable.

Introspection. It should come as no surprise that introspection, paying close, honest attention to one's own emotions and physical sensations, provides clues as to how one fits with other people. Noticing one's internal experience makes it easier to take responsibility for one's actions, for the ways one contributes to relationships. And taking responsibility for the roles one plays in relationships can lead to a number of benefits.

First, teachers who practice introspection and take responsibility for their feelings and behaviors are modeling self-regulation, a skill all students need to learn. Second, they are dissolving tension in themselves and others, an experience that is both relieving and liberating. Third, they are learning about themselves and how they fit with their students and, possibly, making lasting changes in the ways they will interact in the future. Fourth, they might discover actual flaws in the ways they are teaching. And last, they are opening up space in which others can exist and grow on their own terms (more on this in chapter four).

Self-care. Noticing one's emotions also alerts teachers to the necessity of self-care; that is, it provides the following information: "Whoa — I'm feeling terrible. I need to do something about that so I can feel better." Elementary as this information might seem, too many teachers (and caregivers in general) regularly ignore it. But the work of self-care is an essential part of a teacher's job description.

Caring for oneself helps teachers stay in tip-top emotional shape. Being emotionally healthy means teachers are less reactive when enactments surface in the classroom. Being less reactive means teachers can respond to students more calmly and thoughtfully and, hence, more effectively. Effective responses to enactments means students will do more desirable learning.

ATTENTION!
Self-care (and being cared for) is crucial for teachers. Figuring out how to get the care one needs is perhaps the

single most important part of any teacher's (or other caregiver's) job.

So self-awareness points teachers to their own need for self-soothing and rejuvenation, a need that is essential for teachers to satisfy on a regular basis. Self-awareness also invites teachers to read their own emotions and familiarize themselves with their own prongs and outlets so as to take responsibility for their contributions to classroom enactments. Simply turning inward and noticing oneself, doing nothing more, can have far-reaching consequences for teachers and students.

Information about Students' Relational Styles
Self-awareness invites teachers to reflect on themselves, their own prongs and outlets. But it also opens a window into their students' relational worlds, into the fits their students are accustomed to experiencing with other people.

As the notion of psychic structure states, one person's behavior (her prongs) encourages appropriate (and unconscious) responses in others (their outlets). Those responses are both behavioral and emotional. When teachers are caught in enactments — when their buttons are pushed — they are, of course, behaving automatically, in ways that come naturally to them. But their behaviors are also accurate responses to their students' compelling prompts and, as such, complete the enactments in just the ways their students have come to expect.

Enactments, then, are self-fulfilling prophecies. Especially under conditions of stress, when it is difficult to be flexible and forgiving, people seek connection with others in familiar ways. Students who act out in class are literally teaching their teachers (and classmates) how to treat them. Ingrid's insecurity and wandering eyes triggered Mr. Jackson's rejection; Jeannie's whining and manipulation triggered Ms. McNamara's angry withdrawals. Noticing these actions and reactions can give teachers insight into the types of relationships that have shaped their students and, consequently, the types of responses from caregivers that feel most familiar to them.

55

Noticing their students' preferred relational styles can help teachers in a couple of ways. First, it further facilitates stepping back and detaching when their buttons are pushed. If teachers can view themselves and their students as playing necessary and familiar *roles*, as taking on dramatic parts in a play, they can stave off blame and judgment. They might also begin to feel compassion, which is an extremely useful emotion when dealing with students who are hurting.

Second, noticing the roles students compel teachers to play can suggest methods of corrective action. If students expect *this* reaction, how might they respond to a totally different reaction? Using self-awareness to identify relational styles and deliberately considering ways to fit differently and more productively with students is a powerful way to teach.

FOOD FOR THOUGHT

Psychic structures, the prongs and outlets that people use to plug into each other relationally, are not fixed. They develop through repeated interactions with people, and they change through repeated, different interactions. These different interactions have been called **corrective emotional experiences**.

When teachers plan lessons that help their students learn new information and skills, they are enacting corrective academic *experiences. Teachers' acts are designed to* correct *their students' current state of knowing by sharing information with the students and encouraging the students to think and operate differently. Effective teaching qualifies as offering "corrective academic experiences."*

When teachers shift their behaviors to fit differently with their students, to strengthen their relationships and make button pushing less necessary, they are participating in corrective emotional *experiences.*

Teaching, one might say, is the art of participating in corrective experiences. Thinking carefully about how to provide these academic, emotional, and relational experiences can give teachers an invaluable advantage in helping their students develop into educated, healthy people.

[Credit for the term "corrective emotional experiences" to F. Alexander, T. M. French, et al. (1946), *Psychoanalytic therapy: Principles and application*, New York: Ronald Press.]

Information about Students' Emotions

Enactments, or pushed buttons, compel responses that are both behavioral and emotional. When they fit together, people unconsciously perceive how to treat each other to make the fit work. The clues they pick up on are, of course, behavioral. But they are also emotional.

For emotions are contagious. When people successfully plug into each other, they complete an emotional circuit. This connection often induces, or creates, in one person the feelings that the other person is having. What this means for teachers is that what a teacher feels when her buttons are pushed is often *exactly* what her student is feeling. Knowing that one's own emotions might match a student's emotions can help a teacher better understand her student and plan ways of interacting more effectively.

In short, teachers' emotions are an extremely valuable resource, as the following story illustrates.

"FEEL IT FOR ME"

The bell for recess could not have been more welcome to Ms. Foster, a pre-K teacher. She had been growing increasingly frustrated with her students during a math activity that involved manipulatives, which the students found much more interesting to throw than to play with purposefully. She had actually been forced to give Manny a time-out for throwing a Unifix cube at a child across the room. She was more than ready for the 20-minute break the children's outdoor recess would give her.

While most of the children got dressed for recess quickly, Manny was having unusual trouble today. He put his boots on before donning his snow pants. Rather than taking the boots off and starting over, Manny sat on the floor and tried to pull his snow pants over his boots. Once the pants were finally on, Manny could not find his mittens. He insisted a classmate had stolen his hat. Then he had to use the restroom.

Ms. Foster had been getting more and more frustrated as Manny's preparations dragged on and her precious minutes of solitude ticked away, but she snapped when he asked to use the restroom. "MANNY!" she yelled. "What is wrong with you? Get your stuff together and GO OUTSIDE!"

At first glance the information Manny was conveying to Ms. Foster is easily decodable: He was bored by the math activity and too unfocused to dress himself for outdoor recess. And Ms. Foster was understandably frustrated by his annoying behavior. If peace were to be restored, Manny needed to shape up. Case closed.

But a psychodynamic perspective insists that there are good reasons for all behaviors, and that, because people plug into each other, one person's behavior is intertwined with other people's behavior. The psychodynamic perspective also demands that teachers practice awareness to begin untangling the behavioral and emotional interconnections. So from a psychodynamic perspective what could Ms. Foster have done differently?

Ms. Foster's Emotion Work
Ms. Foster could, of course, have practiced emotion work.

YELLOW BELT MOVES
Ms. Foster could have gone into *awareness* mode. She could have noticed, first and foremost, that she was having an extreme reaction to Manny. This realization could have pointed to the good possibility that Manny was pushing a button, that the two of them were involved in an enactment.

Rather than act her frustration out unthinkingly, Ms. Foster could have slowed down and detached from the situation; that is, she could have told herself to observe Manny's behaviors and her own reactions to them. Specifically, she could have used self-awareness to gather emotional and relational data: to look at her own emotions, at Manny's emotions, and at the ways she and Manny were fitting together in this enactment.

"Wow, I'm getting really mad," she could have thought, *describing* to herself what her introspection revealed. "And Manny, who loves recess, is taking an unusually long time to get ready to go outside. Why is Manny acting so uncharacteristically? And why am I so angry about it?"

Then she could take a stab at answering her own questions. This step would involve *looking for the good reasons* for Manny's and her own behavior. Ms. Foster could easily identify one good reason for her anger: She really needed a break, and Manny was systematically frittering it away for her. One immediate yellow belt move Ms. Foster could have made, then, was to disengage from the enactment by retreating from Manny: sitting at her desk and attending to her own business while Manny put on his gear. In so doing, she would have also given Manny a break from *her*, something he might very well have needed.

KEEP IN MIND
An excellent response to getting one's button pushed is to **take a break***. Reacting in the midst of distress rarely does any good and often does more damage. Taking a break to calm down, pay attention, and think through one's response can turn an enactment into a positive learning opportunity. Time-outs can be good for everyone.*
[Credit for the importance of taking a break to D. Stone, B. Patton, & S. Heen (1999), *Difficult conversations: How to discuss what matters most*, New York: Penguin Books.]

But why was Ms. Foster so upset? Losing a few minutes of her break did not justify the level of anger she felt. Such disproportionate emotion implied that, through this enactment, Manny was feeding her some of his own feelings. Perhaps that was why he was acting so uncharacteristically: He was furious at Ms. Foster just as she was furious at him. But why?

Reviewing the last few moments of class could reveal a possible answer: Ms. Foster had given Manny a time-out for throwing a manipulative across the room. He very possibly felt ashamed and angry at having been punished in this way. Come to think of it, the fact that Manny threw the Unifix cube at all was surprising to Ms. Foster, as he tended to be an engaged, cooperative student. Why had he thrown the cube in the first place? What was he trying to tell his teacher?

And what about Manny's preferred relational style? Was Manny teaching Ms. Foster that he was accustomed to being yelled at? This interpretation did not square with what Ms. Foster knew of Manny: that he was an enthusiastic and successful learner who interacted comfortably and appropriately with his teachers and peers. It would seem that being yelled at was more *un*familiar than familiar to Manny.

Ms. Foster was doing a good job of practicing awareness to gather emotional and relational data about herself and Manny. But she was stumped as to how all these data fit together. She needed more.

Defenses

What she needed was understanding of yet another form psychic structures can take, that of the psychological defense.

Defenses, as the name implies, are psychological ramparts that all people erect to protect themselves from anxiety and other negative emotions. The idea is that some feelings are just too difficult to experience consciously and hence must be avoided. Defenses, like attachment styles, are the structures that evolve in each person to shield him from what he cannot bear to experience internally.

DEFINITION

Defenses *are psychological shields people use to protect themselves from emotions that are too difficult to feel consciously.*

To see the defenses that Manny and Ms. Foster played out together, one must dig a little deeper into their emotional experiences. Here, then, is what might have been happening under the surface of their enactment:

Ms. Foster had to discipline Manny for throwing a Unifix cube across the room. That could have made him angry and a little ashamed, just as Ms. Foster had guessed.

But the deeper truth could have been that Manny was frustrated by the math activity. He might have had no idea what the Unifix cubes were for and might have been confused by what his teacher was saying about them. This could have surprised him (just as his throwing the manipulative surprised his teacher), for he generally felt on top of the activities he did in his pre-K classroom. He hated feeling confused and lost.

These emotions would not necessarily have been conscious. Nor was the decision to throw a cube across the room (that is, Manny did not consider any options; he just did what he *felt* like doing). Nor was the anxiety and frustration Manny still felt when it was time to go out to recess. To discharge these feelings (again, unconsciously), Manny began behaving in a way that made his *teacher* feel frustrated. This allowed him to disown the feelings he hated and to give them to someone else: Ms. Foster.

For her part Ms. Foster might have been having her own negative experience. Her math lesson went poorly — what had she done wrong? Was she not interesting enough? Was she not helpful enough? Was she asking too much of these young children? Not knowing where she had gone wrong could have made Ms. Foster feel helpless and inept.

And Manny's slow-motion preparations were perfectly designed to push her over the edge. Not only was the boy who gave her the clearest indication of her failure as a teacher demonstrating unfathomable incompetence, but he was also eating away at her quiet time. Her emotional resources were depleted; frustration and anger surged; she yelled; she felt ashamed and even more doubtful of her value as a teacher. By the end Ms. Foster was the person who was angry and out of control, not Manny.

Projective Identification

Two types of defense were very likely at work in this enactment: *projection* and *identification*. Each of these defenses can function independently, but in this case they came together into the defensive enactment called *projective identification*.

Projection happens when one person (unconsciously) disowns a terrible quality or feeling and attributes it to, or projects it *onto* or *into*, another person. For example, I can project a quality such as laziness (one I particularly dislike in myself) *onto* a student and treat that student as if he were lazy, whether he is lazy or not. Or I can project a sense of panic *into* someone by behaving in a way that induces that emotion in them: by shrieking, say, and slamming doors. This latter type of projection is how Manny pushed his feelings away from himself into Ms. Foster.

Identification (as a defense) happens when a person takes on feelings or attributes of another person and acts out in blaming or hurtful ways. In *projective identification* the feelings one takes on are not just those the other person does not want and therefore projects out; they are also feelings one can easily relate to. This happened when Ms. Foster took on Manny's feelings, added them to her own, and acted out their combined anger.

Ms. Foster *identified* with the feelings of frustration and incompetence Manny was *projecting* into her. By expressing his anger for him, she sheltered him from his true feelings, which were too difficult for him to consciously acknowledge and accept. In short, Manny became overwhelmed and projected his unbearable feelings into Ms. Foster; Ms. Foster identified with those feelings and acted them out for both herself and Manny; and the enactment was complete.

DEFENSES

Projection *is a defense.*
Identification *is a defense.*
Projective identification *is a defense.*
See the appendix for definitions and examples.

Ms. Foster's emotion work would be aided by knowledge of defenses. Once she could hypothesize that Manny's uncharacteristic behavior might be associated with the defense of projective identification, she could make some blue belt moves that would provide Manny with emotional relief. These moves, over and above anything she might do to care for herself, would do more than just solve an immediate problem. Negative emotions, when left to fester, often reappear in further enactments. Addressing negative emotions early on prevents the need for escalation.

FOOD FOR THOUGHT

It is important to note that it is unwise to attempt to breach or destroy psychological defenses; they are, after all, doing important work. Noticing them when they happen, though, can be extremely helpful, as corrective action can be taken not against the defense itself but in response to the emotion that might have activated the defense.

When a teacher suspects a student has erected a defense, her first general guess can be that the emotion underlying it is anxiety. Generally speaking, when a person

feels anxious, he deserves thoughtful, caring treatment —
especially if that person is a student who is struggling to learn.
So a first response to a defense can be caring attention.

But defenses arise in response to all kinds of negative
emotions. The more accurately a teacher pinpoints the emotion
underlying a defense, obviously, the more effectively she can
defuse it. This is where emotion work, especially the first step
of self-awareness, comes in.

Teachers who pick up on their own and others'
defenses and who do emotion work can have a huge impact on
their classrooms. They can alter anxiety-producing behaviors,
facilitate learning, prevent escalation, and, not
inconsequentially, make themselves and others feel better.

BLUE BELT MOVES

So what blue belt moves might Ms. Foster have tried? Having
formulated a hypothesis about Manny's state of mind, Ms.
Foster could share some *guesses* with her student.

- "Manny," Ms. Foster could say, "it seems as if you
  don't want to go outside for recess today"; OR
- "I wonder if you're angry that I put you in time-out
  just now"; OR
- "I'm thinking you might be feeling a little frustrated
  by the math activity today."

Manny might agree, disagree (and give more
information about how he is truly feeling, which would be
extremely helpful to Ms. Foster), or continue to resist.

If it felt useful and appropriate, Ms. Foster could try
some careful *self-disclosure*. In doing this Ms. Foster would
model for Manny an effective way of expressing feelings. She
might also help to collapse his resistance by taking explicit
ownership of her own actions.

- "I didn't like putting you in time-out," she could
  say; OR
- "To be honest, I think I confused everybody during
  that math activity"; OR
- "Right now I'm watching you struggle to get ready
  to go outside, and that surprises me because I know
  how much you love recess."

Again, Manny might have something to say in response
to these statements. *Listening* to Manny's perspective would

cue Ms. Foster to any further blue belt moves she might need to make.

BLACK BELT MOVE

Even if Manny were unable to know or share his feelings, Ms. Foster could end the conversation with a *plan* that implied her tentative understanding of the situation and suggest a collaborative solution: "I'd like to check in with you at our next math activity so you can tell me where I've gotten confusing. Would you be willing to help me in that way?" Checking in with Manny and, by extension, with the entire class would be a black belt move that Ms. Foster could use in all of her lessons, not just math.

Time consuming and labor intensive as this emotion work might seem, it is quite possible that it would have transformed the school day. Manny's response to feeling understood and accepted could have made him buoyant. Ms. Foster's success at connecting with a recalcitrant little boy could have felt as renewing as a twenty-minute break. If there were a way to measure energetic output, this psychodynamic approach might register as *less* emotionally draining than the enactment was, and it might even take less time. Certainly the outcome would be much less disturbing for Manny and Ms. Foster: They would have shed their negative emotions and paved the way for more positive interactions rather than carrying grudges and distrust into the future.

There are many defenses against anxiety and other negative emotions; a partial list appears in the appendix. Manny and Ms. Foster demonstrated three very common defenses: projection, identification, and projective identification. The next several stories illustrate a few others.

OPPOSITIONAL TEACHING

Mr. Apkin, a teacher educator in a liberal arts college, was sitting in a small group of preservice teachers. He had broken his practicum seminar up into these small groups to give the students more time to talk to each other about their student teaching experiences. He happened to join a group that included Sean, an opinionated student who described his learning style as "oppositional." Mr. Apkin's approach to Sean tended to be tolerant even when the

64

student dominated large-group discussions, though he (and the other students in the seminar) found Sean's monopolization irritating and sometimes alarming.

In the small group Sean was talking about his experience in a public high school classroom when he addressed Mr. Apkin directly. "Where do you stand on private versus public schooling?" he asked solicitously. Mr. Apkin immediately launched into an answer to Sean's question. No sooner had he expressed an opinion than Sean opposed it. Mr. Apkin heatedly argued with Sean, continuing even when he perceived that the other students in the room had grown uncomfortable. When the time came to reconvene the larger class in the seminar room, Mr. Apkin was physically shaking with anger and frustration.

What was going on in this interaction? Where was the enactment? Where were the defenses?

The answers to these questions require further backstory. Though Mr. Apkin had no way of knowing it, Sean joined his small group feeling deeply insecure about his student teaching. His supervisor had been critical earlier that day, and Sean felt both ashamed and worried. The small group with Mr. Apkin was a perfect setting for payback: Sean could put an authority figure down and raise himself up simultaneously, thus quelling his conscious concerns about his supervisor's negative opinion of him (though not necessarily touching his unconscious concerns, which had to do with fundamental self-worth and ability).

Of course, as with most enactments, Sean was not consciously seeking revenge; he merely did what felt right to him. He undoubtedly found the question he put to Mr. Apkin interesting, but he got caught up in the enactment, which had less to do with questions and answers and more to do with Sean's need to manage his anxiety and negative self-perception. And it should be obvious that Sean was not alone in the enactment: Mr. Apkin played his part masterfully.

We now turn to the emotion work Mr. Apkin could do to gather the emotional and relational data he would need to understand the defenses both he and his student had activated.

Mr. Apkin's Emotion Work

Mr. Apkin's emotion work could take place in different stages. The first stage would be in the heat of the moment. When Mr. Apkin found himself arguing with Sean, he could have *described* it to himself ("Whoa! I'm feeling really angry! And Sean is being typically obnoxious right now") and *looked for good reasons* for it ("What's this anger about? What is Sean gaining by arguing with me about my own opinion? What am *I* gaining by arguing with *him*?").

An immediate response to Sean, based on these two steps, could have been some descriptive *self-disclosure*: "Hey, Sean, I get the feeling we're fighting, and I'm not comfortable with that. Let's call a truce right now and talk together later about this." Mr. Apkin might have to take some action to cool himself down, though, such as massaging his neck or taking deep breaths, both of which he could do in the classroom.

YELLOW BELT MOVES

Once the seminar was over, Mr. Apkin could undertake the second stage of his emotion work: focused introspection. What, he could wonder, did his uncontrollable anger tell him about himself? One message his anger might have carried was the feeling of being conned. Sean might have asked for his teacher's opinion, but he clearly had no intention of listening to it. Mr. Apkin felt shocked and enraged to have been so effectively set up. And underneath this rage was shame that he had been foolish enough to believe Sean's interest in him was genuine.

Mr. Apkin could also notice that his anger was a response to feeling dominated. Sean's refusal to accept his teacher's opinion felt to Mr. Apkin like stonewalling. Mr. Apkin realized his relentless arguing was an effort to knock down this wall to reestablish a stabilizing sense of connection with his student. But because every attempt Mr. Apkin made to assert himself and win Sean's acknowledgment was blocked, he felt rejected and demeaned.

As it happened, Mr. Apkin recognized these feelings. Having grown up with an intellectually dominating parent, he remembered the need to battle for the right to his own thoughts and ideas and for a sustaining connection that made him feel acknowledged and accepted. Feeling these emotions again — shock, rage, shame, disequilibrium, disconnection, rejection, worthlessness — was extremely difficult for him. But noticing and labeling the feelings helped Mr. Apkin to detach from them. Doing this emotion work also pointed to the necessity for self-care as he recovered from them.

Getting a sense of his own prongs and outlets gave Mr. Apkin a possible glimpse into the nature of Sean's. If Sean was able to plug into Mr. Apkin in such a way that Mr. Apkin's need to dominate flared, could it be that Sean, like his teacher, was accustomed to battling intellectual domination as well? Could Sean, by his opposition to domination, be unconsciously motivating the very response he hated?

And what about Sean's emotions? Mr. Apkin had already identified in himself many unbearable feelings; he knew how much discipline it had taken for him to stay with the feelings so he could describe them to himself. Clearly, Sean did not have that discipline. If Sean was feeling anything like what Mr. Apkin was, no one could blame him for acting out in defense against this intense internal discomfort. Mr. Apkin had, after all!

By practicing self-awareness Mr. Apkin was able to collect some useful information about his emotions, his own and Sean's preferred relational styles, and Sean's possible emotions. But what defenses were teacher and student acting out?

As with Manny and Ms. Foster, *projective identification* is a good possibility: Sean might have projected his sense of shame and insecurity from earlier in the day into Mr. Apkin, who was able to identify directly with the emotions. By arguing as though his life depended on it, Mr. Apkin was able to alleviate Sean's anxiety (by reinforcing Sean's shaky sense of superiority) and to vent his own.

Another defense, called *identification with the aggressor*, might also be present. When a person identifies with the aggressor, he takes on the abusive behaviors he himself has been a victim of. He plays rather than suffers from the abusive role. In this case, arguing with his teacher — dominating the way he had been dominated — could have defended Sean against being victimized intellectually (yet again) himself. The same could, of course, be said of Mr. Apkin.

Two other defenses appear to play a role in this story, *displacement* and *intellectualization*. *Displacement* allows a person to take out his feelings about one person on another who is less likely to retaliate. Since Sean felt anxious about his supervisor's evaluation of him earlier in the day, he might have (unconsciously) chosen to undermine Mr. Apkin's authority rather than his supervisor's. Even though Mr. Apkin was also in a position to evaluate Sean (evidence that defenses are not rational), he was, due to his own prongs and outlets, an apt receptor for Sean's displaced emotions.

Intellectualization happens when people pull into their heads, talking rather than feeling. Both Sean and Mr. Apkin resorted to intellectualization (a defense that is quite common in academic settings) when they quelled their emotions by engaging in an intellectual tussle with one other.

DEFENSES
Identification with the aggressor *is a defense.*
Displacement *is a defense.*
Intellectualization *is a defense.*
See the appendix for definitions and examples.

BLUE BELT MOVES

Given these possible good reasons for Sean's and his own behavior, Mr. Apkin could *plan* the talk he had promised to have with Sean about their enactment. He could lead with a *disclosure* about his own experience as a boy. "You know," he could say, "when I was growing up, I had to fight for the right to have my own ideas and opinions. I obviously still feel that way at times, and I apologize for putting you through my defensiveness."

He could then offer a *guess* about Sean's experience. "You put up a good fight, though! I wonder if you've had a similar experience to mine." Mr. Apkin could seek more information about Sean's classroom experience by asking him directly about it: "What is it like for you to be in seminar, listening to other people's opinions and ideas?" The point here would not be to judge, disagree, or punish but to *listen* carefully to gather more information about Sean, about his prongs and outlets.

Obviously, Mr. Apkin would be deluded if he hoped to control the conversation with Sean. He would have to enter the meeting with a genuine desire to both take responsibility for his part in the enactment and *listen* open-mindedly to Sean's perceptions. Even if he did not like what Sean said ("Yeah, Mr. Apkin, you sure went crazy! All I did was ask a simple question!"), Mr. Apkin could absorb that information ("Ah! Sean is well defended against taking responsibility for himself. He must be more insecure than I thought.") and use it compassionately in his future interactions with Sean.

BLACK BELT MOVE

Ultimately, Mr. Apkin could propose a *plan* based at least on his own self-knowledge. "Sean," he could say, "From now on I'm going to focus in class on listening carefully to everyone's ideas. And as an experiment, I'm going to limit my contributions to comments that either support those ideas or respectfully explore them further. To help me keep on track, I'm going to tell the students that this is my plan and invite them, including you, to enact the same plan themselves — and call me out if I stray from my intentions. If you're as similar to me in this respect as I think you are, then you might get called out by a classmate or two. So consider yourself forewarned!"

The preceding stories have illustrated the basic principles of dealing with pushed buttons, or enactments, in the classroom:

- The psychodynamic perspective looks for relational prongs and outlets and the good reasons for their fits.
- Emotion work, including *practicing awareness, describing, looking for good reasons, making guesses, self-disclosing, listening*, and *making a plan*, helps teachers understand enactments and effect corrective emotional experiences for their students.
- Practicing *self*-awareness is especially powerful because it provides teachers with data about themselves, their students' relational preferences, and their students' emotions.

69

- Enactments can reveal attachment styles and defenses, both of which are legitimate ways of managing difficult relationships and emotions.

The remaining stories apply these principles to a variety of situations that might be familiar to teachers.

Prejudice

Teachers' aversions can be conscious, as in Ms. McNamara's and Mr. Apkin's cases, or unconscious. Prejudices are often unconscious, and they come in many forms. Some teachers might feel repelled by overweight students; some might find children from wealthy families entitled and irritating; others might expect children who live in poverty to be less intelligent than other students; some might abhor any evidence of homosexuality. When prejudices threaten, defenses can take over. And the damage these enactments cause can be extreme.

NOT SO BLACK-AND-WHITE

Ms. Ellis taught high school English in an institution that was mostly white. This year several African-American students from a nearby school opted into Ms. Ellis's school, and some of these students were in her English class. Ms. Ellis, who abhorred racism but had never taught black students before, looked forward to the opportunity to help her new students learn.

One day Ms. Ellis broke the class into groups to work on a project, allowing the students to choose their own partners. She noticed that the black students chose each other.

During the group work Ms. Ellis circulated around the classroom, offering advice, checking on each group's progress, and redirecting attention when the students were off task. When Ms. Ellis came to the group of African-American students, she noticed that they were not doing their work. Rather, she told herself, they were "rapping" with each other. She broke their group up, putting each black student into an all-white group.

One of the black students, Tajheeka, objected strongly. "What are we doing that's so terrible?" she asked angrily. "Everyone in this room is talking, Ms. Ellis!"

"Yes, but not everyone is talking back," *Ms. Ellis responded sharply, and she sent Tajheeka to in-school suspension.*

[This story is inspired by J. E. Obidah & K. M. Teel (2001), *Because of the kids: Facing racial and cultural differences in schools*, New York: Teachers College Press.]

What was going on dynamically in this instance? An important answer involves issues of culture and race.

As a white American woman, Ms. Ellis grew up in a society that is structured to protect her white privilege. This structure, which places white people of all classes above people of all other colors, was absolutely invisible to Ms. Ellis. She had never considered that the privileges she took for granted were not shared by everyone.

In addition to being unaware of how her experience as a white woman differed from the experiences of people of color, Ms. Ellis had unconsciously absorbed attitudes and fears that permeate white America. As mentioned, she benefited from the privileges of being white —automatically being trusted by police officers, salespeople in stores, and mortgage providers, for example — and assumed all people enjoyed the same treatment. Through no direct fault of her own, she carried with her unconscious fears and assumptions: that people of color were criminals; that people of color were shifty and untrustworthy; that people of color were lazy.

Central to all racial stereotypes is a strict division between "us" and "them." The "projection of the not-me," as Toni Morrison puts it, provides comfort and alleviates anxiety by turning a person into an object, then foisting unwanted attitudes and fears on that person-turned-object. If I fear my own anger or lust, for example, I can manage that fear by projecting those traits onto others and reviling *them* instead of myself.

One problem with this move, of course, is that *I* am the angry or lustful one, not the person I am acting out on. Another problem is that, if I am in a position of power (which white people tend to be), the person-turned-object becomes extremely vulnerable to my oblivious abuse.

Creating "others" also, by definition, creates "insiders." Being "in" can make one feel special and safe, and it creates a

71

space in which unquestioned assumptions rule. If I am "in," people I define as "other" are "out." Surrounding myself in my "in" space with people who share the beliefs and assumptions I take for granted can relieve me of the difficult work of understanding people I consider different in one way or another.

Ms. Ellis's story demonstrates how a teacher can utilize *defenses* to manage feelings of anxiety stirred by the presence of "others." First, Ms. Ellis seems to have used *projection*: She projected her unconscious fears or stereotypes onto her black students, then interacted with those students as if the projections were true. Ms. Ellis's fear of "others" seems to have been activated when she saw the black students sitting together talking. Though all the other small groups were racially homogeneous, Ms. Ellis (completely unconsciously) apparently saw this one group as rebellious, conspiratorial, threatening. Rather than accept the black students' talking as a natural element of their work (as it apparently was in the other groups), she interpreted it as "rapping," which she (again, unconsciously) defined as disrespectful and undermining.

FOOD FOR THOUGHT
Language and discourse styles are extremely important cultural markers and are often the first elements of minority cultures that are attacked by members of dominant cultures. There are countless examples, among them the United States' English Only movement and apartheid South Africa's policy that forced black students to study in Afrikaans, the language of the minority white rulers.

The second defense she used, then, was *omnipotent control*; that is, she alleviated her anxiety by controlling the black students, putting them in groups of white students that she felt would foster their learning and stop any "rapping." To be fair, Ms. Ellis believed she knew what was best for her black students; she viewed her decision to break up their group as being instructionally necessary. She had no desire to hurt or insult her black students because she had no conscious awareness of the anxiety they stirred in her.

Yet more anxiety was activated in Ms. Ellis when Tajheeka "talked back." It appears that Ms. Ellis projected her unconscious stereotype of "angry black people" onto her student. Once again, Ms. Ellis protected herself by exerting omnipotent control and banishing the source of her discomfort by sending Tajheeka to in-school suspension.

DEFENSE
Omnipotent control *is a defense.*
See the appendix for a definition and examples.

Sitting together is developmentally appropriate for many students. Objecting to injustice is both appropriate and necessary. Ms. Ellis would probably agree with both of these statements in theory and might even have allowed her middle-class white students to get away with such behaviors. But in this story the black students seem to have collided with Ms. Ellis's stereotyped projections, her fear of the "not-me." They unwittingly triggered her anxiety and were controlled in ways that helped Ms. Ellis, not them.

This story, then, shows how racism, a deep manifestation of anxiety for many people, can result in defensive acts that alleviate that anxiety. From a psychodynamic perspective, these acts make complete sense. As attachment theory suggests, people construct themselves in response to the behaviors, emotions, and attitudes they grow up around. These molding influences come from family members and caregivers. They also come from social contexts: clubs, neighborhoods, schools, churches. And they come from media: television, video games, music, magazines. Culture, that intangible yet powerful shaper of human beings, definitely has an impact on psychic structure. Uncovering this impact by scrutinizing one's unconscious prejudices can be difficult, but the understanding it yields can make a big difference for students.

For acts based on prejudice do grave damage. What this story does not show is the contortions Ms. Ellis's African-American students had to make to accommodate her unintentional insults. Their choices were to comply with her commands and stuff their own sense of pride and personal rights or to internalize her unconscious beliefs about them. Absorbing their teacher's prejudices, also called "internalized racism," would mean swallowing her tacit messages about

73

their incompetence, their untrustworthiness, their threatening otherness. Neither option — denying one's rights or believing the worst about oneself — constitutes sound education.

Ms. Ellis's Emotion Work

So what could Ms. Ellis have done differently? In a nutshell, she could have *practiced awareness*, including making sense of the emotional and relational data self-awareness yielded; *described*; and *listened*.

YELLOW BELT MOVES

If Ms. Ellis needed a starting point, Tajheeka's spot-on objection to her teacher's treatment of the black students would have worked nicely. But Ms. Ellis might have noticed her differential treatment before Tajheeka had to point it out to her. "Wait a minute," Ms. Ellis could have told herself. "This group isn't doing anything differently from that other group, yet I'm tempted to break up the group of black students. What's that all about?" If she could access any of the feelings this group stirred in her, and if she was aware of the possibility that she was projecting these feelings onto her African-American students, Ms. Ellis would already be doing important antiracism work.

"When I look at this group of black students," Ms. Ellis could tell herself, "I'm assuming they're being lazy and trying to avoid doing any work. And it makes me mad that they think they can get away with it." Focusing on the students' language, Ms. Ellis might notice, "These students are enjoying themselves and talking to each other in a shorthand I don't completely understand. To be honest, that makes me nervous. And their way of talking makes me feel 'out' when I'm supposed to feel 'in'! I feel excluded and inadequate. It would be very easy to use my power to make *them* feel 'out' and reassert my 'in' status!"

Noticing these feelings and associating them with racism and expectations of racial privilege might well bring up powerful feelings of shame in Ms. Ellis. A natural response to such "white guilt" can be dismissal or minimization of the problem: "It's not that big a deal!" Another natural response can be overcompensation, bending over backwards to be especially nice, tolerant, and, ultimately, blameless. Guilt and shame are important responses to antiracism work and must be borne and worked through, preferably with supportive help.

But Ms. Ellis would have to put these emotions aside for the moment, for, important as they could be to her own development, they could tell her very little about her students. In fact, Ms. Ellis might realize that her projections actually blinded her to the classroom reality. Her next step, then, would be to gather more objective data about her students' experiences. That would require her to *describe* and *listen* with an open mind.

BLUE BELT MOVES

"I'm hearing lots of talk in this group," she could say to her African-American students, "but I don't know what it means. Are you making headway on the project? What are you finding easy? What are you finding difficult?" Checking in with students, black and white alike, and listening to their answers would give Ms. Ellis an essential reality check. Based on what she learned, she could take appropriate instructional steps, or if the students were doing fine, she could simply let them continue.

The emotion work Ms. Ellis could have done was qualitatively different from the emotion work done by the teachers in the other stories in this chapter. The difference is that her acting out began and ended with her. Initially, her prong fit into her black students' outlets by virtue of their skin color only, not due to any overt behaviors or attitudes on their parts. Tajheeka's resistance to Ms. Ellis, which was a legitimate reaction to Ms. Ellis's defensive behaviors and could have motivated Ms. Ellis to reflect on her actions, only provided more fodder for Ms. Ellis's projections. It would not have happened had Ms. Ellis quelled her impulse to exert control.

Of course, the African-American group's off-task behavior might have been an enactment, but Ms. Ellis could just as easily have taken offense at the talking being done by any of the all-white groups. Attending to the pervasive talking in her classroom would have been a good idea; attending to the *black* students' talking, because it was driven by anxiety, initiated Ms. Ellis's one-sided enactment.

Given her antipathy to racism, Ms. Ellis was a good candidate for antiracism emotion work. But as Jennifer Obidah and Karen Teel point out in their courageous and poignant book *Because of the Kids,* even the most fervently egalitarian white teachers can do great disservice to their students of color by

- failing to deeply question their own attitudes and beliefs about race and ethnicity (starting with their own identities); and
- failing to gather information from their students about the *students'* beliefs about their race and ethnicity (beliefs that are by no means universal or monolithic).

There is more, in other words, that Ms. Ellis could do.

BLACK BELT MOVES

In private Ms. Ellis could examine her own racial and ethnic identities. Who were her ancestors? What culture(s) influenced her family? With what group(s) did she identify? What did those cultures and groups mean to her? She could join or form a group devoted to antiracism or participate in diversity workshops or conferences. She could read about racism and racial identity development (an excellent starting place is Beverly Daniel Tatum's *Why Are All the Black Kids Sitting Together in the Cafeteria?*).

And she could get to know her students better. She could ask them about themselves, invite them to eat lunch with her, attend their extracurricular performances and games, and call home to share positive stories with their parents or guardians. A strong personal relationship with Tajheeka, for example, could have altered Ms. Ellis's perception of Tajheeka's "talking back." Rather than seeing her as defiant, Ms. Ellis could have listened to her student and responded more sensitively and effectively to her legitimate objections.

Any responsibility Ms. Ellis took for noticing her own racial experience and for educating herself about the different racial experiences of her students would at once improve her ability to serve her students and remove from them the burden of teaching her about white privilege. In truth, it is the responsibility of all teachers to educate themselves about

76

racism and its effects on white students and students of color alike.

Enactments among Adults

Students are not the only people teachers have enactments with. In fact, enactments and defenses are ubiquitous forces, at work in all relationships. They are definitely present in teachers' interactions with administrators, colleagues, and parents. The next three stories give examples of each.

FOOD FOR THOUGHT

If one is looking for enactments and defenses, the mother lode is where power differentials exist. Employees to bosses, students to teachers, student teachers to master teachers, teachers to principals — relationships that are reminiscent of the original parent-child bond are exquisitely suited to button-pushing.

TEACHER TANTRUM

Mr. Bloom directed a graduate business program whose burgeoning student enrollment demanded that he hire a new instructor. He chose a teacher, Ms. Wilcox, who had applied for his position many years before and had been turned down. The colleagues who had hired him recommended her as an excellent teacher even if they had deemed her unfit for the director position. Mr. Bloom was happy to welcome her to the program.

Soon after the fall semester began, Ms. Wilcox's behaviors became alarming. She started missing faculty meetings. She overlooked program rules, preferring to make and follow her own. When Mr. Bloom eventually began imposing consequences for her transgressions, she began blatantly courting the students' favor and bad-mouthing him. Mr. Bloom became aware of the students' increasing admiration of her and their waning respect for him and felt utterly impotent. How could he discipline Ms. Wilcox without lowering himself to her level? How could he protect himself from her without compromising, even destabilizing, his program?

Mr. Bloom's Emotion Work

It is one thing to find oneself caught up in an enactment with a student. Such enactments might at times feel permissible. But being persecuted by an adult colleague? Such an experience can be surprisingly disorienting.

YELLOW BELT MOVES

To gain perspective on this volatile and distressing situation, Mr. Bloom could start by *practicing self-awareness*. He would need to examine his own emotions to see what data they contained about himself, Ms. Wilcox, and the ways he and his employee were plugged into each other.

It was not difficult for Mr. Bloom to identify one emotion: shock. Ms. Wilcox had taken him completely by surprise. He had fully expected his new faculty member to follow the rules and share his goal of educating their students to the best of her ability. He was unprepared not just for her cruel treatment but also for his strong emotions. Confusion was one of these emotions, as was helplessness. But much to his chagrin the strongest by far was fear.

Why fear? When he thought about it, Mr. Bloom might admit that the feeling of being out of control at the mercy of someone he could neither trust nor understand was familiar to him, and it frightened him. He might be able to see, either on his own or with the help of a professional, that he was someone who avoided this kind of terrifying chaos by suppressing his own desires to satisfy others'. In this way, he could generally avert blowups and bring temporary peace to his world. The down side was that he was hard pressed as an adult to perceive his own needs or feelings when faced with conflict.

Pushing through to these feelings of confusion, helplessness, and fear would be a major accomplishment for Mr. Bloom. And identifying his coping pattern of erasing himself to appease others would be crucial. By *describing* to himself with some detachment what was happening between him and his employee, he could perhaps see the pattern at work with Ms. Wilcox:

As an adult who valued rules and parameters (as these helped to curb chaos), Mr. Bloom's eventual response to Ms. Wilcox's offenses was to alert her to the consequences of her actions. When she escalated rather than moderated her behavior, and the battle became personal, he felt overwhelmed. He automatically plugged into Ms. Wilcox the way he had plugged into previous troublemakers in his life. What had he done wrong? he wondered desperately. Perhaps he was asking too much of Ms. Wilcox. Perhaps he was being overbearing and unreasonable.

Stepping back from these automatic thoughts, Mr. Bloom noted that his response to the helplessness and fear he felt in the face of Ms. Wilcox's willful chaos was to doubt himself and his integrity and to look for ways to satisfy her. If he could only make her happy, the trouble would go away! But Ms. Wilcox was making it abundantly clear that there was nothing Mr. Bloom could do that would make her happy. In fact, it occurred to him, she was committed to being *un*happy.

This thought interested Mr. Bloom, as it suggested that his emotions might match Ms. Wilcox's. Could it be that she felt surprised, helpless, and fearful? How could that be?

Turning his attention to Ms. Wilcox's situation, Mr. Bloom remembered a significant fact: Ms. Wilcox had wanted Mr. Bloom's position a few years before. What might it be like for her to serve in a program she had wanted to direct? She must have felt shocked to be turned down, Mr. Bloom reasoned, and she probably felt helpless to get what she wanted. She undoubtedly wondered why she had been rejected and could not figure out what Mr. Bloom had that she did not.

In the absence of any satisfactory explanation, Ms. Wilcox, apparently, was doing the only thing she knew how to do to regain a positive sense of herself: She was trying to take away from Mr. Bloom what she herself could not possess. Unable to contain her terrible envy and anger (possibly because she could not recognize the personal limitations that might have made her a poor match for Mr. Bloom's job), she spewed her emotions on Mr. Bloom. Her prong, which looks like a combination of the defenses of *omnipotent control* and *regression*, fit perfectly into Mr. Bloom's outlet, which was his fear of conflict and need to appease.

Regression is the adoption of behaviors and attitudes that characterize a much earlier emotional and cognitive age. In Ms. Wilcox's case it was as if she had returned to the "terrible twos," when toddlers first learn the delights of "no" and tax their parents with their stubbornness. And like a two-year-old,

Ms. Wilcox evidently could not tolerate "no" from her parental figure, Mr. Bloom. When Mr. Bloom imposed limits on her behaviors, she escalated her opposition by turning the students in his program against him. The defense of *omnipotent control* is evident in Ms. Wilcox's extreme and blatantly irrational efforts to manipulate the program rules and students to thoroughly undermine Mr. Bloom's authority and take charge of the program herself.

Mr. Bloom was enacting his own defense, that of *reaction formation*. In reaction formation, a person unconsciously represses one response — say, rage — and enacts its exact opposite, in this case appeasement and caring tolerance. It is notable that Mr. Bloom could not immediately identify any feelings of rage when he practiced self-awareness. This makes sense, as it is the emotions one cannot bear to feel that activate defenses.

DEFENSE
Regression *is a defense.*
Reaction formation *is a defense.*
See the appendix for definitions and examples.

But Mr. Bloom could guess, based on his interpretation of Ms. Wilcox, who *was* enraged and was doing everything she could to convey her emotional state to Mr. Bloom, that he was in fact angry. This was a backhanded gift Mr. Bloom could take from the terrible enactment between him and Ms. Wilcox: Mr. Bloom could notice the absence of a very appropriate response to totally unacceptable behavior and keep an eye out for it in future interactions. As will be discussed in chapter three, anger is an extremely useful emotion that can be channeled for beneficial relational ends.

Mr. Bloom made some strong yellow belt moves here. He *described* to himself what seemed to be happening between him and Ms. Wilcox without judgment or blame. He *practiced self-awareness*, looking for emotional and relational data about himself and Ms. Wilcox, and made sense of these data by *looking for good reasons* for his own and Ms. Wilcox's behaviors. He was now ready to make some blue belt moves.

Once he realized that he was in an unsettling but classic power struggle with a very angry and envious two-year-old adult, he could have approached Ms. Wilcox with his *guesses* and *disclosures*. "Ms. Wilcox," he could have said, "I think I have done you a grave disservice. I have invited you to join a faculty you would much rather have directed. I have put you in the untenable position of having to teach through intense disappointment and anger. I interpret your insubordinate behavior so far this term as evidence of these feelings. Does any of this sound accurate to you?"

Ms. Wilcox's response would certainly be interesting, whichever way it went, and Mr. Bloom would do well to *listen* closely to her. But what would matter most for Mr. Bloom's purposes would be a firm *plan*. If he felt confident that Ms. Wilcox would reform her behaviors, he could put her on a very tight probational leash with clear consequences for the slightest transgression. If he felt or feared that she would not exhibit self-control for the remainder of the term, he could fire her on the spot.

The latter action would certainly cause inconvenience to him and the students. But it would be the type of limit Ms. Wilcox needed to help her learn to be a grown-up in the face of stress. Ultimately, it would be better for the program, as setting clear limits, despite the initial resistance, creates for everyone the kind of safe environment in which people can grow and develop.

Common as enactments might be in power relationships, they also happen between colleagues and even between friends.

TELLING THE (WRONG) TRUTH

Greer was a member of a school committee that had been meeting for several weeks. He and the three other colleagues on the team were good friends and were devoted to the committee's goals. At this particular meeting, though, Greer noticed that Samantha was rushing the team's process, as if her main concern was finishing the task quickly rather than making sure it was done well. Greer called Samantha on her behavior, asking that she allow the team members the time they required to express their thoughts on the task at hand.

Samantha did not take well to this confrontation, and she and Greer began to argue openly. One of their colleagues, Ben, withdrew into tense silence. The other, Tara, threatened to quit the committee if Greer and Samantha continued arguing. "How can you sit there and let our process be hijacked?" Greer asked angrily. "I don't let my students get away with shoddy work; I won't let us do it, either." When Samantha responded sarcastically, Greer stalked out of the room and didn't return. He spent the rest of that day feeling deeply shaken and alienated.

Greer's Emotion Work

The fact that he felt so terrible after this episode made it clear that Greer needed to do some emotion work, if only to help himself feel better. What could he have done?

YELLOW BELT MOVES

First, of course, he could have *practiced self-awareness* with the initial intention of administering some self-care. What, Greer could have asked himself, was he feeling?

He knew he felt angry that Samantha was rushing the committee's work. But why did he care so much? What did Samantha's apparent rushing mean to him? Upon reflection Greer might have decided it meant that the group work meant nothing to Samantha, that she was too good for it. *Describing* this interpretation to himself could have made Greer smile, for he had to know it was not true. Samantha was as committed to the group's work as he was.

So why did Greer interpret her attitude so uncharitably? Some backstory: Greer had personal feelings for Samantha. The truth was that he was secretly attracted to Samantha but had never dared to divulge his romantic interest for fear of being rejected. This fear translated, for him, into a feeling of insecurity around Samantha, a strong sense of inferiority to her. And if he was inferior, then she had to be superior, for, Greer realized, that is how he believed the world worked.

This realization might help Greer begin to uncover basic expectations he had developed as a child: that in times of duress people divided up into superior and inferior beings, and that he was always one of the inferior ones. He might recognize his urge to overturn the hierarchy by making himself superior and putting others in the inferior position; he had, in fact, done this many times in his life. Seeing this long-standing pattern in the interaction with Samantha was illuminating.

Greer might understand that by calling Samantha out he succeeded in accomplishing many unconscious goals: He popped what he perceived to be Samantha's bubble of superiority, which he had, by the way, *projected* onto her; he fought his belief that he was inadequate in Samantha's eyes by taking a leadership role in the group; and he allied with Ben and Tara, standing up for their rights in the face of Samantha's apparent contempt for their process.

When Ben and Tara failed to appreciate his gallant efforts on their behalf, and when Samantha responded to his truth telling with sarcasm, his momentary sense of superiority was destroyed, and anger took over. Swamped with the feelings of shame and inferiority he had felt so often in his life and unable to activate an effective defense against the feelings, Greer had no choice but to flee.

Acknowledging these possible *good reasons* for his own behavior, irrational and off base as that behavior might have been, could have served to relieve Greer of his debilitating shame. From the perspective of plugs and outlets, he could tell himself, he couldn't *help* behaving this way in the heat of the moment; he was structured to respond the way he did. His hope lay in noticing the pattern, understanding it, repairing any relational damage he may have inflicted, and practicing alternative responses in the future.

Forgiving himself for his automatic responses could have paved the way for Greer to wonder about Samantha's. Why was she behaving so uncharacteristically at this meeting? The best way to answer this question would be to ask her.

BLUE BELT MOVES

The blue belt moves Greer could make would fill in this gap in his understanding of the situation. They would also help Greer fix his relationship with Samantha. Approaching Samantha, he could first apologize for his extreme reactions, taking full ownership of them.

"I'm really sorry about the way I treated you and everyone else yesterday," he could have told Samantha. "I've figured out some stuff about myself that helps me understand how I can be so overbearing in situations like that." (Note that Greer would be under no obligation to reveal any details about what he had figured out.) "In thinking about my own behaviors, it occurred to me that your attitude in the meeting was totally uncharacteristic of you. Usually you're focused and thoughtful, but yesterday you seemed preoccupied and worried. I'm wondering if you're okay."

ATTENTION!

Emotion work can uncover some very interesting information about oneself. It can lead to better attuned and more constructive interactions with others. But it does not obligate a person to reveal private discoveries or insights. As with any self-disclosure, sharing personal information can be unfair, unnecessary, and unwise.

Given their friendship and the thoughtful way Greer took responsibility for his actions, Samantha might be tempted to speak honestly about herself. She might reveal, for example, that right before the committee meeting she had received some startling and concerning news. Perhaps the principal had mentioned to her that he needed to see her about a parent complaint but had neglected to tell her who the parents were and what the complaint was. Worrying about this news could have made it impossible for Samantha to focus on the committee work, especially if she was fighting the feeling that she was in big trouble. "I think I really overreacted to you," she might have told Greer.

This information would have fleshed out Greer's picture of the enactment he and Samantha had engaged in. He might recognize Samantha's reaction to him as an example of *displacement* (a defense we encountered in the story of Sean and Mr. Apkin earlier). Unable to discharge the anxiety her worrisome news activated, Samantha apparently took the opportunity Greer provided to act out her negative emotions on him. He plugged into her through *projection*; she completed the circuit by *displacing* her anxiety onto him and reinforcing his projection by treating him as if he were the cause of her worries. Two entirely different internal experiences converging in an enactment that both invited truth telling and obscured the truth simultaneously.

By doing effective emotion work, Greer could realize that the truth he thought he was telling at the committee meeting, that Samantha was rushing their process, was partial and amazingly superficial. Yes, Samantha was rushing. But she was also hurting. Digging down to the level of this deeper truth could have been remarkably relieving for both Samantha and Greer. And it could have transformed a destructive experience into a strengthening one.

FOOD FOR THOUGHT
It can be excruciating to say, "I'm sorry." A genuine apology seems to require a retreat to a position of pure vulnerability and total blame. And who wants to go there? But apologies can be made from a position of strength, where one takes full responsibility for one's own actions and leaves others to take responsibility for theirs. Saying, "I'm sorry for these things that I did" can both relieve tension and invite thoughtful contemplation of the enactment, which is almost always a two-way street.

A significant blue belt move Greer made, over and above his honest apology, was to feel genuinely curious about and open to Samantha's truth. Staying open to one's own and others' truths and thereby paving the way for compassionate empathy is what some call *joining*. Joining is one of the best ways to begin establishing the kind of trust that honest communication and strong relationships depend on. It is also an extremely useful approach for teachers, as the next story demonstrates.

DEFINITION
Joining *is a way of plugging in that requires moving one's perspective around so that one is looking at the world through someone else's eyes. It's like linking arms or looking over someone else's shoulder to better understand how they see things.*

THE CUSTOMER IS ALWAYS RIGHT

It was parent-teacher conference week, a week Ms. Sodolsky, a fifth-grade teacher, anticipated with mixed feelings. While she enjoyed meeting parents, she always went into these first conferences with the jitters. Would the parents like and accept her? Would they be bossy? Would they act as if they knew more than she did? These fears, usually unfounded, did not prepare her for her first encounter with Mr. White, Josh's dad.

Ms. Sodolsky had some bad news for Mr. White. Josh was a very active boy who had difficulty concentrating and obeying even the simplest directives. He wasn't doing well in school, and he wasn't completing his homework. When Ms. Sodolsky suggested she and Mr. White could work together to encourage Josh to be more disciplined, Mr. White refused.

"It's your job to teach Josh," he said stonily. "He's fine at home. It's your class he hates, so it's your class that must change." With increasing anger Mr. White listed for Ms. Sodolsky the many flaws of her school and her teaching. "Why can't you people do your jobs?" he shouted at last. "I'm sick of this place!" Ms. Sodolsky testily defended herself and her school but felt she was making no headway. By the time she showed Mr. White out, she felt so angry she could have cried.

[This story is inspired by Lasky, S. (2000). The cultural and emotional politics of teacher-parent interactions. *Teaching and Teacher Education, 16,* 843–860.]

Ms. Sodolsky's Emotion Work

Ms. Sodolsky suffered through this meeting, and her suffering continued afterwards. She surely did not deserve to feel so hurt! At the very least, she needed to take care of herself. Emotion work would have helped tremendously.

YELLOW BELT MOVES

How could emotion work have helped? First, and importantly, Ms. Sodolsky could have noted the intensity and inaccuracy of Mr. White's attack and concluded that an enactment was under way. His inappropriate responses, especially when directed at someone he had never met, were a sign that he was plugging in with prongs that he had used many times before and that had little to do with Ms. Sodolsky personally.

What could her own emotions tell her about Mr. White and his prongs? Using *self-awareness*, Ms. Sodolsky could easily identify anger and defensiveness. She might also realize that during their meeting she had had no idea what to do to reassure Mr. White or to de-escalate him; she had felt miserably helpless. Noticing these feelings, Ms. Sodolsky would do well to comfort and calm herself. The step of self-care would be crucial if she intended to join, even in retrospect, with a man who had upset her so thoroughly.

When she felt ready, Ms. Sodolsky could wonder about Mr. White: Might he share the distressing emotions she felt? If so, what might he have felt angry, defensive, and helpless about? If she could detach from Mr. White's harangue and think about what it had revealed to her, Ms. Sodolsky could guess that Mr. White had not enjoyed his years in school. Perhaps he, like his son, had had a difficult time concentrating and controlling his actions as a boy. Perhaps he had felt insecure about his ability to learn and avoided doing classwork and homework to preserve his dignity. Perhaps he had had parents at home who did not value school and teachers and therefore had not supported the young Mr. White in his struggles.

In short, Ms. Sodolsky could guess that Mr. White had spent quite a bit of time in school feeling angry, defensive, and helpless. And if he had been a "bad" student himself, what must it have been like for him to meet with yet another teacher in yet another school to hear criticism of his son?

Ms. Sodolsky might realize that this could be a case of *projective identification*, an enactment that involves the clear transmission of one person's anxiety into another. If her guesses were right, the anxiety was Mr. White's, and it stemmed from his own experiences as a youth in school. Ms. Sodolsky, being a teacher herself, simply revived these painful images. Because he was interacting with memories, Mr. White was unable to see or hear Ms. Sodolsky. He was blinded by the upsetting picture he was *projecting* onto her and hijacked by his strong negative emotions.

Unfortunately, Ms. Sodolsky could reason, Mr. White's low opinion of teachers and schools in general tapped right into her fears of being inadequate in the eyes of her students' parents. She immediately *identified* with Mr. White's anger and actually entertained his criticisms as possibilities because of her insecurity. Of course, once she identified with the anger she felt moved to express it, both for herself and for Mr. White. The deadlock they achieved together reinforced Mr. White's negative expectations of teachers, who, in his opinion, were unsympathetic and high and mighty, and left Ms. Sodolsky both furious and wholly responsible for a student whose problems suddenly looked worse than she had originally thought.

This would have been good emotion work. By *practicing self-awareness*, *describing* what she noticed about her feelings and about Mr. White, and *looking for good reasons* for what she observed, Ms. Sodolsky would have been able to *make a guess* about the enactment she and Mr. White had cocreated: that Mr. White was battling bad memories of and feelings about his own experiences as a student (and tapping into her insecurities). Her next step might be to *make a plan* to repair her relationship with Mr. White (and hence with his son) by meeting with him again, perhaps in a nonschool setting.

BLACK BELT MOVE

At this meeting Ms. Sodolsky could try to join with Mr. White by gently prodding at the heart of his emotion. "Mr. White," she could ask, "what was school like for *you*?" *Listening* calmly to his answer could teach Ms. Sodolsky a lot about the sources of Mr. White's anger while simultaneously helping him to relax in her presence, an experience he might recognize as unfamiliar yet pleasant. Keeping the criticisms from his own school days in mind, Ms. Sodolsky could describe for Mr. White how her classroom worked and how the strengths she perceived in Josh (strengths she might well have opened the original conference with) could best be augmented. In this way she and Mr. White could begin to banish distrust and fear and initiate a partnership that could greatly benefit Josh.

Actually accomplishing this joining would not necessarily be easy. Mr. White might continue to resist it. Ms.

Sodolsky might decide neither Mr. White nor Josh was worth the effort. It would be a lot easier for her simply to blame Mr. White for the impasse.

But *not* joining with Mr. White could be disastrous for Josh. Leaving the relationship alone might guarantee ongoing, possibly escalating enactments from Josh and even from Mr. White for the rest of the school year. And these enactments could prevent Josh and possibly his classmates from learning. The choice for Ms. Sodolsky, then, would be between the hard work of connecting with Mr. White and the hard work of surviving endless enactments in her classroom. The latter choice would mean stagnation and, most likely, failure to learn; the former, risky as it would be, could open up relational and educational possibilities that Ms. Sodolsky, Mr. White, and Josh could never have anticipated.

Joining with Mr. White would require self-restraint, understanding, compassion, courage, and dedication. For this reason the final step in Ms. Sodolsky's emotion work would qualify as a black belt move. It is one thing to join with a student; it is quite another to join with an adult who has the power to make a teacher's life very difficult. Reluctance to bridge the gap with Mr. White would be understandable, then; but refusing to attempt to repair the relationship at even the most basic level could be a mistake.

WRAP-UP

The above stories barely scratch the surface of the many ways psychic structures, prongs, and outlets, manifest in classrooms. Indeed, the interactional variations are mind-boggling. Salzberger-Wittenberg et al. catalog just a few of the reactions teachers can have to their students' perfectly understandable attempts to foist the "mental pain" of learning onto their teachers; that is, to enact defenses that alleviate unbearable emotions:

> If [the teacher] is receptive to this [foisting] he becomes the one who feels inadequate, frightened, stupid, helpless, confused, and he in turn may try to escape from this in a number of ways. He may meet fear of his ignorance about the world by a dazzling display of theoretical knowledge, fear of impotence by exerting

power, fear of chaos by a rigid approach to his subject and a rigid control of his pupils, fear of inadequacy and humiliation by claiming superiority and making his students feel small. A vicious circle may be set up in which the teacher reacts to the powerful emotions evoked in him by helping the student to evade inevitable stress or forcing the anxiety back into him. These *are* quick solutions to the problem of mental pain, but in as far as they avoid the inevitable anxieties connected with learning, such a teacher is in fact discouraging the development of a capacity to think. (pp. 57–58)

It is important, then, for teachers to examine their buttons and their button pushers — to investigate their reactions to irritating students and colleagues; their surprising interactions; their prongs, their outlets; their feelings of anxiety, insecurity, and anger; their "mental pain." In other words, they must engage in emotion work: practicing self-awareness, describing, looking for good reasons, making guesses, self-disclosing, listening, and making plans. In doing so they gain perspective on their own and their students' mental pain, the "inevitable anxieties connected with learning," and they have an opportunity to help transform that pain into "a capacity to think" — which is, after all, their job.

CHAPTER ANSWERS

We can now attempt answers to the questions at the beginning of this chapter:

- *What is "a button"?*
- *Where are these buttons located?*
- *Why is one behavior or experience a button for one person and not for another?*

A button is a portal in one's psychic structure, an outlet into which other people can plug to trigger familiar emotions and behaviors. Buttons are located in our fibers, our bones and nerve endings, and the evidence of their existence resides in our enactments. Because our psychic structures are unique, the portals, or outlets, or buttons that we make available in our interactions and the prongs, or button pushers, that we fit with differ from person to person. So one person's button-pushing

90

behavior, while it might enrage me, would not even register on someone else. Through attachment styles and defenses, people plug, or lock, or fit into each other — push each other's buttons — and in the process give each other vital information about themselves, their needs, their fears and doubts, and, for teachers, the paths of their students' learning.

KEEP IN MIND

- *People have **psychic structures** that determine how they plug into others.*
- *When people plug into each other in troublesome ways, they are engaging in negative **enactments** that can cause a lot of suffering.*
- *The **psychodynamic perspective** seeks to understand enactments to effect beneficial change.*
- ***Emotion work** is the steps people can take to understand and influence enactments.*
- *Emotion work consists of **practicing awareness** (of self and others); **describing**; **looking for good reasons**; **making guesses**; **self-disclosing**; **listening**; and **making a plan**. Chapter five contains further discussion of these skills as well as ways to practice them.*
- ***Practicing self-awareness**, a subset of practicing awareness, reveals valuable **emotional and relational data**: information about the self, information about others' relational patterns, and information about others' emotions.*
- ***Defenses** are a type of enactment that protects people from strong emotions that are too difficult to feel consciously (see the appendix for a partial list of defenses).*
- *There is a **glossary of terms** at the end of the book.*

91

CHAPTER TWO

INSULTS AND COMPLIMENTS: TEACHERS AS DEVELOPMENTAL PARTNERS

"You're a bad teacher."

"You're stupid."

"I hate you."

"You don't know what you're doing."

Teachers can receive messages of this sort, sometimes out loud, sometimes silently, from students, parents, colleagues, and administrators. While the impact of such statements can be painful and deeply demoralizing, the advice teachers often get when they are smarting is, "Don't take it personally."

Really?

Don't take it personally? How is it possible not to take such hurtful comments personally?

Amazingly enough, it *is* possible. Even essential. But as this chapter reveals, not taking cruel comments and actions personally can require effort. Figuring out how to handle insults can be difficult but extremely valuable in defusing and even transforming the occasional psychic bombs dropped in school.

And how about these?

"You're the best teacher I've ever had."

"I really want to know what *you* think."

"I want to be you!"

Unlike insults, compliments are friendly and positive. They are honest expressions of how students feel about their teachers. And unlike insults, compliments should be taken personally, as they are sometimes the only reward teachers get for doing such a difficult job. Right?

Wrong. While compliments are sweet gifts that can warm teachers' hearts, taking them personally can be perilous. Yes, they often convey students' perceptions of their teachers. And these perceptions are important and informative. But compliments do not necessarily capture the truth about a teacher. After all, how well do students know their teachers?

Rather, compliments can indicate developmental truths about the *student*. Accepting compliments as enthusiastic offerings is, of course, fine and can make a teacher feel good. But plumbing compliments for what they indicate about students' developmental needs and desires can be invaluable

The trick to not taking hurts, insults, and even compliments personally is in understanding the developmental role teachers can and must play in their students' lives. Whether they like it or not, teachers (and parents) are routinely used by students as *objects* for a variety of purposes. Some of these purposes are dastardly, as when a student treats a teacher with contempt; others are developmentally necessary, as when a student looks up to a teacher. All of the purposes originate in "good" reasons. The bottom line is that teachers are *developmental partners* to their students: objects for their students' *use* along the road to growth and learning.

In this chapter we will consider some object roles teachers routinely play for students. Specifically, we will explore the importance for students of *twinship, idealization,* and *mirroring*. We will look at how *taking it personally* can lead to *reversed roles* that hinder rather than promote healthy development. And we will emphasize the importance of detaching as a means of *not taking it personally* and paving the way to healthy development and learning.

CHAPTER QUESTIONS
- *How is it possible not to take insults or compliments personally?*
- *Why is it important not to take them personally?*

BEING USED
Generally speaking, people don't like "being used." When a friend borrows money and never repays it, I can feel "used." When I meet someone at a party and spend the next half hour listening to him talk about himself, I can feel "used." When I have made dinner for my family, set and cleared the table, and washed all the dishes myself, I can feel "used." These experiences and others like them can be unpleasant. While I might not be conscious or determined enough to avoid them, I

can certainly complain about them. I seem to believe, first, that such experiences should not happen to me and, second, that they are always someone else's fault.

But the truth is that people use each other all the time. The very nature of fitting together, of plugging into each other, means that I am just as active in being used as others are in using me. I may not be conscious of the purposes my actions accomplish for me. I may only be conscious of what others are getting out of me and the negative emotions I feel about that. But I am active in every interaction, even those in which I am utterly passive, for doing nothing counts as a meaningful move in relationships and interactions.

And having emotions counts. It is interesting to note that in all of the examples above being used can accomplish some valuable, "positive" emotional purposes:

- I might enjoy feeling generous and indispensable to my friend when I lend her money. I might also relish, perhaps unconsciously, the belief that I am morally superior to her when she fails to pay me back. Her use of me, then, can feed a positive self-image that I want to maintain because it accomplishes my purpose of feeling good about myself.

- If I expect to be invisible at parties, to be left standing in a corner by myself, I might welcome and even attract people who need to talk nonstop, as if at a wall. The feeling of being needed and occupied could be a great relief. And the sense that I am invisible might also comfort me, as it would confirm a basic belief about myself that previous experiences at parties has helped to shape. Like many relational patterns, this one might be unflattering, but at least it would be familiar.

- Being hyperresponsible and supercompetent is a reward in itself. Unfortunately, earning that reward requires others to be *ir*responsible and *in*competent. Once again, by doing everyone's work, I can feel superior to them, a feeling that my simmering resentment reinforces.

In these scenarios I am certainly being used by others for their purposes. But I am also using them for mine. Some of these purposes are noble; others are undermining. Often they are unconscious, and they are fundamentally emotional. But they are always present, the underlying "good" reasons for why I do what I do.

So the bad news about being used is that I am always complicit, whether I am conscious of it or not. I might want to believe that I am at my family's mercy, that they can "make" me do and feel things, but the truth is that they cannot. I am, in fact, in charge of my own actions and responsible for managing my own emotions. So while I might blame my family for letting me do all the work at dinner, I am the only one I can legitimately blame for, well, doing all the work at dinner. And I can wonder how I am benefiting from taking all this work on.

Whether and How

The good news is that I can make conscious choices about *whether* and *how* I am used. The next time I find myself cornered at a party, I can excuse myself with "So sorry — I've got to go check in with a friend." Or after listening to my conversational partner for 15 minutes, I can ask him to go grab me another Fresca. By making choices about *whether* to be used — "No, thanks" — or *how* to be used — "Sure, I'll do this for you, but you need to do something for me" — I reduce the probability of feeling resentful or shamed. I am also managing reality; that is, I am embracing the fact that people use and are used but that I do not need to be a victim if I do not want to.

There is real danger, though, in deciding whether or how to be used. Standing up for oneself, as those in subordinate positions know all too well, can activate the wrath and violence of those in power. Children, people of color, women, people who are attracted to members of the same sex, members of certain religions, and others who are "different" and disempowered have historically suffered extreme consequences for "being uppity." The choice to resist being used can feel, in these cases, like no choice at all.

Even when the stakes are not life threatening, there is often little incentive to rock the boat. Telling my broke friend a firm "no" could trigger extremely uncomfortable responses: wheedling, the silent treatment, wrath, slander, violence, abandonment. It is not difficult to understand why many people consent to be used rather than face the unpredictable, possibly hurtful, sometimes dangerous consequences of refusing.

Another way of putting this is that it can be easier to "take it personally" (to collaborate with and perpetuate others' use of you) than to "not take it personally" (to decide *whether* and *how* to be used). Taking it personally can result in perpetual repeats of the same galling situation or in impulsive, emotional action that temporarily relieves one person while hurting and confusing others. *Not* taking it personally means detaching, seeing the situation for what it is — an instance of using and being used, pure and simple — and deciding what to do about it.

Let's see what taking it personally might look like in a classroom.

INSULTING INTELLIGENCE

Mr. Greene, a high school French teacher, was explaining to his students some nuances in the use of verb tenses. This was a third-year French course in which Mr. Greene began moving his students toward fluency. Often, Mr. Greene spoke in French, but he allowed his students to use English.

Hiram, an earnest, hardworking student, stopped Mr. Greene in midexplanation. "That's just not right," Hiram said in English. "You're not making any sense."

The truth is Hiram did this a lot: He often questioned Mr. Greene's teaching. And it always enraged Mr. Greene. How dare this student challenge him? How dare he imply Mr. Greene did not know what he was talking about? Why would Hiram repeatedly do such a thing to his teacher?

As always happened, Mr. Greene gave in to his outrage. "Let's see," Mr. Greene said to Hiram. "Who knows how to speak French here? You? Or me? I suggest you spend more time listening to the expert, Hiram, than questioning him."

What is going on here? How did Mr. Greene take Hiram personally?

Simply put, Mr. Greene took Hiram personally when he perceived Hiram's proclamations as attacks on Mr. Greene's intelligence and expertise. He took his student personally when he assumed that Hiram's problem was with *Mr. Greene* rather than with *Hiram*.

So what? So Mr. Greene took Hiram's comment personally. Why shouldn't he? After all, Hiram was being demeaning.

There are at least three reasons Mr. Greene should not have taken Hiram personally. One is that a natural consequence of taking anything personally is the desire to get revenge, to punish. Mr. Greene did take satisfying revenge on Hiram by asserting, snidely and condescendingly, that there was a hierarchy in the classroom where Mr. Greene was on top and Hiram was on the bottom. Putting Hiram in his place in this way could not possibly promote a positive attitude toward learning French in Hiram or in his classmates.

The second reason, related to the first, is that by taking Hiram personally Mr. Greene condemned himself and Hiram to repeating this same type of interaction forever. The two have established a pattern: Hiram criticizes his teacher; Mr. Greene gets mad; Mr. Greene punishes Hiram; Hiram feels confused and hurt; Hiram criticizes and begins the cycle all over again. Clearly, his teacher's sarcasm does not deter Hiram. In fact, there might be something familiar and therefore comfortable for Hiram in these interactions, as tends to be the case with enactments. The fact that this pattern repeats itself implies that Hiram and Mr. Greene are using each other, plugging into each other, for the emotional purpose of venting emotions. But no desirable academic learning is taking place.

A third reason Mr. Greene should not have taken Hiram personally is that he missed crucial information about Hiram and his relationship to learning French. Admittedly, Hiram did a good job of masking this relationship by focusing Mr. Greene's attention on Mr. Greene. As we saw repeatedly in chapter one, such masterful redirection is a primary purpose of button-pushing enactments. "Don't look at *me*," button pushers seem to be saying. "This is all *your* fault!"

But believing that Hiram's difficulty was all his teacher's fault was a mistake. What could Mr. Greene have done differently here? How could he *not* take his student personally? What would he have gained by not taking Hiram personally?

Mr. Greene's Emotion Work

Resisting the automatic urge to take students' insults personally requires discipline and attention. In short, it requires emotion work.

YELLOW BELT MOVES

A useful first step in the maddening moment with Hiram would have been to *detach*. As defined in the previous chapter, *detachment* means stepping back, noticing and describing what one observes, and thinking about it. Detaching in this way allows for continued connection *and* rational assessment and is crucial to not taking students personally.

It bears repeating that detaching does not mean disconnecting. It means *unplugging*, or resisting the impulse to engage in an enactment while remaining curious and attentive to the information offered by one's emotions and students' behaviors. This is an extremely valuable stance, one that is essential to rigorous emotion work.

For Mr. Greene detaching from Hiram's accusation would have given the teacher time to decide *whether* to be used by Hiram: Should he engage with Hiram or ignore him and move on? If he chose to engage, detaching would have helped Mr. Greene think about *how* to be used. And it would have given Mr. Greene time to decide what *not* to do: retaliate.

A useful second step would have been to make time to reflect on this classroom moment later. Exercising *self-awareness* might help Mr. Greene identify the interaction as an enactment. If Mr. Greene had noticed his sudden and extreme emotional reaction to Hiram's button pushing, he could have suspected there was something going on with Hiram beyond a simple, judgmental accusation. He could then search within the enactment for

- information about himself;
- information about Hiram's emotions;
- information about Hiram's preferred relational styles.

Information about himself. Hiram accused Mr. Greene of not making sense when he was explaining French verb

99

tenses. Could there have been any truth to this assertion? Honestly contemplating this possibility would not need to feel insulting to Mr. Greene. Rather, discovering where he might have been confusing could only make Mr. Greene a better teacher. He could return to class the next day and, after acknowledging the accuracy of Hiram's complaint, he could revise his explanation to better reach not just Hiram but his less bold classmates as well.

In addition to contemplating the content of Hiram's accusation, Mr. Greene could benefit from examining his own emotional responses to it: rage and insecurity. Reliving the moment could easily bring up Mr. Greene's outrage that a mere student would question his intelligence and challenge his expertise in French. In attempting to glean information about himself, Mr. Greene would have to explore this strong sense of offense and his belief that his student was undermining him. Could it be that Mr. Greene feared he wasn't qualified enough? Did he find Hiram (or other students) intellectually intimidating? If his honest answer to either or both of these questions was yes, Mr. Greene could then address his need to bolster his qualifications or to manage his sense of inferiority in the classroom, both worthwhile issues to examine.

If, on the other hand, Mr. Greene determined that his credentials did not need beefing up and that his students were far from intimidating, he could consider the possibility that Hiram's accusation was inaccurate — further evidence of an enactment. For example, Mr. Greene could remind himself that he was fluent in French, had spent many years living in and visiting French-speaking countries, and had been teaching to great acclaim for over a decade. He clearly knew his stuff. With this confirmation of his competence, Mr. Greene could entertain the possibility that the insecurity and anger he felt told him less about himself and more about Hiram.

Information about Hiram's emotions. Having guessed that he and Hiram had been locked in an enactment, Mr. Greene could assume that Hiram had *projected* his negative emotions into his teacher as a means of avoiding them. And given how strong the emotions were in Mr. Greene, he could understand how Hiram might want to escape them.

But why might Hiram feel angry and insecure? He was a good student who was dedicated to learning French. And despite his tendency to oppose Mr. Greene's teaching, he was a nice young man. Clearly, Mr. Greene had to *look for the good reasons* for Hiram's surprising emotions.

Much of the time Hiram worked hard and responded positively to classroom exercises and assignments. When Mr. Greene thought about these exercises and assignments, though, he might note an interesting pattern: Hiram seemed most comfortable when he was applying hard-and-fast rules to the French language. He became oppositional — that is, he challenged and questioned in a demeaning way — when rules "changed" or didn't apply consistently.

Could Mr. Greene's anger, his fear that he wasn't perceived as knowing his subject matter, mirror Hiram's anger and fear at not knowing how to manage shifting and inconsistent rules? Could it be that, as soon as Mr. Greene entered the messy realm of *using* language, not just mechanically following rules, Hiram rebelled because he had no idea how to function in this realm? This possibility made sense to Mr. Greene, as Hiram did appear to be rigidly rule oriented and extremely uncomfortable with having to feel his way around in French. It would follow that if Hiram were more left brained than right brained the messy realm of language use would cause him anxiety and concern.

Information about Hiram's relational styles. By making this *guess* about Hiram, Mr. Greene would have identified a possible relational style that Hiram enacted not just with people but with ideas, activities, and subject matter when he was feeling stressed. That is, the way Hiram related to information or activities that felt impossible to him seemed to be to reject them and to escape his negative feelings by *projecting* them into someone else. When Mr. Greene *identified* with Hiram's feelings — that is, when Mr. Greene took Hiram's feelings personally — he helped Hiram avoid academic growth by focusing on the decoy (the perceived insult) rather than the true underlying need for guidance through a zone of discomfort.

Obviously, this enactment can be seen as an example of *projective identification*, a very common and effective defense introduced in chapter one (and defined in the appendix). In the language of this chapter, Hiram seems to have been *using* Mr. Greene as an outlet for his own unbearable emotions. He was *using* Mr. Greene as an *emotional object*, an object to act out on for the purpose of emotional relief.

ATTENTION!
People can be turned into objects for other people's use. Objectification often signals that a defense is at work. For example, projection turns a person into a **screen** *for emotions to be displayed upon or a* **jar** *for emotions to be contained in. Identifying with the aggressor turns a person into a* **punching bag***. The defense of omnipotent control turns people into* **pawns***. At the same time that objectifying others can be relieving for the one who uses, it can be irritating and even frightening or dangerous for the one who is used.*

So what could Mr. Greene have done differently? Based on his *emotion work*, Mr. Greene could recognize the valuable role Hiram was insisting his teacher play. By engaging Mr. Greene in a defensive enactment, Hiram was handing his teacher accurate (if cloaked) information about where he was stuck and what he needed from Mr. Greene to get unstuck. Counterintuitive as it may sound, Mr. Greene could have silently (if reluctantly) thanked Hiram for this information and the opportunity to fine-tune his teaching.

BLUE BELT MOVE
An immediate response to Hiram could have been to *join with* him, to swing around and look at the French lesson through Hiram's eyes. To do this, as has been mentioned, Mr. Greene would have had to detach, or resist his automatic impulse to take Hiram personally. He would have had to feel genuine curiosity about Hiram's experience, and he would have had to believe he could help Hiram learn in spite of — or, more accurately, because of — his resistance. As illustrated in chapter one, *joining with* a perceived opponent can instantaneously melt even the most hostile enactment.

How might Mr. Greene have joined with Hiram? When Hiram declared that Mr. Greene's explanation didn't make sense, Mr. Greene could have asked Hiram for more information. "Here's an important complaint," he might have said. "Tell me more so I can better understand what doesn't make sense to you." Affirming Hiram's confusion would validate for all students their right to struggle in French class; asking Hiram to *describe* his difficulty would have encouraged Hiram to take some responsibility for his experience rather than blaming Mr. Greene for it. His description would also have suggested where Mr. Greene could offer clarification.

In the longer run Mr. Greene could have figured out a way to teach differently to be able to reach Hiram and others like him. A good place to start would have been, once again, with Hiram himself. Having made a good *guess* about the source of Hiram's resistance to the lesson on exceptions to verb rules, Mr. Greene could test out his hypothesis by having a talk with his student.

He could start with *self-disclosure*: "I must admit that the biggest obstacle I had to overcome in learning to speak French was my fear of making mistakes," he could tell Hiram. "I was supergood at doing written exercises and passing French tests, but I got all jumbled up when it came to speaking or writing. I've since learned that this is common for many second-language learners. I'm guessing it's true for you, too."

Listening to Hiram's response could give Mr. Greene a good sense of how he could tweak his lesson plans to better meet Hiram's needs. And let's face it, better meeting Hiram's needs would benefit other students who were perhaps not as brave about voicing their own confusion. Overall, allying with Hiram in a *plan* to work on writing and speaking well could help both teacher and student plug into each other differently to effect linguistic change.

BLACK BELT MOVES

One important outcome of Mr. Greene's emotion work and his talk with Hiram might be the recognition that Mr. Greene's teaching was talk-based rather than activity- or performance-based, more "head centered" (left brained) than "body centered" (right brained). Until now Hiram had flourished in the talk-based, "head-centered" curriculum, where rules could be discussed and applied, where cognition and information reigned. The next step for Hiram and Mr. Greene could be toward activities — skits, student-made videos, in-class improvisations and discussions — that would require spontaneous collaboration between the mind and body. Mr. Greene's goal, in other words, could become to design instruction that would support Hiram and his classmates in using the language and navigating through French-speaking cultures by "feel," not by rules.

A very basic change Mr. Greene could make in his teaching toward this end would be to conduct the course completely in French, no English allowed. Such a shift could raise some insistent feelings in Mr. Greene: *doubt* about whether his students could do it, *fear* that they would rebel, *anxiety* about the amount of work he would have to do, and so on. Such responses could benefit from more emotion work so Mr. Greene could commit wholly to whatever plan he made.

Such a major curricular shift would also bring up emotions in Hiram and his classmates. Insisting that students speak solely in French would throw Hiram straight into his discomfort zone: out of abstract rules and into the actual everyday use of a foreign language. Because such a detour would undoubtedly generate intense anxiety in Hiram, Mr. Greene would have to *plan* ways to support Hiram and his classmates in making mistakes, overcoming self-consciousness, embodying authority, taking risks, playing and having fun with language. Taking this crucial step into performance-based language instruction could be one of the best things that ever happened to Mr. Greene's teaching — and he would have Hiram's "insult" to thank for it.

Emotional and Developmental Objects
The story of Hiram and Mr. Greene illustrates how a student can use a teacher as an *emotional object*, a partner in an emotionally relieving enactment. But it also shows how students can use their teachers as *developmental objects*, or partners in the crucial process of development, of growing and learning and changing. Being the objects of all this use can be extremely irritating; *not* taking students' use personally can demand great tolerance and self-discipline.

DEFINITIONS
*An **emotional object** is someone who is used, or acted out on, for emotional relief.*

*A **developmental object** is someone who is used for another's emotional and cognitive growth and development.*

So being used can be maddening. But it is not necessarily a bad thing. Fitting together with someone in a mutually beneficial way is both normal and desirable. What is *not* desirable is to collaborate in usurious interactions (interactions with excessive costs) unintentionally or helplessly. Here is where learning how to make conscious decisions about *whether* and *how* to be used is essential.

For the truth about being used is *not* that it should never happen in the classroom. On the contrary, being used as an emotional object or as a developmental object can lead to immense discovery and growth. Because teachers are developmental partners for their students, they are, at bottom, objects for those students' use. Teachers *must* be used for their students' growth and development. Teachers *must* decide whether and how best to be used. And they *must* resist taking this use personally.

KEEP IN MIND
Teachers are **developmental partners** *to their students. Therefore, students must be able to use their teachers for emotional and cognitive growth.*

FOOD FOR THOUGHT
You know the classic story of the student who is shocked when he sees his teacher in the grocery store? The possibility that a teacher has a life outside the classroom can seem outlandish! This disorientation makes sense if you as a student see your teacher as an **object** *for your classroom use. Objects have no life; they sit quietly on a shelf when not in use; they have no needs or desires of their own. Who, after all, wouldn't be perplexed to see a stepladder pushing a grocery cart around a store?*

For teachers are stepladders. They are the furniture students pull themselves up on emotionally and cognitively so they can walk with strength, intelligence, and confidence. The assumption that teachers are objects might feel fundamentally insulting. But most teachers laugh when they see the looks on their students' faces in the pasta aisle. This laugh embraces the truth: that students need to see their teachers as somehow inert and all-powerful, as impossibly nonhuman, so they can use

105

these important adults in the ways their own growth requires. The trick for teachers is in playing this necessary object role with wisdom, firmness, and compassion for their students and for themselves.

TEACHERS AS DEVELOPMENTAL PARTNERS

Chapter one shows how students and teachers can use each other as emotional and relational objects through enactments. Any time one person plugs into another, using begins. Although people are always plugging into each other, it is the negative experiences that tend to draw attention. A valuable response to enactments is to reflect on how one is using others for one's own purposes (information about oneself); how others are using objects for their purposes (information about others and their preferred relational styles); and on *whether* and *how* one will participate in being used (what one can do differently).

This chapter takes the concept of plugging in, or using and being used, into the realm of emotional and cognitive growth and development, which is the realm that teachers and students occupy every day. Our discussion draws on the ideas of Heinz Kohut, a psychoanalyst who founded the field of self psychology.

Put simply, Kohut's claims were that people develop, or grow and become themselves, by using others as objects whose qualities are gradually internalized. It is this process of internalization that gives birth to and sustains the unique, individualized self. Kohut claimed that to develop healthily children (and adults) need to *use* other people as *developmental objects* in at least three different ways. They need to seek *twinship* with other people; they need to *idealize* other people; and they need to be *mirrored* by other people.

People seek twinship with others. It is very important, developmentally, for children (and adults) to find "kindred spirits" who remind them of themselves, who dispel the uncomfortable feeling that they are alone and irreconcilably different from everyone else. When a *twin* is around, even the most uncomfortable situations can feel safe.

People need to idealize others. It is also important for people to find others whom they consider to be models, whose qualities they seek to share or develop within themselves.

People who are idealized are routinely referred to as being "on a pedestal," a phrase that captures the object role they play: that of an admired *statue*.

 People need to be mirrored by others. People need accurate reflections of who they are; they need *mirrors*. This need stems, according to Kohut, from children's natural grandiosity and the value of being seen and admired. However, mirroring is not mere praise; it is description that rings true and therefore can be used to reinforce the self.

KEEP IN MIND
For the sake of growth and development, students often use teachers as kindred spirits, or **twins***; as admired models, or* **statues***; and as accurate reflectors of who the students are, or* **mirrors***. All these uses require teachers to play important roles for students, roles that demand deliberate monitoring by the teacher.*

 Because they are developmental partners, teachers need at times to be used by students as *twins*, as *statues on a pedestal*, and as *mirrors*. The following four stories illustrate each type of use by students, but with a twist: The stories also show what can happen if teachers *reverse roles* and take their students' use personally.

Twinship
The following story shows what twinship can look like in a classroom.

"I THOUGHT YOU WERE MY FRIEND"
Geoffrey was a third-year doctoral student in philosophy. His advisor had invited him to assist in teaching a survey course on the Western intellectual tradition. Although Geoffrey had never received any training in teaching, he needed the stipend, so he accepted.

 Geoffrey's responsibilities included attending lectures conducted by his advisor, meeting weekly with his advisor to discuss how the course was going, reading and commenting on student papers, and running a small tutorial of students from the lecture class. He had to admit he did not particularly enjoy the first three duties. The lectures and meetings with his advisor were boring, and Geoffrey shrank from having to make harsh comments on students' papers.

What he really liked was teaching. He and his ten tutorial students had a blast in class, quickly covering the required material in intellectual history and inevitably veering off into topics of more personal interest. Even better, his students invited him every Thursday night to the local pub's Happy Hour. Geoffrey congratulated himself on being such a good teacher. His students clearly loved him.

In the middle of the semester, Geoffrey graded his students' mid-term exams. He was shocked to discover that one of his favorite students, Cal, had earned a D. He was even more shocked when Cal stormed into his office after having received his grade and yelled, "Hey! I thought you were my friend!" To appease his buddy Geoffrey changed the grade to a B+. Cal slapped him on the back and offered to buy him a beer.

Students who view their teachers as "friends," as people who can relate to them, to their strengths and struggles, have found valuable twins. Students can benefit from easy familiarity with teachers who lead them into, and safely through, difficult intellectual territory.

But this story also illustrates how perilous twinship can be. True, the roles Geoffrey played in this situation were potentially powerful. As a student himself, Geoffrey was undergoing his own developmental process. He knew firsthand how risky and stressful learning can be. And he knew what kinds of behaviors and attitudes from his teachers and mentors best facilitated his own growth. As a teaching assistant, Geoffrey became one of these mentors. He could be available to his own students in a particularly empathic way, drawing on his concurrent experience as a learner. Given these two roles, Geoffrey was positioned to be a very effective twin and teacher.

The problem with Geoffrey, it appears, was that he did not distinguish between his role as student and his role as TA. He did not view the students in his tutorial as charges; he evidently saw them as peers. One could guess that he was delighted to be able to *use* these new "friends." Their admiration of him must have helped soothe the feelings of insecurity and incompetence he felt as a doctoral student.

At the same time Geoffrey was a first-time teacher. Worse, he was a first-time teacher with absolutely no training or preparation. As any novice teacher might, he clearly feared actions that invited conflict. He didn't like making comments on papers and disagreeing with or correcting his students in class, actions that might cause his students to retreat from or even attack him. It is not difficult to imagine that Geoffrey felt totally exposed in his tutorial and, even if he knew the subject matter inside and out, could not escape the distressing feelings of anxiety and vulnerability he had as a teacher.

Actually, there was one escape. By downplaying his authority and bonding with the students through their shared student status, Geoffrey could avoid confrontation, mask the feeling that he was constantly teetering on the brink of disempowerment, and win the admiration he needed. He could shrug off the responsibility of being a *developmental object* for his students' growth, a "twin" who could model what it is to learn and know Western intellectual history, and use his students as an *emotional object* for his own relief. He could fulfill the students' desire to use him as a twin and *reverse the role* by using his students the same way.

Where's the danger here? So Geoffrey was using his students; didn't this benefit everyone? It certainly made for a more relaxed tutorial environment, which is better for learning than a tense one. And Geoffrey's casual and friendly attitude made it easier for his students to relate to him. All good, right?

What is ironic about this story is that Geoffrey's role reversal, which quieted his sense of defenselessness, shielded him from conflict, and allowed him to use his students for his own gratification, was precisely what left him vulnerable to his student's attack at the end of the term. Because he chose the role of friend over teacher and because he was not equipped to manage conflict, Geoffrey had absolutely no traction when Cal objected to his grade. His only option was to give in to Cal's demand. There's the danger: A teacher who uses his students as twins loses his authority in moments of crisis.

What could Geoffrey have done differently?

In the Heat of the Moment

In the moment when Cal yelled, "*I thought you were my friend!*" Geoffrey could have exercised *self-awareness* and *described* what he noticed. By staying present to himself and Cal but observant of the situation, Geoffrey could allow for Cal's anger but also protect his own right to be confused and uncertain. And most importantly, he could buy himself some time.

"Hold on, man," he might have said. "You're clearly upset, and I don't blame you. But I'm both your friend and your teacher, and right now I don't know how to navigate these two roles. I need some time to think about what to do here. So I'm going to have to ask you to come back tomorrow with a cooler head so we can figure out how to solve this problem." As mentioned in chapter one, time-outs can be good for teachers *and* students. Geoffrey could use this time to consult his advisor and, given his aversion to conflict, possibly appeal to the campus ombudsman for mediation.

Detaching could also have prevented Geoffrey from taking Cal's anger personally. If Geoffrey convinced himself that *he* was the cause of Cal's anger, he would completely miss the true source of his student's emotion: his terrible grade. Not taking Cal's emotion personally could allow Geoffrey to consider a crucial question: Who was responsible for Cal's grade and, more fundamentally, Cal's performance on the exam? Was the teacher? Or was the student? Talking to Cal about the specific ways he had "earned" the D could help clarify how Cal had failed himself. And examining the ways he had enabled Cal to earn that D would reveal how *Geoffrey* had failed Cal.

Geoffrey's Emotion Work

Here's where extended *emotion work* would come in. Not having the faintest idea that he was using his students inappropriately, Geoffrey would start at the beginning: with his emotions. As recommended in chapter one, he could wonder what his emotions told him about himself, about his students, and about his students' relationship with him and the subject matter. Specifically, he could focus on his boredom in his professor's lectures and meetings, his dread of evaluating

110

student papers, and his relief in chatting and partying with his students.

YELLOW BELT MOVES

Information about himself. Generally speaking, boredom means disconnection and disengagement. Why, Geoffrey might wonder, did he feel disconnected and disengaged? One possibility could be the fact that Geoffrey felt overwhelmed by his first teaching job. Not only had he taken on a difficult assignment, but he had done so with no preparation at all. Shutting down is a common response to chronic uncertainty and insecurity. Acknowledging that he was overwhelmed would not necessarily have dispelled the stress or the boredom, but it could have been a relief to Geoffrey.

Another possible explanation for his boredom could have been that Geoffrey was feeling what his advisor felt. Geoffrey's disengagement from the lectures and the planning meetings might have matched his advisor's disengagement. In short, Geoffrey's boredom might have told him a lot about his advisor's attitude toward the course and, possibly, toward teaching in general. If his mentor lacked interest, enthusiasm, or confidence, why would Geoffrey feel inspired and capable?

Geoffrey's dread of commenting on student papers could have led to many interesting discoveries. Did he dread this task because he feared conflict? Did he dread it because he couldn't stand messes and just wanted to clean up everything his students turned in? Did he dread it because he had no idea how to help his students improve? A yes to any or all of these questions (and others) could have suggested paths for further exploration that would clearly have helped Geoffrey improve as a teacher.

Finally, Geoffrey's cathartic delight in chatting and partying with his students could have suggested to him that he wished to avoid the challenges of teaching and learning. Listing those challenges could have been extremely helpful for Geoffrey. Sometimes, just naming a fear can lead to a sense of mastery over it. Naming challenges can also translate into setting goals. The more explicit Geoffrey could be about his fears and needs as a teacher, the more effectively he could grow into the job.

One upshot of all this reflection would probably have been the realization in Geoffrey that he needed substantial support for his teaching. Where he would find this support remains a question (and is discussed in chapter five). But the very task of looking for support could have redirected Geoffrey's anxious energy away from his students to more appropriate resources.

This stage of emotion work would also have revealed to Geoffrey that he was quite insecure about his teaching. Turning his attention to his relationship with his students, especially with Cal, and keeping awareness of his anxiety in mind might have presented Geoffrey with these insights:

- I feel inadequate as a teacher.
- More than anything, I want my students to like me (even if they don't learn much from me).
- The thought that they might not like me, that they might actually disdain me, is terrifying.
- Having fun with my students is a good way to get them to like me and to hide my terror and sense of incompetence.
- My students show they like me by asking me personal questions, laughing with me, and inviting me out with them.
- It is impossible for me to resist students' questions, humor, and invitations. I am relieved to be able to escape the academic — where I feel inept — for the personal — where I feel appreciated and admired.

These insights could be very helpful for Geoffrey. He could wonder about the seductiveness of his students' apparent interest in him: their questions, their appreciation of his humor, their insistence that he socialize with them. If he were to take this interest personally, he could conclude that his students simply perceived him to be the *mensch* he was. But if he experimented with *not* taking their behavior personally, he could contemplate the possible purposes the students' behavior was satisfying for *them*.

Information about the students' emotions.
Specifically, Geoffrey could wonder if the students' behavior served them the same way it served him: as an escape from anxiety. Could it be that the students were distracting him and thereby avoiding their own fears about the class? By taking

112

their apparent interest in him personally — by believing that they knew and loved him — was Geoffrey missing his students' more practical purpose, to manage the difficult learning his course demanded?

Information about the students' relationship with him and the subject matter. At this point, Geoffrey could afford to take stock. One thing he knew was that he was nervous and insecure about his teaching. And he could guess that his students were nervous and insecure about their learning. An apparent fact was that he and his students liked each other. So perhaps they were all *using* each other to avoid their insecurities. How might they have been using each other? By being overly friendly and intimate.

Aha! Twinship might be at work!

BLUE BELT MOVE

Having practiced *self-awareness*, *described* his emotions and observations to himself, *looked for good reasons* for his own and his students' behavior, and made an informed *guess* about the twinship dynamics of his tutorial, Geoffrey would be ready to take some action. But his *plan* would have to take certain facts into consideration:

- His students clearly wanted to *use* him as a *twin*. This desire was developmentally appropriate and therefore allowable.
- He had to resist his desire to use his students as twins since his need to reverse developmental roles was *not* appropriate or allowable.

The prospect of being a proper teacher with his students, or being available for friendship but aloof enough to be convincingly authoritative, could once again indicate to Geoffrey that he needed support outside the classroom. He could not use his students as twins, but he surely needed help from someone! In his case, then, *self-disclosing* to his advisor, to another professor, or to a trusted peer could be a wise move.

BLACK BELT MOVES

Inside the classroom, Geoffrey would need to teach the students about the line that divided him from them. To this end, more *self-disclosure* might be helpful. "This is a smart and fun class," he might tell his students at their next tutorial meeting.

"You're so fun that I sometimes lose track of our purpose for being here, which is, of course, to learn about Western intellectual history. I know: GROAN!" he could anticipate the students' response to this announcement. "But I'm here to tell you that this stuff is *interesting*. I'm also here to warn you that I'm going to *show* you how interesting it is. Given how smart and fun you are, I'm pretty sure we can do this together. But I need your buy-in."

Here's where Geoffrey could reveal his *plan*. "Tutorial is just one hour long once a week. My goal is to spend the first 45 minutes of tutorial trying to show you how interesting the topic of the week is. In the next ten minutes of tutorial, you get to tell me how I did. In the last five minutes, we can make plans for Happy Hour. How does that sound to you?" Of course, *listening* to students' feedback could help Geoffrey adjust his plan to maximize its chance of success. And listening to their feedback after every tutorial lesson would help him attune his teaching and in the process become a better, more confident teacher.

How Did Geoffrey Know?

Realizing that he and the students were *using* each other was a crucial step toward Geoffrey's breakthrough. And deciding to see this use as an example of mutual *twinship* — of students using him as a twin and of his *reversing the role* and using them as twins — helped him fashion a plan that would respect the students' needs for autonomy and support while redirecting his own needs. But how did Geoffrey know to apply the twinship framework in the first place?

As we saw, describing his tutorial as being overly friendly and intimate proved to be key. Entertaining the possibility that this casualness might be related to underlying anxiety was also crucial. Without the anxiety that prevented him from actually teaching, Geoffrey's relationship with his students could qualify as simply mellow. Add the anxiety, and the relationship became more complicated. Geoffrey learned that combining anxiety with friendship that felt more important than any academic goals probably equaled twinship. Of course, he couldn't be sure, but probing the possibility was worth the effort and in the end turned out to be fruitful.

114

QUESTION: How do you know when you're using students as twins?
ANSWER: When being friends with students becomes more important than teaching students.

Geoffrey could also have anticipated, before he even began teaching, that he and his students might be susceptible to seeking twinship with each other. He might have *guessed* that his students would particularly value him because he was young and was a student like them yet was an authority on the subject matter they were supposed to master. He could have predicted that seeing him as a twin would help his students relax in the face of a curriculum that might otherwise feel alien and intimidating.

Geoffrey could have made similar predictions about himself. Teaching students who were just a few years younger than he could easily tempt him to give up the role of teacher and settle into the role of friend. And with a little introspection Geoffrey could have discovered that he, too, needed help in approaching his teaching assignment. Anticipating these needs for twinship could have helped Geoffrey plan ahead, both for himself and for his students. Put another way, Geoffrey could have made deliberate decisions about *how* to be used by his students.

KEEP IN MIND
*The value of **anticipating** cannot be overstated. Thinking ahead about ways students might use you (or how you might use them) and planning responses that will reduce tension and promote learning can make for extremely effective teaching.*

Taking Twinship Personally
So what precisely are the perils of taking twinship personally, of reversing roles and using students as twins? The overarching answer is that such role reversal is developmentally inappropriate. As learners students are by definition developing, no matter what their age. As such, they are vitally dependent on their teachers for guidance, support, and encouragement. What students need their teachers to be, then, are people who can be used for inspiration and personal growth

precisely because they are strong, confident, separate, informed, and, at best, compellingly admirable; that is, students need their teachers to be *developmental objects*.

There are several more specific dangers in reversing the twinship role. One is the potential for limiting a student's development if it looks as though he might surpass his teacher. A student who serves as a twin for his teacher but who grows beyond that teacher might no longer be able to play the twinship role. The teacher might try to hold the student back to avoid losing him and the valuable role he played. Ironically, a twinship student's success at the tasks his teacher sets for him might cause anxiety in a teacher who is insecure enough to fear the student's learning and growth.

Another pitfall, as Geoffrey demonstrated, is a teacher's inability to play the authoritative role his position of power in the classroom demands of him. Some teachers hesitate to exercise authority because they suspect their students will respond with contempt or even outright rebellion. Better to make the students like you! But too often this goal forces teachers to satisfy the demands of friendship and student approval over academic requirements. Such a role reversal can lead to lower standards and choices that weaken instruction (such as grade inflation, using class time to chat aimlessly, or general permissiveness). In the long run no one gains from such compromises.

A third pitfall appears when a teacher-student friendship becomes erotic. While romantic and sexual desire aimed at a teacher or student is probably more common than some might care to think, it can quickly become problematic if strong boundaries are not in place. Again, as long as two "twins" are student and teacher, the teacher's overriding obligation is to be the student's developmental partner. This means establishing the physical and emotional distinctions necessary to keep the teacher and student roles clear. When teachers begin to have erotic feelings for a student, a second obligation is to work through the feelings to channel them appropriately.

In sum Geoffrey took his students' desire for twinship personally. He had extremely good reasons for doing so, but his teaching and his students' learning suffered as a result. *Not* taking the students' desire for twinship personally would have meant welcoming the students' willingness to relate, taking responsibility to monitor that relating, and finding the help and approval he needed as a teacher elsewhere. It would have meant accepting the students' need to see him as a peer, as a twin whose presence could relax and inspire them, but nevertheless conducting himself as a mentor, as someone who was accessible but detached and comfortable with his authority. Making these changes in himself might have been hard work for Geoffrey, but it was the work he needed to do to become an effective teacher.

FOOD FOR THOUGHT

One of the great pleasures of teaching can be establishing friendships with students. Does Geoffrey's story imply that this is unwise or even unethical? No. Friendship between a teacher and a student can be a powerfully positive developmental and instructional force. Trust, mutual respect and enjoyment, and identification are actually desirable ingredients in a healthy teacher-student relationship. They form just the sort of environment a student needs if she is to flourish personally and intellectually.

But Geoffrey's story does imply that teachers who are friends with students must be especially thoughtful about their role. When a teacher sees a student as a friend, he is (one hopes) acknowledging wonderful traits in that student — maturity, intelligence, special skill or understanding — that the teacher's friendship and support can strengthen. The teacher gains by discovering a kindred spirit in her class who enlivens her teaching and offers the teacher opportunities to learn and grow herself.

But as Geoffrey's story demonstrates, friendship between a teacher and a student still requires distinct roles. Just because a teacher considers a student a friend does not let her off the hook of teacher responsibilities. It does not mean the teacher can ignore her obligation to act as her student's developmental partner, as the authority and guide in the classroom, as a potential object for her student's use. While a teacher-student friendship can be refreshing for a teacher, it must be unquestionably good for the student.

117

Idealization

The same constraints on "twinship" relationships for teachers — remaining committed to being a developmental partner, moving between friend and teacher roles without risking one's authority or threatening the students' integrity — hold when teachers are idealized as well. Once again the danger in the next story is in "taking it personally," or using one's student to bolster one's self-esteem.

Student-to-Teacher Idealization

The following story shows how a teacher can misuse a student's normal idealization of her.

"I WANT TO BE YOU"

Ms. Williams was an energetic and entertaining fourth grade teacher. She generally liked the subjects she taught; she was funny; and she loved the spotlight. She was also very sensitive to her students and often took it upon herself to solve their frequent social problems.

One day two of Ms. Williams's favorite students returned from recess crying. They had had a fight during lunch. While the rest of the class settled down, Ms. Williams helped the girls make up. Feeling noticeably better, one of the girls, Zoe, said wistfully, "Ms. Williams, I want to be you!" The compliment reinforced Ms. Williams's sense that one of her most important jobs and greatest talents was in the area of mediation. Her students, while they could not actually be her, were indeed lucky to have her as a teacher.

As the year progressed, Ms. Williams's involvement in students' quarrels increased. In fact, Ms. Williams insisted that she play a role in solving any relational problem she got wind of, even those outside of her classroom. She kept a special eye on Zoe, who seemed particularly inclined to experience conflicts with her friends and was more than willing to let Ms. Williams step in and help her. Ms. Williams congratulated herself on being such a remarkably influential figure in Zoe's life.

One could not ask for a more direct expression of idealization than Zoe's wistful confession, "I want to *be* you!" She so admired Ms. Williams, her energy, her focused and caring attention, her ability to cut through emotional tangles, that Zoe would have gladly merged with her idol and become "one" with her. This urge is the normal precursor to Zoe's eventually absorbing the admired qualities herself. By relating so wholeheartedly to Ms. Williams — by watching her closely, immersing herself in the feel and being of her teacher, and benefiting directly from her teacher's admirable strengths — Zoe was poised to learn from Ms. Williams.

Unfortunately, Ms. Williams took Zoe's worship personally. She did not realize that Zoe was *using* her as a *statue on a pedestal* to learn about qualities Zoe admired and wanted to possess herself. She did not grasp that Zoe's admiration of her was not about her but about Zoe. And developmentally speaking, Zoe's self-interest was entirely appropriate.

But Ms. Williams, because she needed the type of attention Zoe offered her, *reversed roles* and began *using* Zoe to keep the attention coming. She increased her problem-solving efforts, repeatedly demonstrating her competence and bathing in Zoe's admiration. Unfortunately, by seeking and solving Zoe's problems for her, Ms. Williams held Zoe in an endlessly incompetent position. She denied Zoe the chance to exercise the very skills Zoe wanted for herself. While the student longed to *use* the teacher as an *ideal*, the teacher used the student as a mirror.

Ms. Williams's Emotion Work

What could Ms. Williams have done differently? Of course, she could have started with her emotions and wondered what they told her about herself, about Zoe, and about Zoe's relationship with her.

YELLOW BELT MOVES

Information about herself. In beginning her emotion work, Ms. Williams could have become *aware* of her strong reaction to Zoe's exclamation, *described* the experience to herself, and *looked for good reasons* for it. "Wow!" she might have said to herself. "What a surprising comment from Zoe! It made me feel really good, kind of like a rock star. And Zoe's like an adoring fan. What a great feeling it is to be admired and adored!"

But Ms. Williams might have noticed other emotions in addition to this great feeling of pride and worthiness. One emotion could be uncertainty. What did Zoe's admiration mean? Was Ms. Williams really as wonderful as Zoe thought she was? Another emotion might be fear. What if Ms. Williams wasn't wonderful? What if Zoe was wrong? And desperation might be in the mix. Would Zoe keep feeling this way? What if she stopped admiring her teacher? What could Ms. Williams do to prevent that from happening?

Contemplating these complicated emotions might have revealed to Ms. Williams that she had lost perspective on her fourth grade student. Sure, Zoe's comment suggested that Ms. Williams could be influential and that some students adored her. And yes, such feedback felt great. But Ms. Williams was *hungry* for this feedback. Her insatiability led her to take Zoe's admiration personally, to *use* Zoe in all her vulnerability as a source of self-esteem. Seeing it this way could help Ms. Williams make a *plan* for herself: to explore and address her legitimate and extremely important need for affirmation and admiration with someone who was qualified to help her learn from this work.

Information about Zoe. Committing to pursue appropriate satisfaction of her own needs could help Ms. Williams detach and wonder about Zoe's needs. "Why," Ms. Williams could ask herself, "might Zoe see me the way she does? I mean, I'm *not* a rock star; I'm her teacher. Why would Zoe want to be me?" Reviewing the incident, Ms. Williams might note that Zoe's wistful comment came after Ms. Williams had helped Zoe solve a problem with her friends. She might *guess*, then, that Zoe appreciated Ms. Williams's ability to untangle social difficulties, to help Zoe and her friends make peace and feel better. This might be a skill Zoe especially valued.

Once again Ms. Williams's own emotions could help her understand Zoe's. The fact that her response to Zoe's compliment was so extreme could mean that Zoe's emotions were also extreme, a hypothesis her exclamation — "I want to *be* you!" — would confirm. Extreme admiration is often the same as idealization. A good guess about Zoe, then, would be that she *idealized* her teacher.

Information about Zoe's relationship with her teacher. But what might the purpose of Zoe's idealization be? In truth, idealization can be tricky, as it can accomplish quite different goals:

- One purpose is to use a person as a model for how to be. For this purpose one needs a *developmental object*, or someone whose traits and skills can slowly be absorbed and personalized, leading to personal growth and learning.
- A second purpose is to use a person for temporary emotional relief. This happens when the idealization is a defense (as described in chapter one). With defensive idealization the *statue on a pedestal* is an *emotional object* that is used to manage unbearable feelings, not to promote personal growth.

What happens when a teacher takes either of these object roles personally? We saw in chapter one that completing the emotional circuit of an enactment, or taking the enactment personally, perpetuates it. If Zoe were using Ms. Williams as an emotional object, and if Ms. Williams took this use personally, Ms. Williams would be allowing herself to become a *statue* that Zoe could plug into as a receptacle for her anxiety.

For example, Zoe might have a difficult time connecting with her peers. If such attachment caused anxiety in her, and Ms. Williams was especially good at facilitating those attachments, Zoe could begin to *use* Ms. Williams as a go-between. Her admiration of her teacher would be real — after all, Ms. Williams provided intense relief from social conflict — but it would require Ms. Williams to continue playing the mediator role forever so Zoe could continue to experience this emotional relief.

The up side for Zoe of using Ms. Williams as an *emotional object* would be guaranteed relief in difficult social situations. The down side would be twofold: First, Zoe would need to continue causing conflict with her friends to guarantee Ms. Williams's ongoing help. And second, Zoe would be preventing herself from learning how to relate in a healthier way with her friends, thus trapping herself in social clumsiness.

The purpose of idealization as a defense is the exact opposite of the purpose of idealization as a means of development. Using Ms. Williams as an *emotional object* would simply perpetuate Zoe's weaknesses. In contrast, admiring Ms. Williams and imitating her skills, or using Ms. Williams as a *developmental object*, could lead Zoe to become a competent mediator herself.

In truth, it wouldn't matter very much which purpose Zoe's idealization was serving. What would matter would be Ms. Williams's response. In both cases she would have to figure out *whether* and *how* to be used by Zoe. There might be times, for example, when Ms. Williams would simply opt out of helping Zoe make up with her friends. Occasionally leaving Zoe to her own devices would be essential for Zoe's skill development. At other times Ms. Williams could step in to help, but she would have to be a proper ideal for Zoe, neither a static receptacle for anxiety nor a role-reversing user herself. Her aim would be to enjoy the glow of Zoe's high regard for her but to embrace the developmental process Zoe was inviting her to embark on.

What would a proper ideal, or *statue on a pedestal*, look like? It would consist of Ms. Williams's putting Zoe's admiration into perspective, allowing Zoe to gradually take over her own problem solving, and expecting changes in Zoe's attitude as Ms. Williams frustrated her.

Here's how Ms. Williams might put Zoe's admiration into perspective. "Zoe is a fourth grader," she could remind herself. "Of course she thinks the world of me; that's normal. But she doesn't really know me so cannot possibly reflect me accurately. What I need to do is help Zoe grow into the unique, valuable person *she* is."

FOOD FOR THOUGHT

QUESTION: How do you know you're being idealized?
ANSWER: When students treat you like a rock star. Sometimes you can tell by the things they say: "I want to be you!"; "I want to know what you think." Other times you can tell by your own feeling of importance. If you start imagining you're indispensable to a student, consider the possibility that you are

being idealized and need to step back a bit, to transform yourself from a **statue** *into a* **scaffold**.

BLUE BELT MOVES

Ms. Williams would then have to focus on being a scaffold for her student as Zoe reported her difficulties with her friends. Ms. Williams could step Zoe through similar steps to the ones teachers are encouraged to take throughout this book: becoming self-aware, describing, looking for good reasons, guessing, self-disclosing, listening, and making a plan for future interactions. Given her enthusiasm for relational problem solving, Ms. Williams could even take on emotional literacy as a formal instructional objective in her class, a curricular addition that would arguably be of immense benefit to all students, even fourth graders.

In supporting Zoe to become her own problem solver, Ms. Williams might end up frustrating her student. She might fail to be the perfect mediator; she might refrain from doing exactly what Zoe wanted her to do; she might begin to appear as a real person to her student rather than a breathtaking but inanimate statue.

This could be difficult for both Zoe and Ms. Williams. Admirers can be brutal when awed objects fall from grace in their eyes. And few idealized statues welcome that fall. But feeling and surviving disappointment are essential skills. Allowing Zoe to go through these feelings without withdrawing from her or climbing back up onto the pedestal would be a great feat for Ms. Williams, one truly worthy of admiration.

Of course, sometimes Ms. Williams would make mistakes. For instance, she might misestimate what Zoe was capable of handling on her own. In these cases Ms. Williams could repair with Zoe: She could revisit the original problem and strengthen the scaffolding around Zoe and her friends so they could succeed at the particular social task before them. Above all, Ms. Williams would need to stand firmly in herself as a person, which might mean frequently drawing on the help of peers or professionals whose experience and advice could provide the bolstering Ms. Williams's self-esteem needed.

123

Reversed Idealization

The story of Zoe and Ms. Williams is about a teacher's mismanagement of a student's idealization of her. The next story is about a teacher's reversal of this developmental role when he idealizes a student and condemns others.

"I WANT YOU TO BE ME"

Mr. Birdwhistle was an elementary school band teacher. His students were rank beginners, so Mr. Birdwhistle put a lot of energy into teaching his students how to play their instruments. His ultimate goal was the band's participation in twice-yearly performances, which he took very seriously.

During lessons and rehearsals Mr. Birdwhistle could be quite impatient. In lessons he often chided individual students. "You call yourself a sax player?" he might yell. In band rehearsals he picked sometimes on entire sections, sometimes on individuals. Although he was trying to improve the band's sound, his criticisms could be cutting. "Maybe we should do this concert without the trumpet section, as it appears they don't care enough to learn their parts," he might say.

Mr. Birdwhistle also had favorites, students who showed special musical promise. Mr. Birdwhistle praised these students openly: "Maurice, you're such a fine flute player!" He grandstanded them in front of their peers: "Let's listen to how Maurice plays this line, as he is the only one who can do it right." And he drew close to his favorites, complaining to them about the rest of the band and keeping them after class for friendly chats.

Every year several students dropped out of band. Mr. Birdwhistle saw this as natural attrition and didn't worry much about it. But this year he was shocked when he lost not just a sax player and a couple of trumpet players but Maurice as well.

Let's face it: Mr. Birdwhistle had a difficult job. He had to move young children from total incompetence on their instruments to a public performance in a very short time. And he had to wrestle with the fact that many people would judge his teaching abilities by the quality of the students' playing. This is a recipe for anxiety if ever there was one!

It seems that one way Mr. Birdwhistle managed his anxiety was to foist it on students whose playing was disappointing. Of course, any band director will encounter students who do not play well because they lack talent or motivation or because they resist the challenge of mastering their instrument. There are many good reasons for subpar performances. But the pressure Mr. Birdwhistle felt to provide impressive outcomes made it impossible for him to tolerate anything subpar. Because he couldn't bear his own anxiety, it appears that he spread it to his students.

Another way Mr. Birdwhistle seems to have managed the pressure he felt was to idealize one or more of his students. Mr. Birdwhistle didn't just praise or encourage Maurice; he held him up for all to admire. He raised Maurice onto a pedestal and shone a spotlight on him to inspire his classmates.

How did criticizing students and idealizing students help Mr. Birdwhistle manage his anxiety? On the surface one might guess that Mr. Birdwhistle's criticizing and praising were both forms of projection. By lambasting students Mr. Birdwhistle shared his negative feelings, making his students feel as anxious as he did. And highlighting a student's success might have reinforced a sense of hope in Mr. Birdwhistle; if one student could do it, perhaps the others could, too.

But there's another layer of possibility, one that is a bit more complicated. Let's see how Mr. Birdwhistle might have come to some understanding of the complex forces at work in his band classroom.

Mr. Birdwhistle's Emotion Work

The shock of losing Maurice, painful as it might have been, could have prompted Mr. Birdwhistle to do some valuable *emotion work*. Why did Maurice quit band? Why did his desertion hurt Mr. Birdwhistle as much as it did? As always, a good place to start in seeking answers to these questions would be with Mr. Birdwhistle's own emotions.

YELLOW BELT MOVES

Information about himself. How did Mr. Birdwhistle feel about losing Maurice? Obviously, he felt surprised, even blindsided. He had thought Maurice enjoyed band, and he had assumed Maurice relished all the positive attention Mr. Birdwhistle lavished upon him. *He* would have appreciated his teacher's attention if *he* had been Maurice.

If Mr. Birdwhistle were really attentive, this thought would raise a red flag. "If *he* had been Maurice" implies that Mr. Birdwhistle was using himself as a model for Maurice. He seemed to assume that he and his student shared standards and preferences, that they were one and the same, that Maurice would naturally respond to praise exactly the same way Mr. Birdwhistle would have. Just as Zoe's wish to *be* Ms. Williams implied a desire to merge with her idol, Mr. Birdwhistle here seemed to merge with his student, collapsing the boundaries between them and thus making it very easy to take everything Maurice did personally.

FOOD FOR THOUGHT

Emotion work is not easy. Practicing self-awareness very often uncovers emotions that are not at all becoming. Teachers who discover their jealousy or entitlement or resentment or hatred might be tempted to halt the process by judging themselves harshly or denying such terrible emotions exist in them.

But teachers must resist this temptation! Detaching and suspending judgment are crucial *to successful emotion work. Remember: Emotions are data. They reveal psychic structures and relational patterns, not immutable truths about character. What a teacher should look at ultimately are the actions she takes as a result of facing her difficult emotions. Now that's character.*

If Mr. Birdwhistle had missed the evidence that he had merged with Maurice, he could continue to follow his emotions. Why would he have appreciated his teacher's attention? What would it have meant to him? For Mr. Birdwhistle, perhaps, attention from his band teacher would have provided confidence where there was none. Or perhaps it would have validated what Mr. Birdwhistle already knew: that he was a very good musician. Or perhaps it would simply have encouraged Mr. Birdwhistle and made band a pleasant class for him to attend. Praise can certainly have these effects. But why so *much* praise? What did Mr. Birdwhistle's need to raise Maurice up on a pedestal tell Mr. Birdwhistle about himself?

Once again Mr. Birdwhistle would have to return to the feelings he had about Maurice's quitting band. In addition to feeling surprised, Mr. Birdwhistle might easily notice that he felt hurt. Yes, and a little angry. Very angry, in fact. How dare Maurice abandon him and the band? How dare Maurice humiliate him, as if his regard for Maurice's talent was nothing?

These thoughts might lead Mr. Birdwhistle to the realization that his praise was more than support, validation, or encouragement. In truth, he tacitly expected something back from Maurice. He wanted Maurice to feel grateful to him and to admire him. More accurately, Mr. Birdwhistle wanted to be especially influential for Maurice, to have a particularly significant impact on his development, to be able to take at least partial credit for his talent. He wanted reflected glory.

This realization might have been quite difficult for Mr. Birdwhistle to reach. After all, these feelings are not very becoming, especially for a teacher who is supposed to be concerned about his students' welfare. But if he could admit these feelings to himself, Mr. Birdwhistle would have hit pay dirt.

First of all, Mr. Birdwhistle could explain to himself why he felt so hurt when his star student quit band. Maurice wasn't just lowering the quality of the band's sound; he was rejecting Mr. Birdwhistle. Despite his teacher's immense investment in him, Maurice apparently did *not* value Mr. Birdwhistle's influence and did not seem to care how his abandonment made Mr. Birdwhistle feel. (Or worse, Maurice might have *wanted* Mr. Birdwhistle to feel bad.) That hurt.

Second, realizing that he was angling for reflected glory could have pointed Mr. Birdwhistle to the conclusion that he was *using* Maurice for his own purposes. What might those purposes have been?

- To highlight evidence of his own competence
- To vicariously bask in Maurice's talent
- To appear powerful and influential

Of course, these would all be legitimate purposes, "good" reasons for Mr. Birdwhistle's behaviors in band. But they were all about *him*. They had nothing to do with

Maurice's growth and learning. Could it be that Mr. Birdwhistle's praise functioned to benefit himself more than Maurice? Could it be that, by idealizing Maurice, Mr. Birdwhistle was merging with Maurice and glorifying himself through his student?

Information about his students. How might Maurice feel about Mr. Birdwhistle's praise? It might come as no surprise to Mr. Birdwhistle that he actually had no idea. His knowledge of Maurice was limited to, first, the actual playing he did in band and, second, Mr. Birdwhistle's *beliefs* about who Maurice was: a miniversion of himself. Recognizing the difference between knowing a student as he is and constructing beliefs about a student based on who the teacher needs him to be for the teacher's purposes would have been crucial for Mr. Birdwhistle.

This is how Mr. Birdwhistle's idealizing Maurice and other students became complicated. Mr. Birdwhistle wasn't just projecting onto Maurice; he was fusing with Maurice, turning him into a *statue on a pedestal* that looked remarkably like himself. The fact that he had very little sense of who Maurice actually was could confirm this interpretation. It is very difficult to see a student accurately when all one sees is a reflection of oneself.

Given this remarkable revelation — that he tended to idealize, or merge with, his favorite students to reassure himself of his own worth — Mr. Birdwhistle might turn his attention to those students who irritated him. How did he feel about them?

Irritated! Angry! Appalled! Scornful! It might not be difficult for Mr. Birdwhistle to access these negative feelings. He had high standards for his band and lost all patience with students who didn't share those high standards.

But why so contemptuous? Why not empathic and reassuring? Once again Mr. Birdwhistle might be able to admit that the students themselves had very little to do with his emotions. The truth was he didn't know his sax player and trumpet players any better than he knew Maurice. What he was contemptuous of, he might realize, was not actual students but his *beliefs* about who his students were: lazy, disrespectful, opportunistic, uncooperative.

And why on earth would he view his elementary school students so severely? One possible answer is that Mr. Birdwhistle was *projecting* onto his students qualities he hated in himself. This is often the case when people are judgmental or critical of others: They externalize their own worst qualities and attack those failings in others as they would attack them in themselves. For this reason paying close attention to how one judges others can provide accurate information about what one hates most about oneself.

Another possible answer is that Mr. Birdwhistle might have feared these students. When he saw his trumpet players "goofing off," he did not see struggling musicians but, rather, powerful students who disrespected him. Mr. Birdwhistle appeared to be convinced that these disrespectful students were going to ruin his concerts and make him look bad in front of the school and the larger community. In other words, perhaps parents and administrators would see *him* as lazy, disrespectful, opportunistic, and uncooperative. That scared him.

With all this introspection Mr. Birdwhistle might realize that he was taking his students' behaviors personally. He took his favorite students personally by idealizing them — by merging with them and seeing their talents as reflections of his own — and he took his struggling students personally by demonizing them, or rejecting them as wholly disgraceful.

In a complicated way he seemed to be "splitting" his students into either/or categories: either all good or all bad. (The students in the middle probably didn't attract Mr. Birdwhistle's attention.) In neither case was he relating to real students, just images of them crafted out of his own beliefs and fears about himself and how others saw him. In the process he was surviving some difficult emotions, but he was not teaching optimally.

DEFENSE
Splitting *is a defense.*
See the appendix for definitions and examples.

What could Mr. Birdwhistle have done differently? How could he prevent himself from taking his students' abilities and behaviors personally? Turning his self-awareness into action might take time and a lot of practice, as it would

129

require going against some deep self-protective instincts. But Mr. Birdwhistle's difficult introspection could serve him well in changing the ways he interacted with all of his students.

BLUE BELT MOVE

A first step Mr. Birdwhistle could take, either one-on-one or in small group music lessons, would be to gather data from his students about their attitudes toward band. What did they like about their instruments? What didn't they like? What did they like and not like about band? *Listening* to the students' answers would help Mr. Birdwhistle begin to form impressions not just about who his students were but about the impact his class had on them. Getting to know the students as individuals with particular relationships to music could help him detach and craft better responses to his students' telling behaviors in class.

BLACK BELT MOVES

A very important and, ultimately, more public move Mr. Birdwhistle could make would be to deliberately prepare for difficult student situations. To do this he would have to *anticipate* which student behaviors might goad him into actions he wanted to avoid; *describe* what he noticed; *make guesses* about the students' reasons for these behaviors; and *plan* different responses. For instance, rather than praise or criticize, he could *describe* and, when appropriate, *self-disclose*:

- "I noticed that you got all those notes. That line is an important theme in this piece, so it was nice to hear you play it so accurately."
- "Did you notice that you were all playing in tune that time? It seems that you were listening to each other and adjusting."
- "That's a tough rhythm! Let's slow it down so everyone can get it right."
- "I know how hard it can be to focus on playing your instrument when you're surrounded by friends. Can we agree to do our absolute best through measure 41 and then reward ourselves with a short break?"

Related to preparing would be detaching. Mr. Birdwhistle could commit to stepping back from interactions with his students so he could observe the students and his own reactions with curiosity. Of course, detaching is not always easy, especially when one's instinct is either to fuse with a student or to attack, but it is absolutely essential if a teacher is to resist taking students personally and make himself available for his students' developmental use.

FOOD FOR THOUGHT

QUESTION: How do you know you're idealizing a student?
ANSWER: When the student can do no wrong. And when the student does *do wrong, you feel angry and betrayed and are tempted to disown or dismiss the student.*

The bottom line for Mr. Birdwhistle would be to establish boundaries in the classroom that would prevent him from reversing roles and spoiling his students' efforts to use him as a developmental partner. Setting boundaries is the topic of the next chapter. For the purposes of this chapter, it is enough to point out the various pitfalls of idealization in the classroom.

Taking Idealization Personally

As with twinship, idealization has its benefits. It can feel good to be idealized, and it can feel good to merge with a powerful other. But idealization also has its drawbacks.

One pitfall of idealization, alluded to earlier in this chapter, is the temptation to make a mountain out of a compliment. Teachers need to hear praise, of course, and compliments can be flattering. But alarms should go off when a teacher loses perspective on the value and meaning of a student's compliment. Feeling disproportionately puffed up or obligated to live up to the complimenter's implied standards or feeling worried about the truth of the compliment can be signals that emotion work is needed. Heeding these signals means turning to helpful adults for perspective, not to students.

Another major pitfall that many teachers experience (but may not associate with idealization) is the fear of admitting, "I don't know." Whether students are actively idealizing them or not, teachers can suspect that discovering they are not all-knowing will cause their students to disrespect and condemn them. This pressure to be perfect increases exponentially when a teacher actually knows a student idealizes her, as the fall from a high pedestal can be hard indeed.

Teachers who avoid exposing their ignorance would do well to explore this fear. Do they expect to be idealized? Do they *wish* to be? What would happen if they weren't? What does it mean to not know? What does it mean to *know*? What do they imagine knowing and not knowing mean to their students? How might their students feel about being people who, by definition, do not know? Students have every right to want their teachers to be all-knowing, infallible, perfect — to idealize them. But when teachers take this idealization personally, they can mislead students about the nature of knowing and the absolute necessity of not knowing.

A third pitfall of idealization, the flip side of not knowing, is working feverishly to continue deserving a student's idealization. This is what Ms. Williams did. By trying to be ever present, eternally wise, and all-powerful, Ms. Williams did not just strengthen Zoe's social incompetence but threatened to exhaust herself. Participating in Zoe's use of her as an *emotional object*, or taking Zoe's idealization personally, meant Ms. Williams unconsciously agreed to freeze herself into a *statue* devoted to costly maintenance of an undesirable *status quo*.

The danger of freezing into a static statue applies to students as well. When a teacher idealizes a student, as Mr. Birdwhistle idealized Maurice, he puts the student into a straitjacket and restricts the student's range of self-expression. If all Maurice was allowed to be was a model flute player, for example, he might be reluctant to take risks that would challenge him but would potentially bring him down in his teacher's sight. Or he might thrash about in an attempt to escape the straitjacket, acting out to wake his teacher up.

When teachers define students in constrained terms, reacting to a frozen, idealized segment of the student's personality, they can also cause confusion. "Is that who I really am?" the student can wonder in consternation. "What is this teacher seeing in me that I don't see in myself?" Of course, teachers see qualities in students that are invisible to the students all the time. Such generous visioning can be quite motivating to students. But inspiring visions tend to be expansive, not contracting. Idealizing can contract vision. Any time teachers freeze their students into straitjackets of any sort, idealized or demonized, they are doing them a disservice.

The danger for anyone who is idealized, teacher or student, is the inevitability of disappointing. Ms. Williams, who needed Zoe to admire her skills at mediation, worked extra hard not to disappoint Zoe. Any of Mr. Birdwhistle's favorites could be tempted to contort to fit within Mr. Birdwhistle's limited expectations to avoid disappointing him and losing his regard. Again, falling from a pedestal is never enjoyable. And disappointment is the switch that flips the idealized statue on its head.

The truth, though, is that disappointment is essential; it is character building. Students who use teachers as developmental objects must eventually separate from their idols and employ the skills they have learned from them. Disappointment is an effective way to ease that separation along. In short, teachers who can be idealized and who can fall from the pedestal without taking their students' admiration and disappointment personally — and who remain present and available through the entire process — are being superb developmental partners.

Mirroring

One of the most important jobs teachers have is *seeing* their students: reflecting back to students who they seem to be, what they seem to be saying or doing. Teachers who do this are playing the essential developmental role of "mirroring." And *mirrors*, being merely reflective surfaces, cannot take their use personally. Rather, they simply do their reflective jobs; they see honestly.

But being a mirror is not always easy for teachers. One reason is that detaching, a prerequisite to mirroring, does not come automatically to everyone. A second reason is that students can push back ferociously and demand rigorous emotion work from their teachers. (We will see examples of such pushback in the next chapter.) Another reason is that teachers need mirrors themselves and can seek them in their students. (We saw examples of this in the three stories above.)

What does being a mirror look like for a teacher? In the next story a teacher manages to avoid the temptation to *reverse roles* and see his own reflection in a student's work. Instead, he shifts from a "doubting" stance to a "believing" stance, one that allows him to *mirror* rather than judge his student. [Credit for "doubting" and "believing" stances to P. Elbow (1973), The doubting game and the believing game: An analysis of the intellectual enterprise, in *Writing without teachers* (pp. 148–191), New York: Oxford University Press.]

"I SEE YOU"

Mr. Peterson, a tenth grade English teacher, loved his subject matter and valued the knowledge about literature and writing that he brought to his classroom. He took very seriously his role as a commenter on student writing, trying different approaches to help his students improve their skills.

On this particular day his students had brought in poems they had written on "pride." Originally thinking he would bring the poems home that night to read and comment on, Mr. Peterson decided spontaneously to invite his students to read them out loud. Before he had time to consider the implications of his invitation, his first student volunteer, Wally, had launched into his poem about war and patriotism.

"'And the rockets' red glare,'" Wally read,
"Bullets and explosions everywhere,
Showed the soldiers' national pride
In their eyes opened wide . . ."

When Wally finished reading, Mr. Peterson's mind went blank. The two most honest comments he could have made were "I hate rhyming poems" and "I hate writing that glorifies war." Panicking because he did not know what to say to his student, he closed his eyes and said, "Wally, would you please read your poem again?"

As Wally read, Mr. Peterson consciously took a receptive stance rather than a judgmental one. He detached, muted his critical voice, and joined with Wally, listening to Wally's words and the feelings his student was trying to convey in the poem. When Wally finished, and after the class had applauded, Mr. Peterson was able to offer an honest reflection of Wally's work.

"Wally, you are quite good at rhyming," he said. "That is a skill I completely lack. And I hear in your poem a very deep pride in your country and in the men and women who fight in its wars. Your poem conveys that sense of pride, partly through your effective allusion to our national anthem. Did anyone else hear what I heard? Did anyone hear something else?"

As his classmates shared their own generous responses, Wally actually took notes.

Mr. Peterson's struggle in this story is another common one for teachers: suspending personal preferences to open up to the students' or, put another way, letting students' work be about the *students* rather than about the teacher. In suspending his own preferences, Mr. Peterson became a *mirror* for Wally. How did he do this? And how can this type of mirroring be helpful to students?

Mr. Peterson's Emotion Work

How did Mr. Peterson become a mirror for Wally? He did some *emotion work*.

YELLOW BELT MOVES

First, Mr. Peterson became *aware* of a strong feeling of panic when he realized he had nothing positive to say about Wally's poem. While Mr. Peterson had no time to describe or think about this feeling, he did have the presence of mind to refrain from speaking through his panic — he did not blurt out his first unhelpful thoughts — and to *slow down* the process.

Asking Wally to reread his poem was a brilliant move. It gave Mr. Peterson time to detach, to tuck away his judgmental reactions and reach out to Wally empathically. It gave him time to decide *whether* and *how* to be used. Somehow, Mr. Peterson grasped that his personal opinion of Wally's poem, especially if delivered in a public forum, would not help Wally improve his work. What Mr. Peterson chose to focus on, instead, was Wally: his self-expression, his apparent strengths, the purpose and intended impact of his work, the aspects of the poem that appeared most striking. This is *mirroring*: reflecting back to students what they look and sound like without judgment or ulterior motives.

135

FOOD FOR THOUGHT

The truth is that teachers throughout this book have been mirrors for their students. Any time a teacher takes the steps recommended for emotion work, they are mirroring. Description, *for example, counts as mirroring. "Right now I'm watching you struggle to get ready to go outside," Ms. Foster told her young student, Manny, in chapter one, "and that surprises me because I know how much you love recess." By describing what she saw and noting the difference between the current state of affairs and Manny's past behavior, Ms. Foster mirrored to Manny his resistance.*

Guessing *is also a form of mirroring. "I know how hard it can be to focus on playing your instrument when you're surrounded by friends," Mr. Birdwhistle could have said to the trumpet section, showing them a nonjudgmental picture of their goofing off. "Can we agree to do our absolute best through measure 41 and then reward ourselves with a short break?" In posing this question Mr. Birdwhistle could simultaneously invite his students to take responsibility for and control of the behaviors he described and acknowledge the difficulty of the effort. More subtle mirroring.*

And self-disclosing *can also serve as mirroring. "I must admit that the biggest obstacle I had to overcome in learning to speak French was my fear of making mistakes," Mr. Greene might have told Hiram earlier in this chapter. "I was supergood at doing written exercises and passing French tests, but I got all jumbled up when it came to speaking or writing. I've since learned that this is common for many second-language learners. I'm guessing it's true for you, too." By describing his own experience with learning a language, Mr. Greene hoped to describe Hiram's. Casting an honest light on himself allowed him to illuminate Hiram, mirroring that is all the more powerful because it normalizes vulnerability.*

How Is Mirroring Helpful?

How can this type of mirroring be helpful to students? Surely, a teacher's job is not just to reinforce students' current skill levels. How does mirroring help a student improve?

Here are some answers:

- Mirroring focuses on the student.

136

- Mirroring clarifies responsibilities.
- Mirroring embraces and normalizes reality.
- Mirroring requires seeing.

Each of these answers deserves explanation.

Mirroring focuses on the student. Obviously, school is about students and their work. Of course! But as we have seen several times already in this book, school very easily becomes about teachers (and administrators and parents) and *their* needs. And distinguishing between a teacher's needs and her students' can be difficult, requiring disciplined emotion work.

Mirroring is a powerful way to make this distinction. Even teachers like Mr. Birdwhistle, whose psychic structures plug into certain students by merging with them, can resist this impulse by being a *mirror*. "Did you notice that you were all playing in tune that time?" Mr. Birdwhistle could have said to his band. "It seems that you were listening to each other and adjusting." By *describing* what he observed and *making a guess* as to what his musicians had done, Mr. Birdwhistle would have acknowledged the students' accomplishment — staying in tune — and the work that must have gone into it — listening and adjusting. Even if they had no idea what "playing in tune" meant, the students would be invited by Mr. Birdwhistle's comment to pay closer attention to themselves and each other, an act that could not help but improve their ability to hear and play music together.

Focusing on the students, in other words, allows teachers to notice and respond to students' strengths and needs. Of course, mirroring is just one way to focus on the students, but it is an extremely powerful one.

Mirroring clarifies responsibilities. When teachers allow students to use them as *emotional objects* or when teachers *reverse roles* and *use* their students, responsibilities get muddled. Who should be resolving conflicts with fourth grade friends, Zoe or Ms. Williams? For whom should Maurice be playing his flute, himself or Mr. Birdwhistle? Who gets to resist teaching, Geoffrey or his students? When teachers or students abandon their own or take over others' responsibilities, learning is compromised.

Mirroring, in contrast, fixes roles. Teachers see; students get seen. Teachers describe students' work; students own their work, explain it, improve it. Teachers keep their hands off; students put their hands on. When they mirror, teachers simply cannot do the students' work for them. They cannot use the students for their own purposes, nor can students use them in any way except developmentally. Mirroring, in other words, facilitates competence within one's role and collaboration across roles. It draws a line between teacher and student and helps regulate how each navigates the gap.

Mirroring embraces and normalizes reality. When teachers mirror, they note reality *as they perceive it* without judging it. This can take courage, as the reality one perceives about oneself and others is not always attractive. "I'm both your friend and your teacher, and right now I don't know how to navigate these two roles," Geoffrey could have told Cal when Cal protested his grade. Geoffrey might not have been proud of having blurred these roles, but denying the fact would only have further complicated the situation. Stating the reality, regrettable as it was, could set the stage for reality-based problem solving.

So mirroring embraces, or baldly states, perceived reality about oneself and others. By refraining from judging the reality, mirroring also normalizes it. But why is that good? Why would teachers want to imply that their students' realities are "normal"?

One way of answering this question is to ask another one. Why would teachers want to imply that their students' realities are *ab*normal? Even if a teacher hates a student's actions or attitudes, judging the student's truth as "abnormal" denies the student's reality and is, ultimately, shaming. Dismissing or erasing students can never be good. Imposing one's own version of reality on a student is just as bad. Mirroring is important because it preserves all versions of reality, the teacher's and the student's, yet allows for teacher and student to meet in mutual understanding. The value of this type of meeting cannot be overstated (and will be explored in chapter four).

Mirroring requires seeing. And seeing requires looking. When teachers look at students, at least two things happen. First, teachers get valuable information about the student. Does the student look tired? Has the student been crying? Is the student wan or, conversely, healthy and

138

energetic? Are the student's eyes bright? Looking at students' faces and noting how they move and hold their bodies can help contextualize their classroom behaviors.

Second, looking at students with the intention of seeing them completes a circuit. It is a form of plugging in. It activates relationship and the give and take of learning. Whether or not a student wants to be seen, a teacher who *mirrors* conveys that she is present, caring, and attentive, qualities that students require from their developmental partners. And because it rejects judgment, accurate mirroring can be immensely relieving.

Mirroring is relieving because *being seen* is relieving. Of course, mirroring someone at her best is gratifying: "You played every note correctly"; "You stole the show!"; "You got your hair cut." But mirroring someone at her worst, difficult as it may seem, can be liberating. Why? Because *mirroring focuses on the student*, which gives the student a chance to get her needs met; *mirroring clarifies responsibilities*, which allows for individual competence and collaboration; *mirroring embraces and normalizes reality*, which banishes judgment and shame; and *mirroring requires seeing*, or acknowledging what is true, whether good or bad. These conditions, as we will see in chapter four, free students to be creative, to grow, and to learn.

The bottom line is that mirroring, seeing someone accurately, is deeply affirming.

Mirroring the Negative

But how can a teacher mirror negative qualities to a student without hurting the student's feelings? The key here would be in retreating from the term "negative," which implies judgment. Personal judgments are not mirrors. They are evaluations; they skip the crucial step of simply seeing.

Mirroring is reflecting. And mirroring negative qualities requires acceptance of the fact that reflections are not always lovely. "That must be very confusing — to want my attention but to get it in ways that make me angry at you," Ms. McNamara might have suggested to her difficult student Jeannie (in chapter one). This picture is not necessarily becoming. It's just, possibly, true.

139

The power of mirroring is not in its potential to flatter and appease — that is, to deceive — but in its accuracy. If Ms. McNamara's guess about their relationship resonated with her student, Jeannie would be able to acknowledge the honest picture her teacher painted and seize upon the feeling of being seen and understood. (Of course, if Ms. McNamara's guess about Jeannie was *in*accurate, it would have no power.) Students do not actually need pretty pictures of themselves from their teachers. They need accurate reflections.

Mr. Peterson's dilemma offers an example of one way to use mirroring in the face of negative qualities. If Mr. Peterson had shared his initial impressions of Wally's poem, he would have been viewing Wally's work through his own personal lens and responding judgmentally. "Rhyming poems aren't my favorites," Mr. Peterson might have said. "They seem so childish. And war is a terrible topic for a poem. It's too grisly and depressing. Isn't there something else you're proud of and could have written a poem about, Wally?"

These might very well have been Mr. Peterson's judgments, and stating them out loud might have made Mr. Peterson feel better. But how would they have helped Wally? They would have given Wally a concrete sense of his teacher's personal preferences for poetry, certainly. And Wally could have devoted himself (after he had recovered from his humiliation and disappointment) to writing poems that pleased Mr. Peterson rather than himself; that is, he could have focused his energy on accommodating Mr. Peterson's judgment rather than on cultivating his own skills, aesthetics, and relationship to writing.

By mirroring Wally — by stepping out of himself and letting Wally's poem show him its particular power — Mr. Peterson stripped out the "negative" and the "judgment" and offered Wally a picture he could use. "That's what I was aiming for!" Wally might have exclaimed. "I really am proud of our soldiers, and I really do love my country. I'm glad that came through in my writing." Wally could know, through Mr. Peterson's accurate reflection, that he had accomplished his expressive task.

140

But *Mr. Peterson's* task would have just begun. Wally might have achieved his own poetic purposes, but there would certainly be room for improvement. Here is where Mr. Peterson's judgment would come in. As a professional developmental partner (i.e., teacher), Mr. Peterson would have to decide where he thought Wally needed improvement and how he might help Wally achieve it. Mr. Peterson would have to exercise his judgment not in the sense of condemning or shutting down but in the sense of assessing and opening up possibilities.

In the process Mr. Peterson would undoubtedly apply his personal standards to his instructional goals for Wally. As someone who hated rhyming poems, Mr. Peterson might be tempted to challenge Wally to write a nonrhyming poem. This instructional goal would be an empty one, a mere exercise of Mr. Peterson's self-serving authority, if it was aimed at changing Wally's mind about rhyming; that is, if Mr. Peterson's purpose was to turn Wally into a mini version of himself, a student who agreed with his teacher.

The challenge would be valuable (and, by the way, might work better) if Mr. Peterson's purpose was authentically Wally centered. "You seem to have rhyming down pat," Mr. Peterson might say. "That's quite a skill. But I have a confession to make: I'm a little suspicious of rhyming poems. I worry that poets can lose track of what they really feel when they spend time looking for a rhyme. My own experience is that, when I'm searching for a rhyme, I become more superficial, more focused on sound than feeling.

"So here's my challenge," Mr. Peterson could say. "Write a second version of this poem, a poem that captures your pride in our country, that does not use rhyme. Let's see what the differences between the poems and between your experiences of writing them might be."

Note Mr. Peterson's technique. He acknowledges and reinforces the difference between his own and Wally's preferences by *self-disclosing*, by admitting and explaining his tastes, his personal (and perhaps peculiar) reality. This self-disclosure would be key to the challenge, for it centers on a skill to be developed rather than approval to be won.

141

And Mr. Peterson's opinion about rhyming would come across not as gospel but as a testable hypothesis. "Your mission, should you choose to accept it," Mr. Peterson seems to be saying to Wally, "is to compare two different poetry-writing experiences and report back to me on what you find." Of course, Mr. Peterson would report out to Wally as well, since his response to the two poems would be important data in this experiment.

How might Mr. Peterson then evaluate the outcome of his challenge to Wally? If his job is not to judge, then are all responses valid? If Wally's reality is just as valid as Mr. Peterson's, why bother with a grade?

Once again, Mr. Peterson would be obligated to use his professional judgment to evaluate Wally's progress in his class. This evaluation would be fairly straightforward when it came to right and wrong answers, and it would be tricky when subjectivity was called for. In the case of Wally's poem, where at least two legitimate personal realities (Mr. Peterson's and Wally's) would need to be taken into consideration, a shared set of criteria would smooth the communication and discussion of responses to Wally's poem. Put another way, a rubric — especially one created by all the students in the class — would help mediate between different perceptions of poetry, allowing teacher and students to hold and develop their own responses and, importantly, to understand others'.

BLACK BELT MOVE

Put yet another way, rubrics and class-generated criteria require mirroring; that is, they require accurate descriptions of what a particular reader perceives, then shared discussion of the various meanings of each reader's observations. Far from falling into relativism, such discussions allow thoughtful readers to agree about the positive and negative qualities of a student's work. Grades that are based on this type of collaborative analysis are both meaningful and respectable.

So to review: How did Mr. Peterson become a mirror for Wally? Importantly, he slowed down: He noticed his own response to Wally's work, realized (through his feeling of panic) that his personal response would not be helpful to Wally, and deliberately chose to focus on Wally and what his student was trying to express through his poem. Because he wisely recognized that he was not totally prepared to be Wally centered (because he was concentrating on himself and his reactions), Mr. Peterson asked Wally to reread his poem. This time he could quiet his own response and listen to his student (that is, he could detach). This is the fundamental requirement for mirroring: quieting oneself down, listening to and seeing another, and describing what one hears and sees without judgment.

The example of Mr. Peterson and Wally shows how a teacher might mirror negative qualities of work that can be improved upon. What about plain old incorrect answers? To illustrate this type of mirroring, another story is required.

"I SEE THAT YOU'RE WRONG"

Ms. Moinzadeh taught English to seventh graders. By midyear she felt she knew her students fairly well and enjoyed the discussions they had about the literature they were reading.

Today the class was discussing the play they had just finished about Helen Keller and Annie Sullivan, The Miracle Worker. *Ms. Moinzadeh posed the question, "We read in the stage directions that once Helen learned how to label things Mrs. Keller realized that she had simultaneously gained and lost a child. What did the playwright mean by this?"*

Immediately, Cara's hand shot up, and Ms. Moinzadeh called on her. "He means Helen is no longer a child but Annie Sullivan is now like a daughter to her," Cara answered.

Without hesitating, and feeling quite confident that Cara could handle her brusqueness, Ms. Moinzadeh said, "Wrong." She scanned the class for more raised hands but noticed, out of the corner of her eye, that Cara visibly shrank. Too late, Ms. Moinzadeh realized she had hurt Cara's feelings, and she felt terrible for the rest of the day.

To be fair Ms. Moinzadeh's response to Cara counted as mirroring. "Wrong" is a perfectly acceptable description of Cara's answer. But Ms. Moinzadeh hurt Cara's feelings, and that in turn distressed Ms. Moinzadeh. What to do?

Ms. Moinzadeh's Emotion Work

The first thing to do would be to address the unintended mishap with Cara. The second thing would be to consider alternative ways to mirror wrong answers in the future.

YELLOW BELT MOVES

The distress she felt might incline Ms. Moinzadeh to condemn herself for having been insensitive to Cara. How could she have been so thoughtless? It might take some effort, but backing away from self-blame — detaching from the temptation to judge herself — would be extremely important for Ms. Moinzadeh. After all, hurt feelings are coconstructed. They arise out of a particular fit between two people and cannot necessarily be predicted in advance (unless, of course, one party *intends* to hurt the other). There is no way Ms. Moinzadeh could have anticipated or controlled how Cara would interpret "Wrong." In fact, she had felt pretty confident that Cara would be able to handle her honesty.

Rather than burden herself with blame, then, Ms. Moinzadeh could examine what her emotions told her. Did her distress and guilt reveal anything significant *about herself*? One thing she might notice was her intense worry that she had done something wrong, that she had somehow damaged Cara with her honesty. It wouldn't be difficult to guess that this revulsion toward being wrong might tell her something significant *about her student's emotions*: that Cara shrank in class not necessarily because of what Ms. Moinzadeh said but because Cara felt ashamed to be wrong. In this way Ms. Moinzadeh might have uncovered essential information about Cara's *relationship* with being wrong: It was bad.

And her emotion work would point to the real dilemma Ms. Moinzadeh faced with Cara and other students for whom making mistakes was shameful: creating a classroom culture in which being wrong and mirroring negative qualities would be acceptable, even welcomed. For even if Ms. Moinzadeh could smooth over the hurt of "Wrong" and refrain from using that particular word with Cara ever again, Cara's relationship with making mistakes would remain. The only way to alter that relationship, to change the prong with which Cara plugged into others' evaluations of her, would be to change the rules about making mistakes.

BLUE BELT MOVES

But for now, Ms. Moinzadeh would have some repairing to do with Cara. She could start with some *self-disclosure* and good *guessing*.

"Cara," Ms. Moinzadeh might say the following day, "I suspect I miscalculated yesterday [*self-disclosure*]. Remember when you answered one of my questions and I said you were wrong? I just said it flat out: 'Wrong.' I think I might have surprised you with my frankness [*making a guess*]."

Listening to Cara's response would help guide Ms. Moinzadeh in talking about how it feels to Cara to be wrong. If necessary, Ms. Moinzadeh could continue to *self-disclose*: "When I make a mistake, I can feel terrible, as if I've done some sort of damage. It makes me wonder: What damage is there in making a mistake?"

This, of course, is the heart of the matter. Ms. Moinzadeh could discuss this question with Cara privately as a means of clarifying for Cara why "Wrong" was not meant as a slap. And she could enlist Cara's help and advice in making a *plan* to enlarge the conversation to include the entire class. Ms. Moinzadeh could even explain to Cara that talking about making mistakes, relieving as it might be in the moment, is simply not enough. "We have to make a mistake-friendly classroom," Ms. Moinzadeh might tell Cara, "so everyone can *behave* in ways that support making mistakes and taking intellectual risks." Enlisting Cara's aid in this project could simultaneously help Ms. Moinzadeh hone her plan and empower Cara to embrace this difficult relational shift in herself.

BLACK BELT MOVE

To lay the groundwork for a "mistake-friendly classroom," Ms. Moinzadeh would have to bring the question "What damage is there in making a mistake?" to the entire class. From a consideration of the dangers of erring, Ms. Moinzadeh could move to exploration of the *benefits* of being wrong. Ultimately, the class could agree on individual and collective responses to wrong answers, responses that would constitute the kind of corrective action that all the students could benefit from.

It is quite likely that out of these discussions ideas would emerge for how Ms. Moinzadeh might mirror wrong answers in the future. In fact, making this issue an explicit topic of discussion in class could be very helpful for teacher and students alike. "What's the easiest way for you to hear you're wrong?" she could ask her students. Some suggestions they (or she) might come up with could include the following:

- "Ask for my reasoning."
- "Ask the rest of the class what they think."
- "Have us write down our answers and check with a neighbor before we share."
- "Congratulate us for thinking creatively!"
- "Just say, 'Wrong' or 'Nice try.' We'll know you're not being judgmental or mean."

The point is that there are any number of ways to mirror wrong answers. The key is in achieving a fit between teacher and students and among students in which the mirroring is taken for what it is: an honest reflection of reality without judgment. Mirroring works best in an environment that honors reality and trusts that different experiences are inescapable, meaningful, and, ultimately, enlightening.

FOOD FOR THOUGHT

QUESTION: How do you know when you should mirror a student?

ANSWER: When you sense that a student needs to be seen or heard.

Students broadcast their need to be seen and heard in many different ways, from acting out to being silent and unobtrusive to everything in between. Really, students need to be mirrored all the time, so a teacher can't miss when she decides to act as a mirror.

Taking Mirroring Personally

In truth, mirroring is not as simple as it sounds. While most, and possibly all, teachers are in the profession for the students, they are also in it for themselves. Many teachers, like other professionals, choose their career because it is somehow fulfilling for them. But the path to personal fulfillment is not always considerate of others. In the story above about Mr. Greene and Hiram, for example, Mr. Greene managed his insecurity by taking revenge on Hiram: by punishing him for questioning his teacher rather than noticing and mirroring Hiram's uncertainty about what he was supposed to be learning.

When teachers take what they observe personally, the students' welfare stops being the teachers' top priority. As Mr. Peterson demonstrated, mirroring requires teachers to set aside their own needs and focus on the students; it requires an acute appreciation of and commitment to the differences between teachers' and students' roles and responsibilities; it requires teachers to embrace students as they are, to accept students' realities as legitimate; and it requires accurate seeing and describing.

In general, mirroring means committing to giving the credit for learning and knowing — and for resisting and failing — to the students. It means keeping very clear about one's own preferences and perceptions and those of the students. It means accepting, even relishing, the fact that students must use their teachers. And all of this requires conscious intention. Hence, mirroring is not easy. But it is essential to ongoing development.

And it can be extremely fulfilling. Being mirrored is good for students, yes, but mirroring is also good for teachers; that is, it lifts the pressures of knowing and being everything for everyone off teachers' shoulders. It gives teachers permission to slow down and observe. It opens space for students to show who they are in often surprising ways.

And it feels good. The generosity of mirroring can fill one with satisfaction, and empathizing opens one up to a myriad of such pleasurable emotions as excitement, pride, wonder, and joy. Of course, teachers need to be mirrored as well, and sometimes their students satisfy that need. But ideally, teachers work in their own healthy reflective environment, a place where they are seen and valued by competent and empathic colleagues and administrators.

WRAP-UP
The truth is that being used by students as objects for their own growth is inevitable. And taking students' use personally can

147

be extremely irritating and exhausting. Fortunately, being used can also be personally rewarding and educationally effective, especially when a teacher chooses *whether* and *how* to be used. When teachers play the roles of *twin, statue on a pedestal,* and *mirror* well, students can learn and grow cognitively and emotionally.

In other words, committing to *not* taking students personally means taking one's role as developmental partner seriously. This role brings with it endless opportunities for aggravation and insult, as students will use their teachers ruthlessly. Managing this use by students by doing careful emotion work can be demanding. But as the central adults in the room, the emotional furniture, the developmental partners for all students, teachers simply cannot afford *not* to do this work.

CHAPTER ANSWERS
Here are some answers to the questions from the beginning of the chapter:

- *How is it possible not to take hurtful comments and behaviors personally?*
- *Why is it important not to take them personally?*

Teachers, as developmental partners to students, are often used as objects by their students. Students need twins *to banish their sense of isolation,* statues *to idealize, and* mirrors *to affirm their existence and value, and teachers (as well as parents) are perfect candidates for such use. When students use teachers, they are not thinking about their teachers as people; they are using their teachers as objects. Of course, this use can be inherently insulting to teachers who, naturally, insist on being people. The only way* not *to take such insults personally is to accept the fact that teachers are sometimes used as objects, not because of who they are but because of the developmental role they necessarily play in their students' lives.*

This role is inescapable. And it is powerful. This is why it is important not to take students' hurts, insults, and even compliments personally: because, when teachers do, they miss crucial opportunities to help their students grow and develop. And helping students grow and develop — the definition of being a developmental partner — is the very essence of teaching.

KEEP IN MIND

- *Teachers are **developmental partners** to their students.*
- *As such, teachers will inevitably be **used** by their students as **developmental objects**.*
- *An **emotional object** is someone who is used, or acted out on, for emotional relief.*
- *A **developmental object** is someone who is used for emotional and cognitive growth and development.*
- *Students will use their teachers as **twins**, or kindred spirits who remind students they are not alone or isolated; **statues on a pedestal**, or ideals whose admirable qualities can be adopted by the students; and **mirrors**, or honest reflectors of what appears to be the students' reality.*
- *When teachers take their students' insults or compliments personally, they are in danger of **reversing roles** and using the students for their own purposes.*
- *Even if teachers cannot choose **whether** to be used by their students (as students will use their teachers whether they like it or not), teachers can choose **how** to be used to each student's benefit.*
- ***Detaching**, or stepping back, noticing and describing what one observes, and thinking about it with genuine curiosity, is prerequisite to **not taking students personally**.*

CHAPTER THREE

BOUNDARY CROSSINGS: BEING A "GREAT ENOUGH" TEACHER

Most if not all teachers enter the profession hoping to be great: great at designing instruction, great at conveying content, great at relating to students, greatly influential. Such aspirations are admirable, but they overlook an extremely important fact: Teachers are not alone in the classroom. They're generally accompanied by a large number of students.

If it were entirely up to teachers, of course, every student would learn every lesson immediately. In fact, we are told by those making public policy that great teachers should control their students' learning (or at least their students' scores on standardized tests).

The beliefs that teachers are fully responsible for students' learning and that the best teachers and the best practices can guarantee learning outcomes are based on an important assumption: that *linear* cause and effect rule educational activity. Under this assumption a teacher says or does something to his students, and the students store the teaching in their brains for later retrieval. Paulo Freire called this the "banking" metaphor of education; others have called it the "conduit" metaphor ("open brain and pour knowledge in").

The psychodynamic perspective is based on entirely different assumptions about learning. One of those assumptions is that learning emerges from relationship (we'll explore this assumption further in chapter four). Another assumption, one we encountered in chapter one, is that relationships happen when people "plug into" each other to achieve a "fit." These relational fits are not controlled by one person; they are accomplished through collaboration, both conscious and unconscious. All participants in a relationship, even the "passive" ones, contribute to the connections that allow growth and learning to occur.

Different metaphors are needed, then, to describe the psychodynamic view of learning. One metaphor, used in chapter one, is "circuitry," or the completion of connections through "plugging in" that allow relational "electricity" to flow. Another metaphor might be "symbiosis": where interdependent, mutually adaptive living organisms work together to grow and learn.

Shifting from the banking metaphor to the symbiosis metaphor means embracing the messiness of teaching and learning. It means abandoning the comforting notion of cause and effect and accepting the challenges of negotiating mutually constructed relationships. And it means shifting one's ambition from being "great" to being "great enough."

But what does it mean to be a "great enough" teacher? And how can "great enough" be better than "great"?

In this chapter we will continue exploring the notion of teachers as *developmental partners* by learning what it means to be *great enough*. We will look at the ways in which *limits* and *boundaries* and, by extension, supportive *holding environments* can promote student learning. While rigorous emotion work is always encouraged, in this chapter we consider what teachers can do *in the heat of the moment*, before they have had time to reflect carefully. All along the way we will see why being great enough in the give-and-take of educational relationships is the best way to go.

CHAPTER QUESTIONS

- *What does it mean to be a "great enough" teacher?*
- *How can "great enough" be better than "great"?*

THE "GOOD ENOUGH" PARENT

Psychoanalyst and pediatrician D. W. Winnicott recognized the powerful developmental roles parents and other caretakers play for their children. Obviously, children need their parents for the basics of physical survival. But children also use their parents for emotional development. Ideally, it is through their parents and other caregivers that children individuate into separate, healthy, true selves who are capable of self-knowledge and self-respect but who can also connect intimately and humanely with others. Where both of these needs, the physical and the emotional, come together is in the *holding environment*, or the space parents and guardians provide in which their children's physical well-being and emotional development are nourished.

The Holding Environment

The notion of a holding environment is simple enough. It is a space within which children are safe to grow, explore, experiment, be creative, make mistakes. It is the context within which emotional and cognitive development takes place and within which attachment styles, psychic structures, and psychological comfort zones form.

One can consider the holding environment from the physical perspective of layout, materials, and activities, but one must also take the emotional atmosphere into consideration. For example, emotional development requires abundant, loving interaction between parent and child. It also rests on opportunities for the child to be "alone . . . in the presence of mother" (Winnicott, 1965). To be alone in the presence of mother (or, more generally, of *another*) is to immerse oneself in one's own imagination, the make-believe world within which a child makes sense of the real world, with the absolute certainty that help and attention, should the child need them, are nearby.

DEFINITION

*The **holding environment** is the physical and emotional context within which people are "held" so they can, one hopes, grow and develop safely and healthily.*

FOOD FOR THOUGHT

A holding environment can be as small and intimate as a mother's arms or as broad as a school, a neighborhood, or a nation. And the bigger the holding environment is, the less control an individual parent has. A father might give a mean bear hug but be unable to protect his children from dangers on the playground, on the school bus, or on the street. The notion of "holding environment," then, is not just a psychodynamic one. It is a social, economic, and political one as well.

One of the most important elements of a holding environment is *constraints*. Take, for example, a typical two-and-a-half-year-old boy. Not surprisingly, this toddler needs a

153

safe holding environment: Among many other things, he needs to be supervised when he plays; he needs to learn about dangers in his surroundings; he needs to be stopped from doing himself or others harm. Unfortunately, when faced with these constraints, our toddler often turns against his parents the very word they are using with him: "NO!" And as any parent of a typical toddler knows, the onset of "NO!" can make holding, whether in one's arms or in the environment, just about impossible.

Good Enough and Not Good Enough
As with students, a child's resistance to parental wisdom and guidance often leads to a power struggle. And as do teachers, parents can quickly lose perspective and control.

When parents lose perspective and a sense of control, they can try to pacify the child. They coddle and appease, trying to soften the blow of their "NO!" They make deals, bribe, distract, and simply give in, sabotaging their "NO" by turning it into an apologetic "yes." Winnicott describes such parents as "too good": They are so nice that they bend over backward to avoid their children's wrath. They choose to put off until tomorrow lessons about reality and limitations that their children need to learn today. By being accommodating in the face of resistance, these parents lose perspective on their developmental role and allow their children to call the shots.

Other parents who lose perspective and control get angry themselves. They identify with the rage their child is feeling and give in to their own rage at being thwarted. Rather than model for the child how to manage anger effectively, they actually take over their child's anger and turn it against him, often overwhelming and frightening him with their extreme reaction. Parents who co-opt their children by being fiercer and angrier are what Winnicott calls "not good enough." They, like their overly accommodating counterparts, take their toddler's resistance personally, perceiving disobedience as a personal threat rather than a developmentally necessary and appropriate gesture.

In this chapter we are concerned mainly with "good enough" parents and "great enough" teachers. For that reason, and to simplify the distinction, "too good," overly accommodating parents (and teachers) are put into the same category as "not good enough," co-opting parents (and teachers); that is, they are both "not good enough."

The good-enough parent, according to Winnicott, is one who can "meet" the toddler's bid for power, or "omnipotence," firmly, consistently, and objectively. Good-enough parents understand and accept that children must challenge them for the sake of their growth and development. They know that a daring and disobedient toddler (or teenager) needs not coddling or terrorizing but holding and containing.

DEFINITION

Good-enough parents *expect to be challenged. They commit to both setting realistic and healthy limits for their children and surviving the children's inevitable protests against these limits.*

When parents hold their children, they do two things:
- They set the reasonable parameters, both physical and emotional, within which their children must function for safety and health,

AND
- They maintain those limits consistently, even in the face of inevitable protest.

In truth, it is a child's job to push the boundaries; if she does not push and test, she will not gain the confidence she needs, first, that her parents are in charge (not she herself); second (and related), that she is physically and emotionally safe; and third, that reality, while sometimes disappointing, is manageable and survivable.

The great, almost unbearable risk parents and other caregivers run when they set and maintain limits is their children's disappointment and rage. Too-accommodating, not-good-enough parents recoil from the possibility of hurting their child and, by extension, of earning their child's hatred. These parents tend to interpret the crying, screaming tantrums that often result from a parent's "NO" as evidence of overwhelming internal pain. Out of love and concern (and self-preservation), these parents will do anything to stop that pain, including ignoring their own needs and reasonable restrictions. In doing so, they teach their child over and over that *the child is in control* and that the world ultimately yields to him.

155

For the child this means a number of things: He is in danger (being a mere child, he cannot possibly take control); there is no reality other than his own (because the world is ever yielding); difficult emotions are, in fact, unmanageable; and, when he most needs boundaries, there are none. He will not be securely held. These lessons are deeply handicapping, especially when a child eventually confronts real-world limits and cannot, or will not, adapt to them.

DEFINITION
Too-accommodating not-good-enough parents *protect their children from the suffering caused by realistic limits, in the process teaching their children to be entitled and inflexible.*

Co-opting not-good-enough parents are themselves overwhelmed by their child's strong negative emotions and must suppress them to regain a sense of balance and control. Not understanding the child's reaction to "NO!" and, perhaps, suspecting that their insistence is misguided, they resolve their doubts and intense discomfort by crushing the protest. Even when their intent is to restore peace, co-opting not-good-enough parents teach their child to fear them.

DEFINITION
Co-opting not-good-enough parents *enforce limits by dominating their children, in the process teaching their children to fear them and to hide themselves behind a "false self."*

As teachers who insist on compliance do, co-opting parents help their child develop a "false self," one that is focused not on self-expression and autonomy but on self-effacing appeasement of more powerful others. One result can be an overly developed, anxious external orientation, the constant need for others' approval. Another result can be atrophied self-understanding and awareness. Yet another result can be an ongoing pattern of relational abuse as the child-turned-adult models his own behaviors after those of his parents.

156

Good-enough parents can also be not-good-enough parents at times. There is no "embracing hatred" gene that makes some lucky people serene in the face of a child's anger and disappointment. Two traits that characterize good-enough parents are their willingness to repair when they have over- or underreacted and their ability to tolerate their child's learning process in the face of inevitable frustration.

KEEP IN MIND
Two characteristics that good-enough parents tend to have are
- *willingness to repair relationships after the fact AND*
- *tolerance for their children's frustration.*

Repairing
There are many ways parents can repair mistakes they have made with their children:
- Revisiting a tantrum and explaining their reactions
- Working through a conflict with the child after a cooling time-out
- Taking full responsibility for their own actions
- Apologizing for inappropriate or frightening responses

These approaches to relational repair can be immensely healing because children are reassured when parents (eventually) do not take their tantrums personally: when parents can *detach* and both empathize with their children and represent reality in terms that make sense, that match the children's own experience and that honor that experience as separate and worthy, even if sometimes maddening.

By representing themselves fairly and accurately and accepting their children's different realities, parents model the interpersonal boundaries that are so essential to healthy interaction. Repairing mistakes reinforces the distinction between parent and child at the same time that it strengthens the connection upon which a child's emotional life depends.

157

Tolerating Frustration

The ability to remain calm as a child learns how to manage frustration is a crucial skill for good-enough parents. Whether they like it or not, all parents will eventually frustrate and anger their children. The trick, Winnicott advises, is in frustrating "optimally."

As Winnicott sees it a child ideally begins life with a caregiver who is completely focused on her, experiencing what Winnicott calls "primary maternal preoccupation." After a few months the parent begins to return her attention to her own life, juggling her needs with those of her baby and others. Over time, caregivers respond to the baby's cry a little more slowly than at first, unintentionally giving the baby time to practice self-soothing and to adjust to the awful truth that the world is full of limits, disappointments, and frustrations. This lack of immediate availability provides the baby with "optimal frustration," which she can use to learn the essential skill of self-regulation.

DEFINITION

Self-regulation *is the ability to exert self-control and to soothe oneself in moments of stress.*

Fortunately, the world is also (ideally) full of love, admiration, excitement, and reassuring calm, so frustration and other strong negative feelings can be counterbalanced. But introducing children to frustration, inviting them to feel the terrible emotions of hatred, anger, and disappointment, and showing them that these feelings are survivable — not so terrifying that parents cave in to them and not so threatening that parents squelch them with their own rage — is one of the most important jobs good-enough parents can do.

Put a little differently, in terms introduced in chapter two, good-enough parents recognize that, precisely because they are such influential people in their children's lives, they will be *used* as *objects* for their children's emotional (and physical and cognitive) *development*. Because they must frustrate and disappoint, parents will be tested, fought, disobeyed; they will be destroyed, vanquished, in their children's imaginations; they will be hated. When parents take

158

this object-role *personally*, they can become not good enough: They can assuage their own discomfort by either giving in to their children or overwhelming them. When parents embrace this object role, recognizing that it has little to do with them personally and everything to do with them as *developmental partners*, they can provide the type of holding environment all children require.

From Parents to Teachers

So what does this have to do with teachers? As crucial developmental partners, teachers are subject to the same reactions that parents are when they try to "hold" their children. Teachers are, therefore, akin to good-enough parents.

But valuable as Winnicott's definition of a good-enough parent is, the term "good enough" is not good enough for teachers who want to be great. To avoid the appearance of pushing complacency and mediocrity that a superficial reading of "good enough" might imply, the term we will use from here on out for teachers is "great enough." The great-enough teacher, like the good-enough parent, recognizes her crucial developmental role in the classroom and establishes and maintains a healthy holding environment for her students.

THE "GREAT ENOUGH" TEACHER

Guaranteed, students are going to fight "holding" and constraints. They will pack up before the bell rings, refuse to do homework, distract fellow students, and treat their teachers with disrespect. Because learning is a stressful and uncertain endeavor, students of all ages will fall back on thoughtless, maladaptive behaviors that they would never exhibit in less anxiety-producing situations. As developmental partners teachers are obligated to set limits on these behaviors, to say "NO" and "STOP" and to impose appropriate consequences when necessary. Difficulties come in when teachers skip the step of setting limits and instead enact not-good-enough responses.

Definitions

Great-enough teachers *recognize that they are developmental partners with their students and must establish and maintain a healthy holding environment.*

Maladaptive behaviors *are automatic reactions to stress that are triggered by psychic structures. They are behaviors that tend to work in the short term but, because they are* mal*adaptive, can have negative long-term consequences.*

Limits and Consequences

The following story shows both types of not-good-enough teaching – too-accommodating not-good-enough teaching and co-opting not-good-enough teaching – and considers how to turn such automatic reactions into great-enough teaching.

WHO'S THE BOSS?

Mr. Bonham understood that science was a subject some high school students found difficult to enjoy. Yet he loved science and devoted himself to instilling that love in his students.

For the most part he succeeded. But one student, Brittany, consistently resisted his efforts, refusing to do homework, chronically disrupting class, and even treating him with overt disrespect. He tried every way he knew to explain the content more clearly to her, but she had no interest. All she wanted to do, it seemed to him, was ruin his class.

One day Brittany arrived to class late. Rather than enter the room, though, she hid in the doorway, mimicking Mr. Bonham's actions behind his back. The students laughed, and when Mr. Bonham realized what Brittany was doing, he blushed, smiled coldly, and, in an even but tight voice, invited Brittany to join the rest of the class.

After Brittany took her seat, Mr. Bonham had to remind her to get her science materials out, but Brittany had forgotten them. Mr. Bonham offered her his own copy of the textbook. When Mr. Bonham began the lesson at the front of the room, Brittany suddenly yelled, "You can't teach me! I want someone else to teach me this. I want Ms. Penn to be my science teacher!"

"Too bad!" Mr. Bonham burst out. He grabbed the textbook he had lent Brittany and slammed it down with

160

all his strength on her desk. There was no more acting out that period.

Obviously, Mr. Bonham was not being a great-enough teacher. Rather, he enacted both types of *not*-good-enough teacher, the overly accommodating teacher and the enraged, co-opting teacher.

First, he played nice. He smiled at Brittany's outrageous mimicking and uncomplainingly provided her with the science materials she had forgotten. This is the overly accommodating, not-good-enough teacher. When Brittany's provoking became too much for him, he exploded and became the co-opting not-good-enough teacher. Extreme as his reaction was, it succeeded in defining, at least for the moment, who was the boss and whose anger dominated.

What would a great-enough teacher have done? Of course, *emotion work* is always a good idea. Mr. Bonham could have practiced *self-awareness* by asking himself some fundamental questions about his relationship with Brittany. How did he feel about Brittany, generally and in these moments of astonishing disrespect? What did these feelings tell him about *himself*? What did his feelings and Brittany's behaviors tell him about *her*, her needs and abilities? What did they tell him about Brittany's *relationship* to him and to science class? This type of reflection, because it is engrossing and takes time, is best done after the fact, in private or with the help of an informed professional. And given the hostility between him and his student, emotion work would have been essential if Mr. Bonham were to change the way he plugged into Brittany.

What could Mr. Bonham have done *in the heat of the moment*, though? How could he have resisted his not-good-enough urges and behaved as a great-enough teacher would?

The answer is that Mr. Bonham could have *set limits*, or established and reinforced the constraints that would safeguard his classroom as an effective holding environment for all students, especially Brittany.

Setting Limits

Setting limits on inappropriate behavior actually involves a whole series of moves. Figuring out what limit needs to be set

161

is just the beginning. Anticipating pushback is essential, as is holding the line, or enforcing the limit, in the face of pushback. While students might not throw full-blown tantrums on the classroom floor, they very likely will continue to test the limits, escalating their outrageous behaviors to convey their frustration and anger. The great-enough teacher expects this to happen, even anticipates possible reactions from certain students ahead of time, and prepares for them by making concrete *plans* that allow him to maintain the limit safely and humanely.

Once a limit has been set, the great-enough teacher does not take on the student's anger or rescue the student from her feelings, as leaving her to her own responses is crucial for her development. No student will learn how to manage difficult emotions if she is prevented from feeling them. Caving to a student's emotion is not good enough, and overriding that emotion is not good enough. Rather, holding the student in the midst of emotion and not taking her emotion personally allow the student to feel what she needs to feel and, at the same time, to experience the containment she needs.

Staying present to but detached from students' responses, then, is essential. This alert, genuinely curious, and, importantly, empathic stance is the model students need for managing what seem to be unmanageable emotions. Watching a teacher maintain control in the midst of overwhelming emotion can lay the groundwork in students for their own self-regulation, learning that is crucial to maturity.

Defining Consequences

The flip side of setting limits is defining clear consequences. Ideally, the consequences are "natural"; that is, they result logically from failing to respect the limit. If a student does not turn in his homework, for example, he receives a zero for that assignment. If he does not hand in most of his assignments, he fails the class. The natural consequence of not doing assigned work, in other words, is loss of academic credit.

DEFINITION
"Natural" consequences *are those that result logically from an action. They are preferred over arbitrary punishments meted out by a teacher.*

162

Ideally, consequences are spelled out explicitly ahead of time so there is no confusion, wiggle room, or inconsistency. Explicit rules and consequences are good for students, but they are also good for teachers, as making up rules and figuring out consequences on the fly can be ineffective and exhausting.

But consequences must also be determined on an as-needed basis. Again, the more explicit and natural these outcomes are the better. Consequences that appear to be punishments meted out by the teacher rather than the inescapable results of the student's own behavior can backfire woefully.

The great-enough teacher who does not take students' actions personally bears no grudges. She sets the limit, holds the line, manages her own emotions in the moment, and applies consequences fairly. And she is available emotionally for ongoing use, feeling no guilt or fear of being rejected or hated but, rather, being willing to review the event and *repair* as needed to promote self-understanding and compassion.

Of course, a teacher may have strong negative feelings about an event or a student that tempt her to hold a grudge. These feelings, though undoubtedly legitimate, would have to be worked through and defused for two very good reasons: first, so they would not perpetuate a bad relationship with the student and, second, so the teacher would not continue to suffer from the negative feelings.

Despite all of her best intentions and efforts, though, a teacher might discover that she simply cannot set an effective limit with a particular student or group of students. Rather than consider this a failure, the teacher would be wise to accept the reality and take additional steps. These necessarily involve activating the structural network around her: calling on the school administration for advice and support, appealing to students' caregivers at home, and mobilizing other elements of the school holding environment.

In short, then, a great-enough teacher must
- notice when limits are being tested and detach enough to not take the testing personally;

- recognize that testing limits is normal and developmentally appropriate for students of all ages;
- set or reinforce consistent, fair limits and stick to them (hold the line);
- stay present to, yet detached from, her own and the students' emotions, resisting the urge to rescue or punish the students or take on the emotions for them;
- apply consequences fairly and consistently, anticipating and preparing for pushback;
- hold no grudges but, rather, be available for ongoing academic and emotional use;
- mobilize supportive elements within and outside the school holding environment.

Most of these moves qualify as *blue belt*, as they involve interacting with students. The first two are *yellow belt* moves, as they are wholly internal. The last move, which activates the broader school community (colleagues, administrators, and parents) and others, is a *black belt* move.

FOOD FOR THOUGHT

"NO" sets a clear and extreme limit. Such a **hard limit** *is often necessary. But* **soft limits** *can also be extremely effective. Soft limits sound like this:*

- *"Yes, if . . ."*
- *"Yes, when . . ."*

Soft limits are powerful because they involve compromise. And compromise, by holding in tension the needs of both teacher and student, invites students to take realistic responsibility. Compromise also opens up space for innovation and creativity.

For example, when a student interrupts a math lesson with "Can I go to the bathroom?" the frustrated teacher can calmly respond, "Yes, when I've finished talking about fractions — and that will be in about four minutes. I will let you know when four minutes is up." This soft limit acknowledges the legitimacy of the student's physical need — to go to the bathroom — but insists on a compromise that permits the teacher to accomplish an educational need.

164

When a student complains about a particular assignment, saying, "Can't I do something else?" the teacher can answer, "Yes, if your alternative satisfies my teaching objectives." Working to devise a plan that accomplishes those objectives could be eye-opening and enriching for the student and could result in a project that is much more educational for her. The compromise satisfies the teacher's instructional needs and leaves room for the student's creativity and autonomy.
[Credit for "Yes, if" and "Yes, when" to Perry Good of the Connected Schools Initiative, *http://aconnectedschool.com*.]

Mr. Bonham's Limits

Let us return now to Mr. Bonham and his provocative student, Brittany. How could he have set limits that would have "held" Brittany and allowed the other students in the class to go on learning? What, in other words, could he have done differently *in the heat of the moment*?

YELLOW BELT MOVES

When he caught her mimicking him in the doorway, Mr. Bonham's first move could have been to recognize that Brittany was testing limits. His second move could have been to *detach* from his student's behavior enough to not take the testing personally.

BLUE BELT MOVES

His third move could have been to set an undeniable limit swiftly, firmly, and calmly. "I'm sorry, Brittany, but you'll have to take your mean faces to the office, as this is no place for them," Mr. Bonham could have said. Stating this limit calmly would be crucial, as evidence of emotional immunity to Brittany's antics would deny Brittany the satisfaction of knowing she had hurt her teacher. If he were to order Brittany out of the room angrily, she would have achieved her purpose: to affect her teacher, to rile him up, to make him notice her and feel (perhaps) as helpless in his classroom as she did.

Of course, going to the office could be perceived by Brittany as a form of reward. She hated Mr. Bonham's class, after all, so missing it would likely be a bonus. In addition, being sent out of the classroom would guarantee that Brittany would learn absolutely no science that day. Setting a limit that banishes students, then, is rarely desirable.

But given the basically nonfunctional relationship he currently had with Brittany, Mr. Bonham probably would have had no choice. Sending a student to the office is better than losing one's temper and threatening physical harm. It can also be better for the class as a whole, since removing a disruptive student allows other students to get on with their learning and conveys to them that they, at least, will be shielded from inappropriate behavior.

If Mr. Bonham had failed to set the limit the first time, Brittany gave him a second chance. When she admitted that she had forgotten her textbook, Mr. Bonham could, once again, have noticed that Brittany was testing him: Would he hold her accountable for being irresponsible? His proper response could have been to

- notice that Brittany was testing a limit: the rule that made her responsible for bringing her science materials to class;
- recognize that holding her accountable was developmentally necessary for Brittany;
- state the rule that students had to bring their science materials to class every day;
- resist the urge to rescue Brittany and perhaps gain her favor by lending her his own textbook;
- expect her to adjust on her own by coming up with a solution that did not disrupt class;
- expect pushback from Brittany (i.e., ongoing attempts to disrupt class);
- continue to respond calmly and firmly to Brittany without taking her personally and allowing her to set him off.

It is important to note that setting effective limits does not work in a relational vacuum. Let's face it: Mr. Bonham *did* set a limit with Brittany. He slammed his book down on her desk and halted her shenanigans for the day. The problem is that, given the deeply antagonistic relationship he had with Brittany, his options were limited. Even if he wanted to be a great-enough teacher, the only lines he could draw at this moment were those that would curb Brittany's negative behaviors momentarily but inflame her for the future. Short-term gain, long-term loss.

BLACK BELT MOVE

In the long term, Mr. Bonham would need to establish a positive relationship with Brittany. Doing *emotion work* that would improve the way he felt about and interacted with Brittany, then, would be his next obligation as a great-enough teacher. To this end he would have to seek advice and support from colleagues, administrators, and others who could keep him focused on exploring and overcoming his aversions to Brittany and on forging healthy connections with her. Only in the context of a functional relationship can setting limits have any beneficial long-term effect on teacher and student.

Concrete limits define a holding environment. They are the constraints that clarify for children and students how their safety is going to be assured and how their development is going to be fostered. Though limits tend to be specific and concrete — "You must be in your seats by 8:40"; "You may not throw spitballs"; "Class members agree to listen to each other respectfully" — their impact is pervasive; that is, limits both contain and liberate behaviors, defining a space within which play, creativity, and lasting learning can take place.

Respecting Boundaries

The work of setting limits is actually a subset of a broader and equally essential goal: that of respecting physical and emotional boundaries. Limits are, basically, rules; they help define holding environments by establishing expectations and the consequences of not abiding by or meeting them. Limits are related to the context that teacher and students share. Physical and emotional boundaries, on the other hand, are *personal*; they are *felt*; and they are *flexible*, changing by situation.

Physical and emotional boundaries are personal.
They are intimately connected to the types of interactions that a person finds either comfortable or uncomfortable. If someone grew up in a very formal household, he might require more distance and less familiarity from his peers than someone who grew up in a family that was more physically and emotionally

demonstrative. Boundaries, then, define for each person what feels interpersonally safe.

Physical and emotional boundaries are felt. They are imaginary lines that divide one person from another. Sometimes emotional boundaries correspond to actual physical barriers: a poker face, a fence, a closed door. These physical boundaries are visible and tangible and can therefore be used as effective markers of one's need for emotional distance or privacy. But fundamentally, emotional boundaries are not concrete. They are known generally in the feeling of them and, quite often, in the feeling of alarm when they have been breached.

People feel their own boundaries, and they can sense others'. The feeling of a force field that indicates when one can move closer and when one should keep some distance is a boundary. Of course, some people neither project that force field nor sense it in others — or, worse, do not care — and thus are more or less unbounded. The relative strength or weakness of a boundary is, of course, contextual and can depend on many factors, including cultural background.

Physical and emotional boundaries are flexible. Depending on the situation, boundaries move, creating expanded and constricted comfort zones as necessary. The same person who enjoys cuddling on the sofa with her boyfriend can require much more space and formality in her interactions with strangers. If this person imposed the same rigid boundaries on her boyfriend that she enacted with strangers, she would have a difficult time achieving intimacy in any relationship. Flexible boundaries make for greater diversity and appropriateness in relating.

Boundaries also flex in relation to one's feeling of safety. When a boundary is violated, alarms tend to go off in a person's body, and her boundaries can become firmer, more defensive. If the person who violated the boundary backs off and a feeling of safety returns, boundaries can become softer and more elastic.

It can be helpful to think of boundaries, simplistically, as imaginary circles around people. Each person is responsible for what is inside her own circle, while others must take care of what is inside their circles. When people manage their own emotions, behaviors, and needs without taking others' emotions, behaviors, and needs personally, they are staying within their circles, or boundaries.

Emotional boundaries *are*
- *personal;*
- *felt;*
- *flexible.*

They are the imaginary lines that constitute the **circle** *around every person.*

Staying within one's own circle, or having well-bounded relationships, does not mean one must give up being generous, empathic, or caring. Human beings are by their nature interdependent. We fit together in ways that challenge our independence for better and for worse. Love, kindness, understanding, and healing and helping acts challenge our independence by drawing us into positive relations with others. Dysfunction and pathology challenge our independence by trapping us in harmful relations with others. The key is not to withdraw from others in order to be fully responsible for oneself but to connect with others in healthy ways that promote growth and reduce suffering for all concerned.

Of course, not everyone can be perfectly well bounded all the time. It is unrealistic to expect students, those well-seasoned limit testers, to respect their own and others' boundaries. But what about teachers? The next three stories explore three common ways teachers can overstep their boundaries and become not good enough.

Not-Good-Enough Teaching
The following story describes a teacher who is all too willing to step into a student's "circle" and do his work for him.

WHOSE WORK IS IT, ANYWAY?
Ms. Psacharopoulos was a big fan of project-based learning. All students benefited, she felt, from multiweek projects, even students as young as those she taught: second graders.

But Ms. Psacharopoulos did not simply assign a project and send children off on their own to do it. She scaffolded her students the entire way. She helped them plan the project; she sent explanations home to parents with the expectation that they would help; she offered support during lunch and recess; and she gave students plenty of time in class to do their work.

This year, however, one student, Gabe, managed to sidestep all of this help on a big second-grade project, a detailed map of a continent. He masterfully avoided all of the supports Ms. Psacharopoulos provided. Although she agreed to work with him during lunch several times, Gabe barely began drawing the outline of his continent. Notes and phone calls home were ignored. When Ms. Psacharopoulos insisted Gabe stay in during recess to work on his project, he went to the restroom — and stayed there until recess was over.

The day before the projects were due and the students were to present their continents to all the other second graders in the school, Gabe had barely started his assignment. Feeling panicked and extremely angry, Ms. Psacharopoulos finished sketching out Gabe's continent for him and added some geographic details so that he would have something to present the next day.

At the presentation Gabe beamed as he showed off his poster to his peers. Ms. Psacharopoulos alternated between happiness for him and seething fury.

Gabe is one resistant student. He went to great lengths to avoid doing any work on his continent project. But his withdrawal from Ms. Psacharopoulos does not seem to qualify as a boundary crossing. It feels more like an escape attempt! Where is the boundary violation in this story?

Importance of Emotion Work
Before attempting an answer to this question, it must first be noted that understanding Gabe's resistance, or doing *emotion work*, would be crucial in decoding this experience. This was true for Mr. Bonham, and it is true for Ms. Psacharopoulos. As we will see in chapter four, doing emotion work and making sense of resistance would uncover some good reasons for

170

Gabe's refusal to work on the continent project and suggest ways to respond to it.

Emotion work is always recommended for understanding and repairing difficult experiences with students. But emotion work generally takes time and privacy. Noticing boundary transgressions and setting limits can be done *in the heat of the moment* and, at the very least, can serve to contain both teacher and student until emotion work can be done.

Drawing Circles

So to detect the boundary violation in this story, let us draw a circle around Gabe and a circle around Ms. Psacharopoulos and look closely at their interactions.

When it came to the continent project, Gabe wanted to have nothing to do with his teacher. He avoided all contact with her, even resorting to hiding out in the restroom when her influence seemed unavoidable. While there was undoubtedly a very good reason Gabe refused to work on his project, Ms. Psacharopoulos had no idea what it was.

While Gabe's circle was filled with resistance, Ms. Psacharopoulos's circle was filled with anxious determination. Her success as a teacher, she seems to have believed, depended on his success as a student. She was, therefore, committed to changing Gabe through kindness, cajoling, controlling, and anger. When these approaches failed, she was left with a choice: leave Gabe to the fate he had brought upon himself, or continue trying to save him. She chose to save him for reasons that very likely had little to do with Gabe.

From the standpoint of boundaries, the proper choice would have been to leave Gabe to his fate, to allow him to suffer the natural consequences of his actions. Ms. Psacharopoulos had already done everything in her power (short of doing emotion work) to help Gabe complete the project on time. There is just so much one person can do for another.

But from the standpoint of emotions, the choice of letting Gabe suffer the consequences appears to have been absolutely impossible for Ms. Psacharopoulos. The relational "fit" she had achieved with Gabe threw her into such turmoil that her only path to relief was to merge with her student, to step inside his circle, and to use him for the purposes of alleviating her confusion and maintaining her self-respect. In other words, Gabe's problem became Ms. Psacharopoulos's problem because she took it personally. Boundary violation.

Boundary violations are not usually simple matters of taking one step too far. They often involve fairly complicated — and usually unconscious — confusions of reality. Here, for example, are some of the feelings and beliefs, some conscious, some unconscious, that Ms. Psacharopoulos might have had about the situation with Gabe:

- Gabe is intelligent and capable but, for some reason, chooses not to live up to his potential. This means he'll probably be a failure all his life.
- I could — in fact, I *should* — help him live up to his potential to save him from becoming a failure.
- When Gabe does not do his work, I am furious; when he allows me to help him, I am resentful and sarcastic.
- If Gabe fails, it is my fault, and I am a terrible teacher.
- If Gabe fails, it is his fault, and I should give up on him.
- I should let Gabe experience the natural consequences of his actions; that is, I should let Gabe fail.
- If Gabe fails, he will have nothing to present to his peers. He will be filled with shame, and he will be unnecessarily miserable. And I will be just as miserable.
- If I let him fail and he *isn't* miserable and ashamed, I will be angry because I *want* him to feel miserable and ashamed for refusing to do his work.
- If I do his work for him, he will learn that he can get away without doing anything for himself.
- If I do his work for him, I will feel justified in my self-righteous anger.

It is difficult to distinguish between Gabe's reality and Ms. Psacharopoulos's reality in these statements. Where does Ms. Psacharopoulos end and Gabe begin? Ms. Psacharopoulos's beliefs are filled with assumptions ("He'll probably be a failure all his life"), either/or dichotomies ("If

172

Gabe fails, it is my fault; if Gabe fails, it is his fault"), impossible binds ("When Gabe does not do his work, I am furious; when he allows me to help him, I am resentful and sarcastic"), and fusions ("If I let Gabe fail, he will be miserable, and I will be just as miserable"). The bottom line is that all of Ms. Psacharopoulos's beliefs end up reflecting *her* point of view. Gabe's is erased. Boundary violation.

Cutting through these contradictory and palpably agonizing beliefs are at least two related themes: Ms. Psacharopoulos's grandiose expectations for herself and the fact that Gabe and ambivalent students like him are damned if they do and damned if they don't.

Grandiosity

When people are grandiose, they believe themselves to have greater powers than reality warrants. They believe this for any number of "good" reasons, including a desire to be helpful, an overdeveloped sense of responsibility or competence, a lack of faith in other people, an ingrained habit of self-reliance and self-blame, an irrepressible need to control situations. Grandiosity is often a reaction to historical experiences of others' failures: inadequate caregiving, chronic uncertainty and chaos, boundary crossings that demanded from a child premature responsibility and reversed roles.

DEFINITION

Grandiosity *is an inflated, unrealistic sense of one's responsibility and power to change others.*

Grandiosity can be seen as an excellent adaptation, as it transforms intense anxiety due to perceived helplessness into a satisfying, if exaggerated, sense of competence and control. It also requires a departure from reality, as it places on one person's shoulders responsibilities that do not belong to her. As happens whenever someone denies reality for long enough, the responsibilities grandiose people bear can wear them down. They can begin to feel resentful, angry, confused, and totally trapped, and they can blame others. (They can also experience debilitating physical symptoms.)

In stepping into Gabe's circle and doing his work for him, Ms. Psacharopoulos exercised grandiosity.

Damned if You Do, Damned if You Don't

And Ms. Psacharopoulos's grandiosity jammed Gabe between a rock and a hard place. If Gabe did not do his work, she felt angry (and possibly contemptuous) that he was trying to get away with being irresponsible. If he asked for help with his work, she felt resentful and self-righteous for having to, once again, save the day. If he did nothing on the project and felt misery and shame, Ms. Psacharopoulos (who had fused with him) would suffer emotionally. If he got away with doing nothing on the project and did not feel misery and shame, Ms. Psacharopoulos would need to punish him to instill in him the proper feeling of repentance.

In short, once Ms. Psacharopoulos took Gabe's resistance personally, Gabe actually disappeared. And Ms. Psacharopoulos, whose identity rested on the maintenance of her grandiose belief in her competence, responsibility, and ultimate power to rescue and control, took center stage.

Gabe's persistent resistance implies that he was trying to *use* Ms. Psacharopoulos; that is, he was offering her repeated opportunities to set limits on his behavior. He was also inviting his teacher to wonder about his pattern of resistance and ask him about it. Because she took his resistance personally, however, interpreting his behavior as incompetence and designating herself as his savior, Ms. Psacharopoulos began *using* Gabe. In other words, she saw his resistance, sensed him to be a student she could rescue, and merged with him as a means of preserving her sense of self.

This not-good-enough teacher move did not help Gabe; in fact, it effectively eliminated him. In this light, one might wonder if Gabe's remarkably tenacious resistance was to the continent project or to Ms. Psacharopoulos: to her failure to see him and the ever-escalating signals he was sending her.

Ms. Psacharopoulos's Boundaries

What could Ms. Psacharopoulos have done differently? Perhaps the hardest step she could take would be to retreat to her own circle. There she would need to wonder about her urge to merge, and she would have to tolerate the anger, frustration, and, possibly, deeper emotions that her boundary violations allowed her to avoid. And Ms. Psacharopoulos would have to

174

resist taking Gabe and his problem personally, allowing him to occupy his own circle independently from her.

This step would require some *emotion work*, which Ms. Psacharopoulos would best do in private or with someone who was qualified to help her work through her complicated feelings and beliefs. But what could she have done *in the heat of the moment*?

YELLOW BELT MOVES

There are at least two answers. The first answer relies on the necessity of noticing when students are testing limits and declining to take the testing personally. Gabe's ongoing refusal to do anything on the continent project was a massive test of Ms. Psacharopoulos's classroom limits. While she could have attached individual consequences to each of Gabe's breaches, the ultimate consequence was simple and very "natural": Gabe would have no project to present to his classmates. Not taking Gabe's testing personally would have meant accepting this consequence ahead of time. This move might have been extremely difficult for Ms. Psacharopoulos, but it would have been developmentally fitting for Gabe.

A second answer addresses the end of the story, when Gabe's choices landed him and his teacher in somewhat dire circumstances. Here is where Ms. Psacharopoulos's boundaries would have to be quite firm, as she would have to resist the urge, one last time, to save him; that is, she would have to

- reinforce the project rules, reminding Gabe that he was ultimately responsible for getting the work done and accepting the help he was offered;
- stay present to yet detached from Gabe's emotions, refusing to protect Gabe from failure; resist the urge to take on Gabe's emotions *and* to fill him with her own;
- allow Gabe to experience the natural consequences of having no continent poster to share;
- observe Gabe and his reactions, making herself available to help him process, and hence learn from, them.

What might these moves have looked like? Here is one possible scenario:

When Ms. Psacharopoulos discovered that Gabe had nothing to present to the other second graders, she could have become *aware* of her strong emotional response, stepped back from it, and *mirrored* Gabe through *self-disclosure*:

"You know, Gabe," Ms. Psacharopoulos could have said, "I have to confess that I'm feeling a little panicked that your project isn't finished. Do you feel that way?" Wondering about Gabe's feelings would be essential, as it would separate her reaction from his, thereby establishing a boundary. It would also give Ms. Psacharopoulos valuable information about Gabe's experience.

If Gabe's response was "not really," Ms. Psacharopoulos could simply *listen* and nod. Her job would be to accept his attitude toward the project, even if it opposed her own (and the attitude she wanted him to have). In fact, curiosity about this young man might be awakened as she considered how different his stated expectations of himself were from hers.

And she could *describe* for him, calmly and with no judgment, the *consequences* of his attitude. "Okay," she could say, "just so we're absolutely clear: Tomorrow you won't have a poster to show your classmates, so you won't be able to participate in the presentation. I feel bad about that" — honest, off-loading *self-disclosure* — "as I worry that you'll feel left out tomorrow. But there's obviously nothing I can do about your decision. Do you have any questions about what's going to happen tomorrow?" Asking this would allow Gabe to engage with the issue (if he chose to) and, possibly, share more enlightening information with Ms. Psacharopoulos about his resistance, information she might be able to use in untangling future interactions.

If Gabe's answer to Ms. Psacharopoulos's question, "Do you feel that way?" was "Yes, I do," then Ms. Psacharopoulos would have a good sense of what was filling Gabe's circle at that moment: panic. This could help her to feel compassion rather than rage at Gabe. And it could help her to embrace the role of developmental partner, the person Gabe needed to *use* for understanding and problem solving, for holding.

"Oh, boy, if you're feeling the way I'm feeling then you're feeling pretty bad," she could say. "But there might be a way for you to make yourself feel better." Without making any assumptions and without once again taking control, she could ask, "Gabe, do you want to have something to present to the other second grade classes tomorrow?" If his answer was "yes," she could ask what he was willing to do with his remaining time to complete a version of the project they could both live with. If his answer was "no," she could state the consequences just as she did above, without judgment or anger. In the first case, she would be channeling Gabe's immediate energy to help him accomplish his task; in the latter case, she would be allowing Gabe to feel the natural consequences of his actions while being available to help him process his feelings in hopes that he could learn from them.

This is an important point. When gripped by grandiosity, Ms. Psacharopoulos is tempted to believe that Gabe's learning is dependent solely on his completion of the continent project. Her perspective is rigidly dichotomous, on or off, win or lose. If Gabe finishes the project, he will learn about his continent and feel good about himself (as will she). If he procrastinates or fails to finish the project, he will feel terrible (as she will) and will take one step closer to fulfilling her pessimistic prophecy about his future.

By setting a boundary between herself and Gabe, Ms. Psacharopoulos could position herself in the middle ground between these two poles. Whatever move Gabe made, she would be available to respond. If he wanted to pursue the project, she could be there to help him execute. If he wanted to reject the project, she could be there to help him process the emotions this choice might bring up. There would be valuable learning in either move. And learning the latter lesson — that is, living through the emotional consequences of not having a project to present — might help Gabe make different academic choices in the future.

In effect, Ms. Psacharopoulos could have "let Gabe fail." Sensible as this policy sounds on paper, it can be extremely difficult to carry out. Even if she were able to resist the seductive pull of grandiosity, Ms. Psacharopoulos might still have to fight a fear of outrage from Gabe's parents for having given their son a failing grade.

If Ms. Psacharopoulos was, in fact, worried about the reaction of Gabe's parents, she would do well to alert her school administrators to her situation. Their approval of her tactics with Gabe could have been a great relief to her. And knowing that crucial players in the school supported her actions and that they would defend those actions as necessary would have been invaluable to the work Ms. Psacharopoulos was trying to do with Gabe.

Enabling

There is a name for the role Ms. Psacharopoulos played with Gabe: "enabler." In the face of Gabe's persistent and anxiety-producing behavior, Ms. Psacharopoulos unconsciously yielded to her old, unbearable sense of powerlessness and acted for Gabe; that is, she stepped over the boundary between her and Gabe and did Gabe's job for him, allowing him to participate happily in the presentation to his peers without experiencing any negative consequences for his irresponsibility. She encouraged him to resist by rewarding him for it. And ultimately, it was she who suffered: While she was happy that Gabe enjoyed the presentation (or, more accurately, that she had been able to provide this joyful experience for him), she also seethed, wallowing in strong negative feelings for him and for herself.

DEFINITION

Enabling *is a type of relational pattern, a common way people fit together. Enablers tend to be supercompetent and grandiose. They tend to be attracted to people who act less competently: people who are self-destructive, passive, insecure, passive-aggressive. When they fit together, the enabler gets to take control and the incompetent one gets to lose control. Ultimately, no one wins.*

Enabling is a very common way to overstep boundaries. And it takes two to enable. While Ms.

Psacharopoulos can be seen as *using* Gabe to alleviate her anxiety about his project, he was also *using* her.

He was the habitual resister; she was the enabler. He avoided intense negative feelings about himself by pulling his teacher into his circle through passivity; she attempted to protect him and herself from these terrible feelings by taking action for him, by, in effect, denying or counteracting his destructive behavior. He repeatedly invited his teacher to set limits on him so he could experience the natural consequences of his actions (or, in this case, inaction); she took his apparent incompetence personally. He ended up feeling fine about the project (though his suppressed negative feelings about himself could not have changed); she ended up feeling angry (a possible reflection of Gabe's own feelings about this complicated situation).

But she also felt competent and powerful, and it was this feeling that kept her engaged in the cycle. This type of relationship, also called "codependent," is one that tends to prevail between addicts and their partners, caregivers, and even children. It is a pattern that protects the addict from feeling and growing and traps the enabler into denying what is true and committing to doing the impossible.

Another name for this type of behavior in the classroom is overly accommodating not-good-enough teaching.

Envy

Enabling is one type of boundary violation that teachers can enact. Another way for teachers to overstep their boundaries is to *dis*able, or actively take someone down for a perceived offense. The next two stories illustrate two forms of disabling, or co-opting not-good-enough, teaching.

WHO'S THE TEACHER?

Cecilia was a student teacher in Ms. Wade's high school physics class. For the first few weeks of her internship, Cecilia observed, worked one-on-one with students, and taught a few individual lessons. By the middle of the semester, Cecilia was ready to teach on her own for one week straight. She worked hard on her lesson design with Ms. Wade and with her program supervisor and came into school on the Monday of her solo week both nervous and excited.

Cecilia began class differently from the way Ms. Wade usually did, which Cecilia felt was quite dry and traditional. Hoping to pique her students' curiosity from the get-go, Cecilia asked the students to call out what they already knew about the topic she was introducing, vectors. "What the heck is a vector?" Cecilia asked. The students' enthusiastic responses — some serious, some silly, but all focused on the question — surprised and gratified Cecilia. She was establishing the momentum and interest she needed to move the students into the mini-lecture she had prepared.

To Cecilia's shock, however, Ms. Wade interrupted the rollicking brainstorming session. "These answers are getting a little too ridiculous," Ms. Wade said. "I think it's time to move on to the lecture." Cecilia obediently drew the brainstorming to a close and continued with her lesson plan. Not three minutes into Cecilia's mini-lecture, Ms. Wade jumped up and took over. Cecilia, feeling confused and ashamed, watched Ms. Wade teach for the rest of the period.

Where is the boundary violation? If we draw a circle around Cecilia and fill that circle with authority over the physics lesson, we can easily see that Ms. Wade, by first undermining and then completely taking over Cecilia's role, breached a boundary. She poked a hole in Cecilia's circle and let her student teacher's authority drain completely out.

As a mentor teacher Ms. Wade's responsibility was to sit back and watch Cecilia, noting her creativity and success as well as the areas in which she needed improvement. As Cecilia's developmental partner Ms. Wade was supposed to be available to Cecilia as a support and an honest and empathic advisor. But for reasons of her own, Ms. Wade could not stand to be used in this way. Instead, she *used* Cecilia to assuage her own uncomfortable feelings.

What might those uncomfortable feelings have been? One of them could have been envy. Watching Cecilia's evident success with the students, especially while implementing an

180

entirely different teaching style, could have activated insecurity and fear in Ms. Wade. Would the students like Cecilia better than they liked her? Was Cecilia a better teacher than she was? To ensure that both answers would be "no," Ms. Wade cut Cecilia down, first by chastising her publicly and then by teaching for her, implying that Cecilia was incapable of doing the job. Rather than allow herself to be used for her protégé's (and the students') betterment by waiting to offer helpful feedback on the entire lesson, it appears that Ms. Wade used Cecilia to relieve her uncontrollable fear, insecurity, and envy.

DEFINITION

Envy *is an emotion that often spurs boundary crossing, as the envious person seeks to deprive others of what they have. It is as if the envious person is saying, "If I can't have it, neither will she." Envy is generally hateful and destructive and is, hence, a truly terrible emotion.*

And because the best way to appease one's own envy is to wreak havoc for someone else, boundaries are inevitably transgressed. People's circles are invaded and trashed, and especially if those who are envied permit the invasion, the unwanted feelings of insecurity in the person who envies subside — until a new threat arises.

Triangles. A complicating element in Cecilia's story is the *triangular* nature of the interaction. Triangular, or three-way, social structures are inherently unstable, as two-person alliances can so easily form and the "third wheel" can feel left out. Ms. Wade's envious reaction to Cecilia took place in front of, and was undoubtedly influenced by, the students in the classroom. The possibility that the students were allying with Cecilia (and vice versa) — and their enthusiastic response to Cecilia's lesson plan implied that this might be the case — could have been read by Ms. Wade as personal rejection. Being evidently unable to withstand the natural need for her student teacher and her physics students to bond, Ms. Wade broke the connection by inserting herself into the relationship and pushing Cecilia out. In satisfying her envy Ms. Wade readjusted the social dynamic, activating her bond with the students and making Cecilia the one who was left out and rejected.

181

But it seems that Cecilia's response to Ms. Wade's not-good-enough teacher move surpassed a feeling of rejection. As a student herself who was dependent on her mentor teacher for perspective and approval, she actually felt humiliated and full of self-doubt. Was her lesson plan flawed? Was her teaching that bad? What did her mentor teacher think of her? What did the students think of her? How could either of them possibly respect her? What on earth was she doing in a teacher education program? Unlike Ms. Psacharopoulos, who enabled Gabe to be incompetent, Ms. Wade *dis*abled Cecilia, preventing her from being and feeling capable. Of course, this effect is the exact opposite of what learning, developing students need. Ms. Wade's boundary transgression had the potential to do lasting damage to her student teacher.

Ms. Wade's Boundaries

What could Ms. Wade have done differently? *In the heat of the moment,* she could have *detached* from her emotion and committed to observing both herself and Cecilia with curiosity. In this way she would have honored the boundary between them and collected valuable emotional and relational data that she could sort through later when she did some *emotion work.*

YELLOW BELT MOVES

Note that Ms. Wade's move would not have been to deny her feelings. Rather, it would have been to watch them, to take note of them. This she could have done in the moment given her convenient obligation to sit back and watch her student teacher. What better time to *practice self-awareness* than when one is in the classroom but out of the spotlight?

Making the effort to remain in her own circle would have been an impressive feat. Even better, if Ms. Wade could have mustered in herself excitement for Cecilia and the physics students and reminded herself that good teaching appears in many guises — Cecilia's and her own being just two — then she could have accepted and even participated in enjoyment of the lesson.

Cecilia's Boundaries

Ms. Wade clearly had some important emotion work to do if she was to act as an effective developmental partner to her student teacher. But what about Cecilia? As the lead teacher in this classroom instance, she supposedly had ultimate power over the lesson. But as the student teacher she was totally beholden to Ms. Wade, one of the evaluators who determined whether or not Cecilia became eligible for certification. Given the power dynamic of this situation, what could *Cecilia* have done differently?

In the heat of the moment, very little. Setting limits with an envious mentor teacher in front of an entire class of students could have been professional suicide. At the very least Cecilia would have initiated a power struggle Ms. Wade could not allow her to win. At worst she would have made a very influential enemy.

YELLOW BELT MOVES

But Cecilia could engage in *emotion work*. As always, *self-awareness* would have been a good first step. Cecilia could have noticed her reactions to Ms. Wade's invasion and *described* them to herself. "Wow, I am feeling terrible," Cecilia could have said to herself either during Ms. Wade's impromptu lesson or after school. "I feel rejected, hurt, really embarrassed — ashamed, actually. I feel shocked! And because I cannot fathom why Ms. Wade would have done something so thoughtless and humiliating, I feel as though I must be a horrible teacher. And that's the worst feeling of all!"

Reviewing the story of what happened could provide Cecilia with some material for analysis. "The students and I were having a great time — I *thought* — brainstorming prior knowledge about the word 'vector.' I designed this part of the lesson ahead of time: I wanted students to have a chance to make a personal connection with the new unit. My supervisor *and* Ms. Wade approved of this approach.

"When it got a little noisy and enthusiastic, Ms. Wade told me to move on. I did; I began my mini-lecture on vectors. I prepared this lecture but was also able to weave into it some of the students' ideas from the brainstorming session. This part was also approved by both Ms. Wade and my supervisor. I barely had time to get into the topic before Ms. Wade stood up and almost literally pushed me out of her way as she took over talking to the students."

With this thought Cecilia might have felt a surge of anger at the way Ms. Wade treated her in front of the students (a feeling that was long overdue). "Wait — why did she have to take over?" Cecilia might have wondered to herself. "I was doing exactly what I had told her I would do. The students seemed to be engaged and cooperative. I know I'm not a wizard teacher, but I can't see that I was doing anything wrong. Isn't the solo teaching week all about giving me a chance to fly and possibly fall on my own? Why couldn't Ms. Wade let me do this?"

This process of introspection could have helped Cecilia reinsert the boundaries that Ms. Wade had vaporized. Now that she could honor her own perspective on the lesson and verify that she had made no glaring mistakes, Cecilia could turn her attention to Ms. Wade's circle. "Why couldn't Ms. Wade let me do this?" would be exactly the right question to ask at this point. It would prompt Cecilia to look for the *good reasons* behind Ms. Wade's behavior, not for the purposes of judging and condemning her mentor teacher but for the purposes of understanding and taking enlightened action.

It is important to mention that Cecilia would not have to do this reflecting on her own. Being a preservice teacher, she would have a supervisor, and depending on the quality of that relationship, Cecilia could *use* her supervisor as a sounding board.

BLUE BELT MOVES

Cecilia and her supervisor could make any number of *guesses* about Ms. Wade's motives. "Maybe Ms. Wade couldn't stand the noise," Cecilia could suggest. "Maybe she approves of progressive teaching techniques in theory but not in practice. Maybe she couldn't stand to see me fail and wanted to rescue me. Maybe she has a control issue. Maybe she doesn't like me." The possibility that Ms. Wade was envious of her might never occur to Cecilia, but the supervisor could throw out that guess for consideration.

Cecilia would have to weigh the guesses against what she knew of Ms. Wade based on their prior history together. In any case together she and her supervisor could come up with a feasible — and compassionate — interpretation of Ms. Wade's actions and a *plan* for how to proceed.

But proceeding with a plan would require acute sensitivity, as the entrance of a supervisor onto the scene would create yet another triangular relationship. Any whiff of conspiracy between Cecilia and her supervisor could make Ms. Wade defensive and therefore extremely difficult to work with.

Part of the plan Cecilia and her supervisor could devise, then, would have to take this legitimate fact into consideration. Again, the goal would not be to judge or condemn or to give Ms. Wade a taste of her own humiliating medicine. Rather, the goal would be to *repair* the relationship so it could function well for Ms. Wade and, especially, for Cecilia. Ideally, Cecilia would lead the repair work (and her supervisor would support her), as this skill is crucial for teachers at all levels to practice.

A possible *plan*, then, would be for Cecilia to call an emergency meeting with her supervisor and Ms. Wade. The purpose of the meeting would be to discuss Cecilia's solo teaching and how best to facilitate it. In fact, the triad would be discussing how to create an adequate *holding environment* for Cecilia; that is, they would need to agree on the specific conditions that would keep Cecilia safe to learn while student teaching.

BLACK BELT MOVES

An important objective for Cecilia and her supervisor would be to *join with* her master teacher at this meeting. From the perspective of boundaries, joining with an adversary means committing both to accurately *describing* what is inside one's own circle and *listening* with respect and curiosity to what is inside the other's. This detached yet compassionate stance would be more likely to melt Ms. Wade's envy and defensiveness and permit productive collaboration.

Cecilia's first act in the meeting, then, could be to *describe*, briefly and objectively, what happened on her first day and to ask Ms. Wade what had prompted her to intervene twice in the lesson. (Note that it would be unwise for Cecilia to offer a guess as to Ms. Wade's state of mind at the time, as Ms.

185

Wade could easily see this as insubordinate and condescending.) If Cecilia had adequately worked through her initial responses to Ms. Wade's co-optation, she could carry this phase out calmly. Equanimity would greatly assist her cause.

Next, Cecilia (and her supervisor) could *listen* to Ms. Wade's answer to the question about her behaviors and work empathically with her explanation. No judgment — just data collection in the service of understanding.

At some point Cecilia might want to *self-disclose*, sharing with Ms. Wade how the interventions made Cecilia feel. The beauty of honoring boundaries by describing one's personal experience without any hint of accusation is that no one can argue with it. If Ms. Wade was unable to sit with Cecilia's description and attempted to, once again, blur boundaries by denying or minimizing her student teacher's experience, Cecilia (and her supervisor) could gently return her to reality: that Cecilia was describing *her own* experience, which is nonnegotiable.

One could hope that this meeting would strengthen the relational bonds among these three players in Cecilia's education, but the ultimate purpose would be straightforward: to agree on the specific *limits* that would govern Cecilia's solo teaching stints. While Ms. Wade might not gain any insight about herself as a result of the meeting, she should be able to see the value of restricting her role in Cecilia's teaching while at the same time making ample room for focused feedback after the fact. Whether she did or not, though, the rules and consequences governing this threesome's interactions would need to be quite explicit, as would the understanding of how the agreed-upon limits would be monitored and enforced.

Ideally, this meeting would pave the way for Cecilia to complete her student teaching obligations effectively. If Cecilia had to continue to adapt to Ms. Wade's insecurities, ongoing conscious awareness of *whether* and *how* she chose to accommodate — with help from her supervisor — could smooth the process.

Applying the elements of *setting limits* to Cecilia's case is quite tricky because of the power dynamic between her and Ms. Wade. The risk of offending her mentor teacher and therefore jeopardizing herself would be great. But the costs of *not* setting limits could also be high, and these costs could have long-term negative effects. To the extent that her actions with Ms. Wade plugged into dysfunctional relational patterns and beliefs, Cecilia could leave her student teaching experience quite handicapped.

In the interests of creating a useful holding environment, then, Cecilia and her supervisor could set limits on Ms. Wade by

- understanding that Ms. Wade had *good reasons* for her boundary violations;
- setting consistent, fair *limits* on Ms. Wade's behavior; that is, making the parameters of the solo teaching experience concrete and specific;
- agreeing ahead of time with Ms. Wade on how to *hold the line*, or monitor and enforce these parameters;
- tolerating Ms. Wade's attempts to diminish Cecilia's experience and needs; deliberately choosing *whether* and *how* to be used by Ms. Wade;
- staying present and firm but not activated; observing with detachment;
- holding no grudges but, rather, lowering expectations of Ms. Wade's ability to be *used*; consciously resisting the temptation to take Ms. Wade's negative behaviors personally; strengthening boundaries (in this fairly unsafe learning environment); and responding to "alarms" by Cecilia's calling her supervisor.

Even though this story involves a teacher (Ms. Wade) and a student (Cecilia), it is particularly complicated because the student is also a teacher. Both Ms. Wade and Cecilia are supposed to be authorities in the classroom. But how are they to share that authority? Add a supervisor — another teacher with authority — and the relationship negotiations become even more delicate.

Navigating this complex triangular relationship by the seat of the pants could be perilous. Being deliberate and explicit about limits, consequences, and boundaries, while labor intensive, could ultimately help make the threesome's interactions more efficient and educationally rich.

Getting Revenge

Unfortunately, Cecilia's preservice experience is fairly common. Another quite common table-turning, co-opting boundary violation is shown in the next story, which tells of a teacher's revenge.

WHO'S GOING TO BE HUMILIATED?

Dr. Digilio, a college history professor, handed back his students' midterm exams. After a couple of minutes, during which time the students had a chance to look over their tests, he was ready to begin the day's lecture. Midbreath, he noticed a hand shoot up. It belonged to a "nontraditional" (read: "older") student named Jackie, one of Dr. Digilio's least favorite students because she constantly interrupted his talks to ask niggling questions. She had also handed in an alarmingly poor exam. "Yes?" Dr. Digilio asked.

"I'm sorry, but I have a question about one of the test items," Jackie said. "I think your correction is actually incorrect."

Dr. Digilio was stunned, first, that Jackie would interrupt his lecture class to ask about her exam and, second, that she would accuse him of being incorrect, especially in front of all the other students. He wanted desperately to teach her a lesson about proper behavior in his class.

Gesturing impatiently to her, Dr. Digilio allowed Jackie to approach him with her test and show him the "incorrect" item. "No, I'm sorry," he said smugly. "My correction stands." He proceeded to explain Jackie's error to the whole class, making no effort to hide his contempt for her ignorance. "Please study before the next test," he sighed as she walked back to her seat. "I really don't want to have to waste any more of my time reading exams like that one."

What was going on with Jackie? On the surface, she had a question about a correction Dr. Digilio had made on her exam. Asking for clarification of a point made during a lecture or on a test constitutes, of course, legitimate *use* of a teacher.

But Jackie's choice of a particularly inopportune time to ask the question and her decision to ask it in front of the entire class imply that she might have been feeling some aggression under the surface. Perhaps she was intent on popping Dr. Digilio's rather large and, apparently, thin-walled ego bubble, and she aimed to pop it in the most humiliating circumstances possible.

Or perhaps Jackie was entitled, self-absorbed, and unaccustomed to considering others' rights or needs before her own. Maybe she was just plain oblivious. She demanded Dr. Digilio's attention when she did simply because she felt the unfiltered need to. In any case, Jackie definitely *tested* the *limits*, the unspoken rules that defined the roles in Dr. Digilio's lecture class. In stepping out of her expected role of quiet, respectful student, she put Dr. Digilio on the spot, pressing insistently into his circle.

Dr. Digilio's excessive response to Jackie's question points to the probability that he did, indeed, perceive her interruption to be a *boundary violation*, an invasion of his emotional and intellectual space. Clearly, *emotion work* would have helped him in this situation, for it could have illuminated for him what his outrage meant. What Dr. Digilio did instead was to violate Jackie's boundaries. He invaded her back.

Let's look at how the boundary violations worked in superslow motion:

First move: Jackie has a question about her test grade. It is possible she is anxious about it. She might also feel some aggression toward Dr. Digilio. She seeks help at the perfectly wrong time, activating her professor by testing his limits.

Second move: Dr. Digilio feels uncertain. "Did I really make a mistake when I corrected her paper?" he wonders. "Am I going to have to admit to that in front of the entire class? Can I survive that humiliation?" These questions happen in a flash; he is barely conscious of them. Feelings of insecurity, uncertainty, and fear of humiliation flood him, but what he is most conscious of is outrage.

Third move: Dr. Digilio defends against his terrible emotions by treating Jackie in precisely the way he fears being treated himself: He publicly humiliates her for having made a mistake. The viciousness of his response to Jackie suggests the magnitude of his own insecurity. He is *projecting* his feelings into her in order to avoid having them himself.

In effect, Dr. Digilio *took revenge* on Jackie for *using* him in a way he could not bear. In the words of chapter two, he chose *whether* to be used by Jackie, and his choice was: *not*. His actions served to punish her, to disable and neutralize her.

For the moment, at least. Once she recovered, Jackie could very well continue the cycle, activating Dr. Digilio in increasingly mortifying ways.

This desire to make students pay for how they "make" a teacher feel, detestable as it may seem, is nonetheless quite common. It is another way teachers can violate students' boundaries. As we saw in chapter two, it is normal for teachers to take their students personally: to want to rebuff students' irritating attempts to use them by using the students back. Even the most loving and patient person can, when slapped, slap back.

It is in resisting this impulse to slap back that great-enough teachers distinguish themselves.

KEEP IN MIND
Taking revenge *on students who are hurtful or insulting is a common way that teachers violate their students' boundaries.*

Dr. Digilio's Boundaries

So what could Dr. Digilio have done differently? His first act *in the heat of the moment* could have been to *detach* from his response, exercise enormous self-restraint, and stop the boundary crossing by immediately *setting a limit*.

"Jackie, that question is inappropriate at this time," he could have said. "I will be happy to discuss your exam with you during office hours." As in the previous two stories, boundary transgressions, though easily attributed to one person, are actually cocreated. The only way Jackie could invade Dr. Digilio's circle was if he let her in. By stating the limit and protecting his boundaries, he would have foiled her attempt on him and resumed class.

YELLOW BELT MOVES

Once on his own, Dr. Digilio could have done some *emotion work*. He could have wondered about Jackie's behavioral pattern, of which this latest violation was just one instance. What did her behavior tell him about *her*? Clearly, she could use an explicit statement of Dr. Digilio's class expectations and the consequences for breaching them. If she could not discern his rules on her own, he had to tell her what they were and warn her ahead of time what would happen if she could not respect them. In the process of working out these rules and consequences, Dr. Digilio would be learning something about *himself*, what *he* needed to do his best teaching, a task that could be quite valuable for him as well as his students.

BLUE BELT MOVES

For example, he might realize that a *good reason* for his hating interruptions was that they derailed his train of thought, which confused and panicked him. One of his rules, then, would have to discourage interrupting. He could introduce this rule to Jackie by *self-disclosing*:

"Jackie," Dr. Digilio could tell his student during office hours, "because I'm someone who loses track of his thoughts very easily, I get impatient with interruptions during my lectures. I know you have lots of questions, though, and I want to have a chance to answer them. What I need you to do is write down your questions and wait until I have finished lecturing before you ask them." In setting this *limit*, Dr. Digilio would have taken full responsibility for his past impatience with Jackie (the contents of his own circle) and given her a concrete way to manage the anxiety she expressed in the form of pressing questions (the contents of her circle).

And of course, Dr. Digilio would have to state the *consequence* for violating the rule. He could say, "If you raise your hand during a lecture, I will have to ignore you, difficult as that might be for both of us. I hope that, when your arm starts getting tired, you will remember this rule, lower your hand, and write your question down."

BLACK BELT MOVES

It would be wise to share this rule and consequence with the entire class so students other than Jackie could benefit from it.

And if the limit were to work, Dr. Digilio would have to follow through on it by making time after every lecture for questions. If he failed to respect the rule he had set, Jackie might, too; she would likely go back to her old irritating ways to get what she needed.

This is the difficult work of *setting a limit* and *holding the line*, either as a teacher or as a parent: remembering where the limit, or line, is; reminding oneself and others, without fail, of its existence; and imposing consequences calmly and consistently for any transgressions.

Dr. Digilio's first impulse when dealing with Jackie might have been vengeful, but he didn't need to leave it at that. Working through his reaction using the skills of *emotion work* could have helped Dr. Digilio see his relationship with Jackie more clearly and, based on this understanding, *plan* a more measured response to her that would facilitate the learning she needed to do. This would have been an example of *repair*.

Of course, doing emotion work would have been helpful but might have taken more time than Dr. Digilio had in the classroom. Once again, the most important great-enough teacher move he could have made *in the heat of the moment* would have been to immediately *set limits* by

- noticing that Jackie was, as usual, testing him;
- stepping back from the gratifying urge to punish her;
- understanding that Jackie's limit-testing was normal (note that Jackie was an adult herself but, as a student, easily fell into the toddler/teenager role with her teacher, her developmental partner);
- setting consistent, fair limits (rules) that allowed Dr. Digilio to do his best teaching, then holding the line (imposing consequences);
- tolerating Jackie's anger and possible attempts to renew her assault and letting her feel her emotions without punishing her for them;
- staying present and firm but not activated; observing with detachment;
- applying consequences fairly and firmly but also consistently providing time for Jackie's needs to be met;

- holding no grudges: being available emotionally and willing to talk about Jackie's (and his own) classroom experiences;
- seeking outside help in managing his fear of being caught in a mistake and humiliated.

The desire to *take revenge* on students can be irresistible. When anger flares and an easy scapegoat is available, it can be difficult to prevent the very satisfying spew of emotion. It can also be difficult to bear the self-accusation afterward. An effective way to prevent angry outbursts and to survive self-blame after a mistake is to do supportive emotion work. But in the heat of the moment, when there is no time to process thoroughly, the best way to minimize the damage of boundary crossings is to stop them dead in their tracks.

Knowing When Boundaries Are Crossed

A teacher cannot set limits if she's unaware that they are being tested; she cannot protect her own boundaries or respect others' if she does not detect that they are being violated. How can a person know?

The answer has two parts. One part has to do with noticing when one's own boundaries are being invaded. The other has to do with figuring out when one has transgressed someone else's boundaries. And while the above stories illustrate three common ways boundaries are violated in the classroom, there are innumerable possibilities for boundary crossings that arise out of the unique ways people fit together in relationships.

Invasion

How does anyone notice when one's own boundaries are violated? For some, the alarm is physical. They might feel jumpy or electrified; their stomach or jaw might clench; they might feel tension in their back, as if their "back is up." Becoming familiar with these physical signals is a good way of training oneself to know when one's boundaries are being crossed.

There are also emotional signs. Defensiveness is one; withdrawal can be another; fear, anxiety, diffidence, insecurity are all possible signals. For people who have a pretty clear sense of their boundaries, or the sanctity of their physical and emotional circles, anger can be a sure sign of invasion. Again, paying close attention to one's emotional responses when others cross into one's circle will reveal which signals mark the moments when limits need to be set.

The term "invasion" provides a useful metaphor for others' violations of one's boundaries. What does it feel like to be invaded? What is it like to be (or feel) attacked? Anger, fear, uncertainty, tension, flight — all the normal responses to danger — are possible signals of boundary breaches because, in fact, boundary breaches *are* invasions. They may not be visible or tangible or empirically provable, but they are disturbing at best and dangerous at worst. And the way to identify them is to know what they *feel* like.

FOOD FOR THOUGHT

Contrary to what some might believe, anger is an extremely valuable emotion. It indicates that something is not right. It does not tell us what *is not right — that generally requires some investigation — but it does announce in no uncertain terms that something has impinged on us in a negative way. Noticing anger and stopping to figure out what the impingement might be can be immensely helpful.*

Not everyone readily exhibits or even feels anger, though. When it comes to discerning boundary violations, the inability to get angry can be a handicap. Tolerating infringements into one's circle can certainly keep the peace, but chronic invasion can be demoralizing and destabilizing. When unacknowledged emotions build up, they can (and, one might argue, should) explode. And explosions can be both difficult to control and dangerous (as Mr. Bonham demonstrated in his story above).

So "stuffing" anger can mean loss of crucial information about possible boundary violations (and other injustices). And indulging anger, or taking revenge, generally leads to boundary violations of one's own. Neither extreme is useful if the goal is to have healthy relationships. Rather, feeling, paying attention to, and working through anger are highly recommended. When utilized in this way, anger is a crucial signal that must not be ignored because it can be so richly informative.

Seduction

Being impinged upon is like being invaded; crossing boundaries, or stepping into someone else's circle, is more like seduction. There is something *seductive* about the option of doing others' work for them, of feeling supercompetent, of getting what one wants at others' expense, of blaming or accusing or insulting others rather than sorting through one's own feelings and responsibilities. Not that boundary crossing always happens consciously; most often it does not. But there are signals people can become aware of that might indicate they have expanded their own circle and invaded someone else's.

There can be a physical pull toward others that is irresistible. One might feel an itch to get something done or to do it "right" rather than let someone else do it wrong. One might relish the opportunity to solve others' problems, to advise them or take action for them. One might feel the urge to fill a void, to provide a service or satisfy a need, that lies outside one's circle. The thrilling, seductive pull toward competence that aggrandizes oneself and erases the other is a sure sign of boundary transgression.

Or one might be drawn to exploiting others to satisfy a need or fill a void inside oneself. Boundary crossings, in other words, can also result from a sense of personal deficit. People who manipulate others to get what they want — to get others to do for them what they will not or believe they cannot do for themselves — are usually violating boundaries. They are seducing others to serve them. (Think of the friend who borrows money and never pays it back.) Again, when the focus is on oneself at the expense of another, boundary violations are most likely to happen.

Importantly, the simple presence of a need does not imply a boundary transgression. People satisfy each other's needs in mutually affirming ways all the time. A sign of invasion is loss of perspective on the other person: the inability to acknowledge or accept the person's capabilities, self-knowledge, physical integrity, or emotional rights. And invasion means loss of perspective on oneself: either the grandiose belief that one can take on more responsibility, more work, than one should or the self-undermining belief in one's own incapacity or entitlement.

When trying to discern their own boundary crossings, teachers should look for signs of anger, both internal and external. Of course, a teacher might cross a boundary because *she* is angry (about someone's incompetence, passivity, unfairness, etc.). That's internal anger. But a teacher who perceives her *students'* anger would do well to look closely at circles and wonder about who is standing where.

FOOD FOR THOUGHT

QUESTION: How do you know when boundaries are being transgressed?
*ANSWER: When you feel **invaded** or when you feel **seduced** into acting for or on someone else.*

When you feel invaded or attacked, you can guess that someone else is crossing the boundary into your circle. When you feel tugged to fill a void or do someone else's work for her, chances are good that you are the one doing the invading.

External signs of anger can be obvious: outbursts, rudeness, swearing, accusations. Brittany's anger at Mr. Bonham falls into this category. But signs of anger can also be masked in passivity and resistance, as Gabe demonstrated in his story. Whatever initiated Gabe's avoidance of the continent project in Ms. Psacharopoulos's classroom, it is quite possible that her anxious and invasive response to his passivity fed his anger, prompting him to retreat even further from her and the project. Classifying Gabe's avoidance as anger could have helped Ms. Psacharopoulos stop to think about the *good reasons* for his passive aggression and how she might be plugging into it.

So once again, anger, both the teacher's and the students', can be a sign of boundary violation. Other emotions that can accompany a teacher's boundary crossings are anxiety and, more fundamentally, fear: fear of losing control, fear of being unsafe, fear of trusting others, fear of taking responsibility, fear of being unneeded, fear of being alone, fear of seeing the truth. The anxiety that arises from such fears is often intense and hence is usually not consciously felt before the impulse to cross the boundary takes over. A signal that one might be violating a boundary, then, is that impulse: the urge to take over, to *act* so as to reestablish equilibrium.

Note that "equilibrium" does not necessarily mean "balance." With boundary violations, "equilibrium" tends to mean *im*balance: a dynamic of superiority and inferiority, of power differences, of one-up and one-down. The key to understanding equilibrium is to consider how *familiar* the relational pattern is, not how fair and equitable it is. When it comes to relationships, as we saw repeatedly in chapter one, familiar means comfortable, even when "comfortable" is keenly unpleasant.

DEFINITION

Equilibrium *in relationships does not necessarily mean "equitable" or "fair." It often means "unbalanced." Equilibrium occurs when people plug in and fit together; it is a relational state that is familiar and, hence, feels comfortable even when it is unpleasant or maladaptive.*

There is one more emotion that can indicate that a person is overstepping boundaries: resentment. Resentment tends to occur when a person feels that she is bearing an unfair burden, that others are getting away with something. The good news about resentment is that it is generally very accurate: The emotion simply does not arise when a relationship is well balanced. The bad news is that resentment invites one to change the distribution of responsibility, which quite often means retreating from other people's circles and setting limits on oneself. Making such drastic personal changes can be extremely difficult.

Dangerous Change

Why is personal change so difficult? The answer has to do with *psychic structures*, with fitting together in familiar ways. If a certain unbalanced fit feels familiar, if it qualifies as "equilibrium," then that imbalance will be sought automatically, especially in times of stress. To behave differently to achieve a new, unfamiliar balance is to go against one's instincts, instincts that have been honed over years of experience.

Take, for example, the overly accommodating not-good-enough teacher who allows students to walk all over him, as Mr. Bonham did when Brittany first mimicked him. Anyone who is comfortable being invaded is probably someone whose boundaries have been transgressed regularly. People who are accustomed to being invaded have internalized (unconscious) beliefs about themselves and other people that justify and reinforce the ongoing use and abuse.

"I can take it" is one such belief. "I would be a cruel and unfair person if I said 'no'" is another. "The other person wouldn't be able to handle it if I stood up for myself." "I would get in trouble if I didn't give in." "I wouldn't be loved." When the stakes are this high, making behavioral changes that invite terrifying and destabilizing consequences can seem downright foolish. Sticking with the familiar and letting the invader in can seem a whole lot more sensible.

Or take the over-accommodating not-good-enough teacher who enables student incompetence. The comfortable fit Ms. Psacharopoulos sought with Gabe had to do with her need to control outcomes in her classroom. As a supercompetent person, Ms. Psacharopoulos expected to *make* her students perform to her standards. (Note how *linear* this expectation is: that a teacher's acts will directly cause predictable effects.) Fitting perfectly with her passive student, Ms. Psacharopoulos enacted some central grandiose beliefs: "I can change him" (positive grandiosity) or "It's all my fault if he doesn't change" (negative grandiosity). In either case the stakes were high for Ms. Psacharopoulos: Either she succeeded in changing Gabe and took the credit or she failed at changing Gabe and took the blame. Although she was trapped in this impossible dichotomy, it was familiar to her. No other options were imaginable.

DEFINITIONS
Positive grandiosity *is the belief that you have more power over circumstances or other people than you actually do (or possibly can).*

Negative grandiosity *is the belief that others' unhappiness or failure is your fault.*

Dr. Digilio's beliefs had to do with responsibility and blame. When he took Jackie's interruption personally, he felt hurt and insulted (and, at bottom, threatened). Rather than remaining in his own circle and taking responsibility for his emotions, he sought equilibrium by letting off steam. "It's better to blame Jackie for my bad feelings than to feel the emotions and deal with them on my own" is one way of stating what seems to have been Dr. Digilio's unconscious and automatic belief. Experiencing negative emotions even for a second can seem worse than foisting them on someone else.

To expect Dr. Digilio to change his behavior by respecting the boundary between him and his student would be asking him to go against his self-protective instincts. To contradict Ms. Psacharopoulos's beliefs about her ability to control other people would be to risk upending her worldview. To encourage Mr. Bonham to refuse to "take it" and instead to set firm, fair limits on every one of Brittany's transgressions would be to invite consequences he might rather avoid.

Personal change is difficult because it can feel so dangerous. Yes, continuing to behave in familiar ways can be frustrating, but it is automatic and safe; that is, not coincidentally, it tends to lead a person away from the emotions she most wants to avoid. Trying something different can mean heading directly into those unbearable emotions. And feeling unwanted emotions can seem incredibly dangerous.

Consider what happens when a person changes behaviors that tend to protect him from feelings he would rather avoid. If, for example, doing others' work for them protects a person from anxieties about doing his *own* work — writing a novel, say, or changing careers or losing weight or starting a family — then retreating from others' circles and staying within his own circle will expose him to those anxieties. And those anxieties will be intense! Teachers who take on personal change, then, must expect pushback not just from their students but from themselves. And again, that can feel extremely dangerous.

Yet personal change is one sure way to affect students — and oneself —positively. As Ms. Psacharopoulos showed us (and contrary to the apparent assumptions of many policy makers), teachers simply cannot *make* their students change. Teachers' best bet is to change their own behaviors and see how the ripple effect of that shift affects their students. Teachers who have the courage to enact unfamiliar behaviors, to reset their sense of equilibrium to respect their own, their students', and others' boundaries, take the risk of facing difficult emotions. They also risk witnessing remarkable, even miraculous, changes in classroom relationships and learning.

WRAP-UP

Limit testing and boundary violating are normal behaviors that crop up in classrooms regularly. Why? Because all learners need to *use* their teachers, who, as *developmental partners,* are the main guardians of the classroom *holding environment.* Teachers must assure their students that they are safe to grow and that their inevitable insults (and compliments) will not be taken personally. Teachers need to assert that they are the adults in the room who will offer corrective experiences to students who need containment. By safeguarding their own and their students' circles, teachers model the type of well-bounded relationships that allow for responsible behavior and reality-based learning.

Being a thoughtful developmental partner, or a great-enough teacher, is demanding work, though. Noticing and correcting one's own boundary transgressions require astute awareness, dedication, and courage to make the "dangerous changes" that can promote healthy relationships and desirable learning. Responding to students' boundary violations means honoring one's own alarms and immediately setting limits no matter how unnatural or unfamiliar that might feel. Surviving student pushback without taking revenge depends on tremendous self-restraint and commitment.

Of course, engaging in rigorous *emotion work* is crucial to being an effective teacher. A key to responding to attacks *in the heat of the moment*, though, is deciding to deal with the fallout of one's actions later — ideally with supportive professional help. If, after feeling an initial pang of shock and fury or noticing the urge to fill a void created by a student, teachers focus on the single task of setting limits, they can prevent ongoing escalations and buy themselves valuable time for after-hours reflection. Following up limit setting with emotion work makes surviving student fallout easier and strengthens teachers in managing future tests and violations.

Overall, setting and living within boundaries can be extremely fulfilling. This is true in part because boundaries allow everyone in an interaction to show up and play his or her part. If I refuse to enable you, or if I say "no" to a request that will make me resentful, or if I hold you to a standard that is within your grasp, then I am living inside the parameters of reality, which can be relieving, and you are left with the feelings and responsibilities that you must learn to manage. If I live within my boundaries, I do not erase you by either merging with or objectifying you, and I do not burden myself with responsibility that is not mine and is, in fact, impossible for me to shoulder in a healthy way. Boundaries, by acknowledging and enforcing separate but connected roles and responsibilities, are fulfilling because they can be so clarifying. And clarity can make interacting a whole lot more effective.

The bottom line is that students use teachers in a great many ways. They need teachers to set limits and survive pushback and resistance. They need teachers to model well-bounded interactions. They need to be able to use teachers as twins, as statues on a pedestal, as mirrors. They need teachers to establish and maintain a holding environment in which they can safely grow emotionally, physically, and intellectually. They need teachers to know, see, and hear them, to take them very seriously, but not to take them personally. And when teachers prove themselves to be merely human through their mistakes — their tempers, their enabling, their revenge, their own needs — students require thoughtful, empathic repair.

Once again, being used as a developmental partner can be extremely difficult. And few teachers, when they signed on to help children learn, were told that this was the work they had to do. Yet it is inescapable. And it is monumentally important. Embracing the role of being used while simultaneously remaining rooted in one's own rich circle — holding students while respecting the boundaries that keep them safe and healthy — provides the stability teachers need to deal with the myriad behaviors they encounter in the classroom.

And the goal is not perfection, not unquestionable greatness. The goal, as Winnicott so aptly conceived it, is to be "great enough."

CHAPTER ANSWERS

It is time to answer the questions from the beginning of this chapter:

- *What does it mean to be a "great enough" teacher?*
- *How can "great enough" be better than "great"?*

A "great enough" teacher is one who understands that perfection is impossible and that self-indulgence — either by being "overly accommodating" or "co-opting" — is all too easy. The great-enough teacher aims at providing a healthy holding environment by setting limits and honoring boundaries despite the good chance of protest from students. When they have over- or underreacted to student behaviors, great-enough teachers revisit the incident to repair with the students; when students escalate their dysfunctional behaviors or express disappointment or frustration, great-enough teachers survive the pushback without taking revenge. In general, great-enough teachers are those who accept that they and their students are human, that relationships are messy, that students will inevitably use their teachers, and that effective learning depends on boundaries that allow for the type of connected separation or separated connection that student growth and development depend on.

"Great enough" is better than "great" because it is more realistic. As we have seen, being great enough means working through grandiosity, envy, and the urge to take revenge — all of which can stem from a need to be recognized as great — to make room for students to succeed and, possibly, fail. Whereas "great" might include "best" teaching practices, "great enough" always involves awareness, negotiation, and flexibility, qualities no textbook company or educational researcher can ever impart.

KEEP IN MIND

- *The **holding environment** is the physical and emotional context within which people are contained so they can grow and develop safely and healthily. Classrooms are holding environments. So are schools.*
- ***Too-accommodating not-good-enough teachers** are those who have a hard time setting and maintaining limits and thus allow their students to "walk all over them."*
- ***Co-opting not-good-enough teachers** are those who rule the classroom with iron-fisted limits, overriding students' authority (and anger) with their own.*

202

- *Great-enough teachers* expect to be used. They commit to **setting realistic and healthy limits** for their students and **surviving the students' pushback** against these limits. They also value **repairing their mistakes** and **tolerating their students' frustration** with learning and growing.

- *Limits* help define holding environments by establishing rules and the consequences for not abiding by them. Limits are related to the context that teacher and students share.

- **Setting limits** and **implementing consequences** are not always easy, but they are essential skills that can be developed. Setting limits is especially useful **in the heat of the moment**, when there isn't time to do thoughtful emotion work.

- **Emotional boundaries** are **personal**, **felt**, and **flexible**. A simplistic way of thinking about boundaries is to picture them as **circles** around people. Individuals are responsible for what is inside their circles, not for what is inside someone else's circle.

- Teachers can expect students to use them for developmental purposes. Some (but by no means all) ways teachers can reverse roles and hinder student development is through **enabling**, **acting out envy**, and **taking revenge**.

- Teachers must **look for signals** either that their boundaries are being violated — that they are being **invaded** — or that they are crossing over someone else's boundaries — that they are **seduced**. If their boundaries are being violated, teachers must immediately set a limit. If they are doing the violating, they must figure out how to get out of their student's circle and back into their own.

- **Personal change** can be difficult because it abandons what is familiar and safe and creates a whole new sense of **equilibrium**, or comfort zone, which can feel dangerous.

CHAPTER FOUR

POWER STRUGGLES: THE THIRD IN THE CLASSROOM

Picture this scenario: Teacher enters classroom. Students chime, "Good morning, Teacher." Every single student passes last night's homework forward. Teacher smiles and introduces lesson of the day. Students listen respectfully, maintaining eye contact, sitting still, and raising their hands for permission to speak. No one is disengaged; no one makes fun of incorrect answers; no one speaks loudly or talks over someone else. Students learn. Teacher administers test. Students pass with flying colors. Teacher goes home feeling great about her job.

What is wrong with this picture? Obviously, it is not realistic. Teachers do not have absolute control over their students' behavior and learning. Students, being autonomous agents, do not always comply with their teachers' desires. Teachers do not always know what is best for their students and, even when they do, do not always act with their students' best interests at heart. More often than not, teachers go home worrying about their students and, sometimes, kicking themselves for things they did or did not do that day.

Here is a potentially more accurate picture of a moment in the life of a teacher: Teacher enters classroom. Students are talking loudly. Teacher tries to get students' attention. Students ignore her. Teacher raises her voice. Some students quiet down; others continue to ignore her. Teacher loses patience and yells at the troublemaking ringleader. Ringleader undermines teacher for remainder of period. Teacher finishes class feeling frustrated and demoralized.

While moments of cooperation certainly characterize all classrooms, so do moments like this one: moments of *power struggle*. And power struggles can be exhausting and discouraging for everyone involved. Why do power struggles arise? What can a teacher do about them?

By now the answers to these questions should be obvious: Power struggles arise because of the ways in which

205

teachers and students plug into each other. And as with all enactments, teachers can do emotion work to defuse them.

But power struggles are worth investigating a little more closely. For one thing, they are a category that many classroom enactments easily fall into. While few teachers end the day thinking, "My, what a lot of enactments I survived today," most teachers can readily identify the power struggles they engaged in. Not surprisingly, several of the stories told in the previous three chapters are stories of power struggle.

For another thing, power struggles are exquisite examples of the phenomenon this chapter is about: the Third. When power struggles arise, the Third is squelched. When power struggles are avoided or resolved in mutually respectful ways, the Third can emerge.

But what is the Third? And why does it matter?

In this chapter we examine answers to these questions through the familiar concept of the *holding environment* and the unfamiliar concept of *potential space*. Along the way we will look specifically at *compliance* and *resistance*, both of which are associated with power struggles. We will consider the perhaps counterintuitive proposition that compliance is not always desirable in a classroom while resistance can be a positive force. Ultimately, this chapter hopes to show that the whole point of doing emotion work is to facilitate the Third. And that matters quite a bit.

CHAPTER QUESTIONS
- *What is the Third?*
- *Why does it matter?*

EMERGENCE

Generally people are tempted to think of reality as being absolute. The "reality" is that it is cold outside. The "reality" is that my son has to do his homework right now. The "reality" is that life is not fair. In fact, these statements represent particular angles on "reality," angles that do not necessarily capture the whole story.

For example, at the molecular level it really is not cold outside. Atoms are simply moving more slowly, and temperature is neither felt nor relevant. From my son's perspective he really does *not* have to do his homework right now. He can finish building his Lego project and do his homework later. A Buddhist monk might argue that life is neither fair nor unfair, that fairness is an illusion. At the very least, then, the definition of reality depends on the point of view of the observer.

But there is more to reality. Sure, one could compose an ever more accurate representation of reality by compiling as many viewpoints as possible, but the difference between "reality" and our *experience* of reality might still be glaring. That difference can exist in part because of a phenomenon called *emergence*, or the arising out of interactions of an experience, a potentially ineffable reality — not my reality, not your reality, but a *third* reality — that is related to the interactions but not reducible to them.

The expression "the whole is greater than the sum of its parts" refers directly to emergence. An easy mechanical example is the bicycle. Some promising parts — a couple of tires, some gears, a chain, a seat, and a handlebar — compose a nifty whole when put together, or "summed up," properly.

But a person cannot possibly appreciate the whole of a bicycle, the entirety of it, until he has experienced riding one. Exhilaration, fear, purposefulness, strength, all these feelings can arise from riding a bicycle. They are dependent on the bicycle, for sure, but they cannot be attributed, or reduced, to any particular part or aspect of the bicycle. And the experience, or reality, that emerges from bicycle riding is unquestionably greater than the sum of the bicycle parts.

The same is true of a relationship: The whole can be greater than the sum of its parts. To what can we ascribe love, for example? Our beloved's eyes? His kindness? The experience of love emerges from the fitting together of two people, each of whom could be reduced to a list of attributes, including beautiful eyes and supreme kindness. But the experience of love implies a profound grasp of a whole, of a person who is much greater than the sum of his parts.

And when two people talk of the love they share, reality gets even more complex, for now these two wholes, each of whom is greater than the sum of his or her parts, experience something that is greater still when they are put together. Emergence. Ineffable experience that is shared but somehow independent, a third reality that is coconstructed yet greater than the people who cocreate it.

THE THIRD

The concept of the Third is not at all easy to define. It is not a thing or a place or an entity; it is not even necessarily grasped consciously. In terms used in chapter one, the Third is related to the electricity that is sparked when two or more people fit together in beneficial ways. The Third emerges from healthily attuned interactions, an experience of connection that is greater than the sum of its parts, greater than the people interacting, greater than the individual actions they take.

An example from the classroom is a good discussion. What are the components of a discussion? At bottom a teacher, a group of students, and a topic. In a good discussion a student, having fit in some way with the topic, makes a comment. Another student comments on that comment. Another student, inspired by the previous comments to make an observation he had never thought of before, adds his novel contribution.

In no time the class is discussing the topic at a level that no individual, not even the teacher, wholly contains in herself but that everyone has some handle on. The distributed, or coconstructed, knowledge is greater than the sum of the knowledge each class member has. And it is not knowledge that is easily catalogued. It is directly related to the interactions of the teacher and students but not necessarily repeatable and definitely not attributable to any particular person or comment.

Definition of the Third

While this example is a good illustration of the Third, it does not quite capture the idea of the Third. For again, the Third is not a thing; it is not knowledge, for example, or a good discussion. Rather, it is a fertile and compelling *experience* that emerges out of interactions that include healthy connections, generous mirroring, and strong boundaries.

The Third emerges out of interactions that include healthy connections. If the Third is a by-product of the energy that flows when people fit together optimally, then it is dependent on the kind of relational attunement discussed in chapter one. In a nutshell *enactments* tend to destroy the Third; respectful, well-managed relationships tend to sponsor it.

208

The Third emerges out of interactions that include generous mirroring. One of the most powerful ingredients of mirroring, as we saw in chapter two, is *detachment*, the stance that allows simultaneously for connection and curiosity. When people are invested in each other *and* seeing and hearing each other, the Third has a very good chance of arising.

The Third emerges out of interactions that include strong boundaries. Ironically, it is when people respect their own and others' circles without trying to invade or manipulate them that the Third tends to emerge. What is ironic about this is that the Third, as a shared and coconstructed reality, can feel very intimate and boundless.

Showing Up

As the name implies, the Third depends on two entities: a first person and a second person, both of whom have the chance to represent themselves. In other words, $1 + 1 = 3$: One person's reality plus another person's reality, experienced and tolerated generously, can generate a third reality. As soon as one of those realities is eclipsed, the Third disappears.

Of course, the term "the Third" comes from the psychoanalytic field, where it is generally two people who cocreate a third reality. In classrooms, where there are usually far more than two people, the term refers to a more complex phenomenon. Given the innumerable relationships being enacted in every classroom, a better term might be "the Nth," as there are any number of realities being cocreated between and among class members.

But the term "the Third," numerically inaccurate as it might be, honors the limited power and perspective of the teacher. Whether the teacher is engaging in relationship with a student or a group of students (including the whole class), she is 1 who is collaborating with another 1 (an individual or a group) in hopes of achieving a shared experience (the Third). Regardless of the actual number of people involved, a teacher's job is to foster, not to squelch, coconstructed realities with students and with groups to the best of her ability. She cannot be responsible for "the Nth" — that is, for everybody's personal and shared realities — but she can do her utmost to facilitate "the Third" between her and her students, individually and collectively.

What this means is that teachers must *show up* in the classroom; they must be willing to know themselves and stand their ground in a great-enough way. And they must allow their students to show up. Possibly the most effective way for teachers to sponsor all this showing up to help cultivate the Third is to do emotion work.

KEEP IN MIND
There can be no Third if teachers do not **show up** *in a great-enough way.*

That is, teachers must practice awareness, describe, look for good reasons, make guesses, self-disclose, listen, and make plans if the Third is to emerge. They must interrupt enactments. They must allow themselves to be used as developmental partners. They must set limits and respect boundaries. And when students cannot or do not show up themselves or when they show up in self-limiting ways, teachers must model this crucial skill for them.

The context within which teachers and students show up is the *holding environment.* As a space within which healthy interactions, mirroring, and strong boundaries predominate, a reliable holding environment provides the structural foundation for the experience of the Third. Think of the holding environment as the bicycle and the Third as the experience of riding the bicycle: When all the components are working together optimally, it can be a thrilling ride.

DEFINITION
The Third *is the shared "third" reality that can emerge out of interactions that include healthy connections, generous mirroring, and strong boundaries — that is, interactions that can happen in a reliable holding environment. Put another way, the holding environment is the bicycle, or classroom structure, and the Third is the experience that is greater than the sum of the classroom's parts.*

Control
But students are not bicycle parts, and classrooms are not machines. How can any teacher hope to control the holding

environment so as to foster the Third? It's hard enough just to teach; why bother with the Third at all?

A quick answer to the first question is that no one can completely control the holding environment. No teacher can fully control students, or the administration, or parents, or textbook companies, or state and federal legislators. In these areas the amount of actual control any teacher has is negligible.

What every teacher can control is herself. If she does that, she can have a mighty impact on the holding environment of her classroom. Focusing on emotions and relationships will strengthen the relational structure of the holding environment. Designing thoughtful, effective instruction will provide an academic structure. A teacher need not actually bother with the Third; what she need bother with is relationships with people and subject matter and the emotion work required to align them.

In truth, no teacher can force the Third to happen. All any teacher can do is fortify the structure out of which the Third can arise. Broadly speaking, that structure is the classroom holding environment. In chapter three we saw why the holding environment is so important: It is the context within which human beings develop emotionally, relationally, and cognitively. This chapter expands on the definition by introducing yet another term, *potential space*, that ties the notion of the holding environment to the notion of the Third.

Potential Space

The same man who encouraged parents to be *good enough* came up with the concept of *potential space*. With this concept pediatrician and psychoanalyst D. W. Winnicott showed how good-enough holding environments can foster both emotional and intellectual development. Specifically, such holding environments allow *play* to take place.

Play, according to Winnicott, is not just child's play (though child's play is the essential developmental "work" of children): It is basic creativity, the ability to make meaning for oneself through interacting with the world and other people. In potential space children learn about themselves, about their limits and the breadth of what they can do; and they learn about others, about the "not-me."

211

In learning about the "not-me," children who develop within potential space, or the "third area," move between inner reality and external reality. In potential space they learn that they are separate from other people, yet also connected to them. In other words, they learn that they are legitimate and valued subjects, agents of their own lives and experiences, and, importantly, that others are as well. In the absence of potential space, the "not-me" can be threatening; human subjects can become objects for inappropriate use; and demeaning enactments such as bullying can occur.

This development of a sense of the self and of others as legitimate, healthily bounded agents is crucial if children are to grow into creative adults. And one could argue that the ultimate outcome of the educational enterprise is creative adults. In potential space creative adults can make art; they can innovate; they can hatch new ideas. For Winnicott potential space is where culture emerges. For a nation it is where discovery and invention can take place. For teachers it is where transformational academic learning can happen.

While Winnicott talks of potential space as a realm of play, creativity, and culture, he also sees it as a place of self-realization, of psychological and cognitive growth, of safety and attunement with others. It is a place in which people and ideas are seen and heard as they are, in which people represent themselves and work out their overlaps and differences as valued individuals (Gentile, 2001). In sum, potential space is the space in which desirable learning and growth can happen.

DEFINITION

Potential space *is characterized by healthy boundaries and respectful interactions. It is a space where people can appreciate the "me" and the "not-me" and, importantly, safely explore new possibilities for what to think and do and who and how to be.*

FOOD FOR THOUGHT

Not everyone shares the assumptions inherent in the concept of "potential space" and the Third. Expressions such as "Father knows best" and types such as the "tiger mother" imply that development relies on dominant parents and obedient children, not on well-bounded, mutually respectful negotiation that supports emergence of a "third reality."

Hierarchical, authoritarian parenting and teaching models differ markedly from the approach taken in this book. Still, there is value to any family or cultural system that supports children's growth with love and caring attention — as long as the children recognize the adults' behaviors as, in fact, loving and caring and not dismissive or abusive. And the truth is, no model, hierarchical or not, conveys these essential qualities. Only people can.

What is the relationship between the *holding environment*, *potential space*, and *the Third*? For the sake of simplicity, let us consider the *holding environment* to be the structure teachers provide within which students move physically, emotionally, and intellectually. It can be adequate (meaning consistently safe) or inadequate (unsafe or inconsistent). The goal for teachers is to construct an adequate holding environment that includes healthy connections, mirroring, and strong boundaries. These qualities open up the *potential space* within which students are safe to be themselves and to respect others' rights. If such a space is created and maintained, *the Third*, the experience of a coconstructed, shared reality that is greater than the sum of its parts, can emerge.

KEEP IN MIND

Because **potential space** *and* **the Third** *are abstract concepts that can easily be seen to overlap, they are used here more or less interchangeably. "Opening potential space" and "opening the Third" can be read as meaning basically the same thing: providing a holding environment that sponsors creativity and meaning making, arguably the whole point of education. When "crushing" or "squashing" or "collapsing" potential space or the Third is mentioned, they mean that conditions exist in the holding environment that hinder or prohibit desirable academic learning.*

So far we have seen how teachers can help create potential space: They can work through enactments, decide whether and how to be used by their students, and establish and

213

respect limits and boundaries in their classrooms. When teachers do this work, they set the stage for the Third to emerge. Specifically, then, one can make the following statements about the Third:

- When teachers and students engage in enactments and complete dysfunctional circuits,
- when teachers reverse roles and use students for their own purposes,
- when teachers or students transgress boundaries in the classroom,

the Third is *not* present.

On the other hand,

- when teachers plug into their students in informed, sensitive ways,
- when teachers allow themselves to be appropriately used,
- when teachers mirror their students,
- when teachers respect boundaries,
- when teachers repair,

they facilitate the Third.

So what does all this have to do with power struggles?

POWER STRUGGLES

Power struggles are a certain kind of enactment in which one person or party tries to dominate another. When one person wins a power struggle, the other person is forced, at least psychically, to disappear. It is as if the losing party is erased. It should go without saying that being erased ruins the chances for the Third to arise and prohibits healthy development and learning. Understanding how power struggles evolve and how they can be defused can have a profound effect on classrooms.

DEFINITION

Power struggles *are a type of enactment in which one person or party attempts to dominate or control another person or party who is unwilling to be dominated.*

FOR MY OWN GOOD

Mr. Leonard was a high school history teacher who particularly struggled with classroom management. An older man without any children of his own, he had little patience for immature behavior. He found noise and classroom activity disorienting and exerted a great deal of energy trying to keep his students quiet and on task. He was regularly taken aback at how disrespectful young people could be to their elders. Still, he was drawn to high school teaching as a way he could indulge his love of history and current events and, he hoped, do some good.

On this day the students in seventh period were in small groups for the third day in a row. And it was Friday. The decibel level in the classroom rose well above Mr. Leonard's tolerance level (and, he feared, the tolerance level of roving school administrators), and he lost his patience. He got the students' attention, gave them individual seatwork to do, and told them they had to be utterly silent for the remainder of the period. Anyone who said even one word would get a detention. This drastic move was for their own good, as they clearly were unable to be responsible for themselves today.

Of course, some students immediately tested Mr. Leonard's resolve. One student started tapping a pencil against the desk. Another student said, "What's that noise?" and a third student replied, "A jackass." Mr. Leonard gave all three students detention slips and sent them to the office.

What is going on here? From the psychodynamic perspective of potential space, quite a lot.

It should be readily apparent that Mr. Leonard found himself in a power struggle with the three disobedient students at the end of the story. But the power struggle really began when the noise level in the room exceeded Mr. Leonard's tolerance level. At that point, it appears, Mr. Leonard began seeing his students as threats to his personal and professional well-being. His anxiety spiked, and Mr. Leonard made a preemptive strike. He shut down all social interaction and in the process collapsed potential space and destroyed any hope of the Third.

Mr. Leonard's Limit

As we know, setting limits is an appropriate way to prevent or contain classroom chaos. When students grow loud, teachers need to quiet them down. But Mr. Leonard's story illustrates that the character of the limit matters. In chapter three, we considered limits that established reasonable rules and consequences and respected people's circles. In Mr. Leonard's story we witness a limit that is quite different.

For one thing, Mr. Leonard's limit, that the merest word would result in a detention, assumed the impossible: first, that his students could transition from noisy to silent instantaneously and, second, that none of them would question this rather draconian display of authority. For another, his limit completely denied the students' reality, whatever that was. Were the students on task? Were they talking about last night's party? Mr. Leonard had no idea. Asking the impossible and denying others' realities combined in this case to initiate a power struggle.

The reality Mr. Leonard was acting on was his own, and it appeared to be dominated by anxiety. Had he been able to slow down, detach, and become *aware* of his feelings, he might have noticed that he felt out of control or overwhelmed and frenzied. He might have noticed a sense of foreboding that someone in authority would look in on his class and judge him negatively. He might even have noticed fear of his students, whom he didn't understand and therefore felt alienated from.

The bottom line for Mr. Leonard, it seems, was that he felt insecure about his performance in the eyes of the school administration and he felt insecure about his ability to manage or relate to his students. Rather than flail about in these desperate emotions, Mr. Leonard cut off what he believed to be their source by insisting on silence in his classroom.

In fairness to Mr. Leonard, he demanded exactly what he craved: complete and instantaneous compliance. He did his best to get what he needed even if he rationalized it as "for the students' good" (in fact, the rule was for *his* good, not theirs). But he set himself and his students up for failure; his inflexibility, based on his insecurity, invited rebellion.

So three students conspired not just to test him but to show him what a "jackass" he was being. They called his bluff. Given the choice between amnesty and consistency, Mr.

216

Leonard chose to enforce his impulsive rule and ended up meting out a punishment that was way out of proportion to the original crime (being noisy during group work). If the students complained to their parents and their parents complained to the school administration, Mr. Leonard might find himself facing the disapproval he had cracked down on his students to avoid.

FOOD FOR THOUGHT

Not all teachers, who are themselves figures of authority, have the healthiest relationships with authority. Remember Mr. Apkin, who had to fight in his family for the right to his own opinion? He, like Mr. Leonard, was a teacher who brought a personal "issue with authority" into his classroom.

It is interesting to consider that some people who had bad experiences as students nonetheless choose to become teachers. Of course, many teachers want to be like mentors who inspired them or saw them for who they were. But some are also returning to a site of victimization and suffering. Sometimes the grade level a teacher ends up teaching is precisely the place where her own development went awry. It is as if we are rewriting our own histories by resolving to do it better than our teachers did for us.

The problem is that, too often, teachers teach the way they were taught. Enter psychic structure. The prongs and outlets that teachers present to their students have necessarily been shaped by influential experiences of teaching and learning in their own past. This can mean that, unless they make a conscious effort to change themselves, teachers can often unconsciously repeat the approaches and mistakes of those who shaped them.

So teachers (as well as all other professionals) have good reasons for going into their profession, but those reasons can be a very mixed bag. As with Mr. Leonard, some of those reasons, such as the desire to do good, are praiseworthy. But others, such as doing unto students what was done unto him, are not (even if they are unconscious). Furthermore, for many teachers, the classroom can be a place of great insecurity precisely because of the issues they are unconsciously hoping to work out: issues of authority, of intelligence, of competence, of appreciation.

Feeling insecure in the classroom, then, is perfectly normal. And as we explored in chapter one, negative feelings such as insecurity often go unnoticed, announcing themselves more in defenses than in actual sensations. But unmanaged insecurity, as we have seen with Mr. Leonard, can play a significant role in destroying the chances for the Third. As such, it is an enemy to teaching and learning. Any insight teachers can gain into the insecurity they feel in school can help tremendously in opening potential space and supporting growth in themselves and in their students.

Mr. Leonard's Emotion Work

It appears that Mr. Leonard's insecurity helped to bring on the collapse of the Third. But what about the students' behavior? Surely that was unacceptable and deserved to be punished. Yes: to the extent that the content — the student's use of the word "jackass," for example — was offensive, the students' behavior needed to be curbed. But from the perspective of psychodynamics, these students' opposition was a gift to Mr. Leonard.

Resistance

How could opposition ever be considered a gift?

YELLOW BELT MOVES

The short answer to this question is that, as with other enactments, student *resistance* offers an opportunity for reflection. Had Mr. Leonard been in a psychological position to *listen* to his students and wonder about the *good reasons* for their snide behavior, he might have been led to examine the reasons for his own behavior. Coming to grips with his insecurity through *self-awareness* and practicing alternative behaviors over time could have made a world of difference for him and his students.

The long answer has to do with the role resistance can play in the life of the Third. To put it simply, when a teacher eclipses the Third, students have two general options: *compliance* and *resistance*. Compliance often means the death of the Third, while resistance can represent a last gasp of air in potential space.

218

In Mr. Leonard's example the three students who resisted were accomplishing at least two things. First, they were protesting Mr. Leonard's self-serving and, to them, meaningless rule. And second, they were inviting him to engage with them. They were asking him to *show up* one way or another, either as a great-enough teacher or as an ongoing not-good-enough teacher.

To be sure, this invitation was unconscious, potentially self-destructive, and unpleasant. As with any enactment, the three students plugged into Mr. Leonard without forethought. In doing so they risked dire punishment. Unconscious or not, the emotions driving this enactment were probably negative: anger, frustration, a desire to test, hurt, and humiliate. Resistance and power struggles are rarely pleasant.

But they are informative. The very act of protest meant the students themselves were willing to show up. By doing so they gave Mr. Leonard an opportunity to turn the classroom situation around and open up potential space. Any discussion of the three students' behavior and the rule they were breaking, any connection that recognized the students' as well as the teacher's different realities, could have led to mutual understanding within the space of a coconstructed third reality.

BLACK BELT MOVES

"Well, now," Mr. Leonard might have said. "I believe you just called me a jackass." "We didn't call *you* a jackass," the students might have said defensively. "But you well could have," Mr. Leonard might have replied. "I just laid down a pretty stupid rule. Anybody out there agree?"

Mr. Leonard could then have *repaired* the situation. He could have explained his controlling impulse and enlisted the students' aid in keeping the classroom noise level down. He could also have taken this opportunity to ask the students how the group projects were going. And if he felt really brave, and if the students were especially receptive, he could have apologized for his somewhat brutal knee-jerk reaction to his anxiety.

It is not difficult to imagine how much warmer the atmosphere in Mr. Leonard's classroom could have been had he acknowledged the legitimacy of his students' reaction to his rule, explained his own legitimate needs, and worked with his students on possible solutions.

Of course, like Mr. Bonham in chapter three, who slammed a book down on a resistant student's desk, Mr. Leonard had foundational emotion work to do. If he had any hope of resolving this situation and making way for the Third in his history classroom, he needed secure, trustworthy relationships with his students individually and with his classes as a whole. The better these relationships, the easier it would have been for him to manage this power struggle.

Compliance

So resistance can be seen as a gift, as an opening, however narrow, to mutual engagement that can revive the Third. Compliance, on the other hand, can mean the end of the Third. We can see this in Mr. Leonard's story. Those students who immediately shut their mouths also tacitly agreed to shut down the Third. To be sure, they were wise to protect themselves from their teacher's punishment. And most students are neither foolish nor brazen enough to protest against the center of power — the teacher — as the three sarcastic students in Mr. Leonard's class did.

But forced compliance can do a triple whammy on students. First, it makes them accomplices in the death of the Third, which is directly counter to their best interests. Second, it denies their vital subjectivity by making them objects of their teacher's manipulation as he reverses roles to lessen his anxiety. And third, it dismisses their reality. Being in a room where one's personal experience is denied can, at best, force it underground and, at worst, cause intense confusion about one's right to exist in the world.

TERRIBLE SECRET

At age 14 Raphael was a strong athlete and a good student. He had many "friends" — that is, he knew a lot of kids, and they seemed to like him. But they did not know him. For Raphael was attracted to boys, a fact he could not share with his family or friends and that he himself refused to accept. Keeping this secret to himself, he was socially aloof and ever vigilant lest someone discover his truth.

One day in school, Raphael was walking down the hall to English class with one of his "friends," Jason. An unathletic boy named Marco passed Jason and Raphael going the other way. Jason bumped into the boy and cried out, "Watch where you're going, faggot!" Marco hunched his shoulders and hurried away, and Jason laughed. So did Raphael.

"What a gay boy," Jason said to Raphael. "Yeah," Raphael agreed, a little too loudly. "Loser! Faggot! He's worthless!" The boys headed into English class, passing their teacher, Ms. Copeland, in the doorway. She had seen the entire exchange and said nothing.

Later that day, after school, Raphael attacked Marco, fighting so viciously that it took two adults to pull him off. Jason and several other boys were watching, cheering Raphael on.

In any act of bigotry, a power dynamic prevails in which there is room for only one person: the bully. In this case Jason needed to dominate Marco, to erase him. And, as in any act of bigotry, Jason's need most likely stemmed from deep fear of the "other," the "not-me." Because his fear of homosexuality and unclear gender identity was so intense, Jason *projected* it onto Marco (turning Marco into a screen), then destroyed it by ridiculing Marco. (It is quite likely that Jason himself had been a victim of bullying and was also *identifying with the aggressor*.)

With the full weight of his heterosexist culture behind him, Jason defined Marco in self-serving, narrow terms, denying Marco (and Raphael) the right to be himself in all his multidimensional fullness. Seizing power through cruelty, Jason decided Marco *would not* be known. Such an act, though verbal and emotional, is unspeakably violent.

Jason's blatant bigotry, one can guess, put Raphael into a terrible bind. Seeing just what people like Jason could do to people like him, Raphael had to make a choice: resist by defending Marco or comply by joining with Jason. For a 14-year-old boy struggling with his sexuality, this amounts to no choice at all. Not only did Raphael join with Jason but he did so ferociously, hoping to bury his identity through vehement overcompensation.

But there is more to the bind. Raphael had to discharge his own fear and self-hatred, first by attacking Marco verbally and then by attacking him physically. The ferocity of the fight suggests the degree of Raphael's self-loathing; that is, it appears that he was enacting on Marco what he felt for himself.

Complicity with the destruction of the Third, then, was deeply harmful to Raphael. It reinforced his commitment to living a terrible lie; it deepened his alienation from himself and others; it strengthened his sense of self-disgust and self-hatred; and it led to the sort of violence that, in too many instances, can end in physical injury and even death.

Teacher as Bystander

What about the teacher in this story? Though she played a seemingly small part, Ms. Copeland actually had a huge negative impact on Raphael. By failing to comment on the boys' homophobic bullying, she effectively condoned it, thereby complying with the collapse of potential space and the crushing of the Third.

There are many possible "good" reasons for Ms. Copeland's failure, of course. She could have been actively homophobic and supportive of the boys' hateful attitudes. She could have been passively homophobic, unable to perceive the boys' cruelty because it felt so familiar and normal to her. She could have been afraid to confront the boys; or she could have been focused on keeping to her classroom schedule; or she could have decided this was an issue for parents to handle.

What all of these "good" reasons ignore is the teacher's fundamental responsibility as a *developmental partner*: to support the cognitive and emotional development of all of her students, to foster an adequate, respectful holding environment. This includes sensitivity to ethics and identity development. If Ms. Copeland had been more aware both of the boys' violence to Marco and of her own complicity in it, she could have made moves to *repair* the damage.

Ms. Copeland's Emotion Work

In the face of such dangerous homophobic bullying, what could Ms. Copeland have done differently?

Ms. Copeland could have started by acknowledging to herself the violence of the interaction in the hallway with Marco. This would have involved noticing the students' actions and her reaction to them. This step can be extremely difficult when an adult tacitly approves of a student's negative behavior, so becoming *aware* is not necessarily as easy as it sounds.

Describing to herself what she had witnessed could have helped Ms. Copeland sort out the issues and establish priorities. "I just saw two boys insult a third boy because of his supposed sexuality," she might have said to herself. "They ganged up on him and bullied him. Bullying is absolutely not acceptable in this school. That is school policy. If I let this go, the bullying will either continue or get worse. And I would not be doing my job."

Of course, it is not difficult to imagine what other thoughts might have run through Ms. Copeland's head. "But we've got so much to do today! And we're behind because of yesterday's assembly. It's also my job to teach subject matter, for heaven's sake. And I don't want to take on Jason and Raphael — they're popular boys, and who knows how the class would respond? They could just as easily attack me as that boy in the hall. . . ."

Making the choice to open the potential space required for proper cognitive and emotional development is not always easy. It can involve curricular detours, student resistance, administrative concern, and, for the teacher, a great deal of courage. It also takes time; Ms. Copeland would have been wise to bring these thoughts home with her so she could carefully *plan* a response to Jason and Raphael – but not before she spoke privately with the boys, expressing her concern about their treatment of Marco and her intention to address it in class the next day.

Ms. Copeland's plan would have had to include, of course, deliberate design of the actions she would take in her lesson and the actions she would ask her students to take. Planning instructional actions is a crucial element in opening potential space and making way for the Third.

These actions would have to meet with the explicit or tacit approval of the school community: parents and administrators. If Ms. Copeland's school had adopted an explicit approach to bullying, her planning could conform to the program's parameters. In fact, applying anti-bullying advice to actual instances of bullying can help students transform the advice into effective response. If the school had no particular anti-bullying policy or if discussing controversial topics such as gender and sexual identity was frowned upon, Ms. Copeland would have to be especially creative in her instructional design. She might also need help in planning and implementing her anti-bullying activity.

Part of her planning, whatever approach Ms. Copeland chose to take, would require *anticipation*. Ms. Copeland would have to think about not just what her students might do in the lesson but what they might feel and, importantly, how *she* might feel. In preparation for the strong emotions a conversation about bullying or homophobia would undoubtedly raise in herself and her students, Ms. Copeland would have to commit to being a great-enough developmental partner to all of her students. Thoughtful instructional design and deliberate cultivation of a stable yet flexible emotional stance would be two necessary ingredients to success.

What would this emotional stance be like? Once she made the brave decision to *show up* and address the bullying in class, Ms. Copeland would have needed to muster curiosity about the encounter in the hallway. This would have required her to step back from it, to suspend her judgment, and to genuinely want to hear different perspectives. Her stance would have needed to be one of *detachment*, a stance that almost literally opens up the potential space between a teacher and her students, permitting the Third to emerge.

BLACK BELT MOVES

Ms. Copeland's next step, then, would have been to create an opportunity for her students to talk about what had happened. She needed to structure a discussion about homophobia and bullying. In this way, she — and Jason and Raphael — could hear their "good" reasons for what they had done. Not only would Jason and Raphael have a chance to talk, but other students who had tacitly condoned the behavior, who had *complied* with the crushing of the Third by remaining silent, would be able to explore their experience as well.

In order to have an open discussion about such a sensitive subject as homophobia and bullying, Ms. Copeland would need very strong *boundaries*. She would have to

- expect students to test limits by being squirrelly, disrespectful, and distracting;
- detach from the students' behaviors so as to not take them personally;
- agree on rules and consequences (limits) that would govern the classroom discussion;
- stay present to yet detached from her own and the students' emotions (possibilities could include fear, sadness, anger, contempt), resisting the urge to rescue or punish the students, to take on the emotions for them, or to discharge her feelings on them;
- apply consequences for breaking the discussion rules fairly and consistently, anticipating and preparing for pushback (such as resistance, ridicule, yelling, withdrawal);
- hold no grudges but, rather, be available for academic and emotional use during and after the conversation;
- mobilize supportive elements within and outside of the school holding environment for herself and, if necessary, for her students.

In this particularly difficult discussion, Ms. Copeland would have to know and contain her own opinions, feel genuine curiosity about her students' opinions, and respect her students' rights to their attitudes, whatever they might be. Once again, she would have to stay detached enough to let her students speak for themselves but interested and connected enough to empathize with them without necessarily agreeing with them or trying to rescue or change them. All this would depend upon her strong boundaries.

Facilitating this discussion would require a good deal of self-assurance. Ms. Copeland would have to feel secure in allowing students the freedom to be honest and possibly hurtful, to function outside her total control. Her job, as with any free-form discussion, would be to hold it, to contain it, so that all of her students could be safe in their self-expression.

225

Some of the ways she could prepare this holding environment would be

- to set *ground rules* for the discussion before it took place;
- to structure the discussion around *open-ended questions* and *thought experiments* that would expand students' thinking about the topic and avoid spotlighting the culprits;
- to channel the discussion into a *plan* that would include agreed-upon rules for student behavior in the future.

Ground Rules

Many teachers set ground rules for class discussions at the very beginning of each school year, a wise practice, especially if it is done in collaboration with the students. In this case, Ms. Copeland could either ask students to brainstorm a list of rules and consequences or review the list they had already come up with. "Think before you speak" might be a good rule. "Speak for yourself, not for anyone else" might be another. "Celebrate people who take huge risks" might be yet another.

Ms. Copeland would have to ensure that students were clear on what the consequences for breaking or following these rules would be. For example, students might agree to curb impulsivity by giving speakers five whole seconds to reflect on and, if necessary, revise what they just said. They might encourage students to begin sentences with "I" rather than "you" to keep their statements responsible. And they might decide to clap when someone said something that seemed especially honest or brave. In addition, students could agree on a signal that any one student could use to indicate the conversation was getting too uncomfortable, at which point the whole class would stop and reassess.

Setting specific parameters would help create a safe context for this potentially exposing discussion; that is, it would define the *holding environment* out of which the Third, or the experience of cocreating and sharing understanding, could emerge.

Open-Ended Questions

What, specifically, would such a discussion look like? Here is one possible scenario: Ms. Copeland could begin class by writing the word "homophobia" on the board. She could invite definitions and guide the students toward the correct meaning, writing "fear" in big letters on the board. She could then ask the open-ended question, "Why might people be bullies?" Here is one way this part of the discussion might unfold.

WHEN ALL ELSE FAILS, DISTRACT

"Why might people be bullies?" Ms. Copeland asked her class. After a long silence, students started offering answers. "They're mean." "They're unhappy." "They have a lot of power." "They want people to be afraid of them."

Ms. Copeland wrote down each answer without comment. When the students ran out of possibilities, she asked a follow-up question: "Why might these feelings -- 'mean,' 'unhappy,' 'powerful' – lead to bullying?" When students looked confused, she said, "Well, there are lots of ways people can act when they feel mean or unhappy or powerful. They can yell, for example. They can cry. They can use their power to help someone or to stand up for what's right. What makes a person want to hurt someone else?"

In truth, Ms. Copeland did not know the definitive answer to her own question. She had some ideas, but she was not an expert either on hurting or on the psychology of a bully or homophobe. Asking a genuine question, one she needed the students' help to answer, felt extremely risky to Ms. Copeland. She knew what her next guiding question was – "What impact does bullying have on other people?" – but she had little idea of how she and her students would get to it.

The students' answers started out innocently enough. Again, "they're just mean" was one ready answer. "They don't know what else to do with their feelings." "They don't like the person." Wanting to go deeper, Ms. Copeland asked the students to say more, to describe the connection they sensed between their answers and the act of bullying. She wondered what the connection between

227

bullying and the "phobia" in homophobia might be. Again, she received the students' explanations without judgment.

Finally, sighing mightily, Jason added his contribution: "Some people are just gross. I mean, come on! Why should we be nice to dorks?" Several students broke into laughter. Others nodded their agreement.

Jason, sensing he had the class's attention, began capering around the room, flopping his wrists flamboyantly and describing the boys around him in flattering terms using an exaggerated lisp. "I'm not a homophobe!" he cried. "I'm a homo!" The students responded with laughter and mimicry of their own – though Raphael was notably silent.

Ms. Copeland felt a rising sense of panic that she was losing control of the discussion. She also felt intensely irritated at Jason. No, it wasn't irritation. It was fear. He was wielding power over the class and Ms. Copeland was afraid she would be unable to stop him.

Noting these emotions, Ms. Copeland took a moment to examine them. What was going on right now? Jason was distracting the class, asserting his power just at the moment that his classmates were discussing bullying, a form of domination he clearly utilized. What an interesting coincidence! How could she use it to her advantage?

The first thing she had to do was get Jason's attention. Putting her body right next to his, she said in a firm voice, "Jason, sit down. Right now. SIT." She made it quite clear that she would accept nothing short of immediate obedience.

Once Jason was in his seat, Ms. Copeland remained right next to him and addressed the class. "This was an amazing coincidence. Here we were, discussing bullying and homophobia, and Jason graced us with demonstrations of both. What I saw was Jason making fun of gay men in a highly simplistic and stereotyped way, and I saw him take control of the class against my will and, I'm guessing, against your will, too.

"What's more, most of you helped Jason express his contempt and fear of homosexuality by going along with *him. Together, we just acted out an incident of bullying and bystander complicity. Congratulations! Now we can try to understand what happened.*

"Please take out a piece of paper and write absolutely silently on this prompt: 'All of you just had a lot of power. What was it like to make fun of another person?' You've got two minutes." When students finished, she gave them another two-minute prompt: "Now switch roles and write about this question: 'What is it like to be the target of public ridicule?'" She assured them that their writing would remain private unless they chose to share it with the rest of the class. And she wrote herself for the full ten minutes.

This story is important to include here because it is wildly unlikely that a conversation about homophobia or bullying will run smoothly, especially in a classroom within which an active homophobe and bully reside. This is a particularly interesting story, as it both illustrates how a teacher can keep the Third open in a discussion but also what a teacher can do when the Third suddenly collapses.

What did Ms. Copeland do to keep the Third open in this difficult discussion? First, she asked *open-ended questions* to which every student could offer an answer. She recognized that true open-ended questions require a release of control, a flexibility based on faith that the discussion would wend its way to her next open-ended guiding question. Second, she asked *authentic* questions, questions she did not have ready answers to, and she took her students' thinking on them seriously. Third, she valued each student's answer, hearing it without judgment. Fourth, she requested elaboration where appropriate and with real curiosity, encouraging the students to explore the answers' meanings and underlying assumptions without fear of criticism or evaluation. In other words, she *detached* and maintained *healthy boundaries* so her students could think and interact safely in potential space.

Ms. Copeland did have a problem, though, when the Third collapsed. Unable to engage in a democratic discussion, Jason took over with his condescending and stereotyped imitation of a gay man. He cracked through the veneer of seriousness to the underlying tension all of his classmates must

229

have felt and offered comic (if insensitive) relief. Because of his own discomfort, he stopped the discussion and initiated a *power struggle*.

FOOD FOR THOUGHT
Comic relief does not necessarily disrupt the Third. Release of tension through laughter and healthy silliness can, on the contrary, fortify the Third. This is true only if *the shenanigans strengthen, rather than undermine, the relationships on which the Third depends.*

More Emotion Work

When teachers take the kind of risk that Ms. Copeland took – the risk of addressing issues and behaviors that foreclose on potential space and the Third and, ultimately, on cognitive and emotional (and identity) development – they invite the additional risk of losing control of their classrooms. Indeed, opening up potential space can feel chaotic, especially if teacher and students are unaccustomed to the experience. Fortunately, the discomfort that can arise when the Third is crushed *and* when potential space is opened can lead to very effective emotion work.

MORE YELLOW BELT MOVES

What emotion work did Ms. Copeland do? As we saw, her immediate response to Jason's homophobic behavior was panic. Fortunately, she was *self-aware* enough to notice her feelings and to stop herself from reacting instantly. Rather, she slowed down and wondered about the sudden turn of events, looking for the *good reasons* behind Jason's actions. Recognizing Jason's antics as distractions was important, but taking very seriously his need to distract when students were exploring the emotions that led to bullying gave Ms. Copeland the data she needed. Whatever Jason was feeling during this discussion, it was apparently uncomfortable enough to prompt him to resort to a familiar pattern: fighting his own sense of powerlessness by dominating others.

What led her to this realization? Her *awareness* of her own sense of powerlessness allowed her to *guess* that Jason might be feeling the same way. Her fear mirrored his fear, and his fear needed containment. In order to *set limits* on Jason's behavior, Ms. Copeland needed to *show up* and contest Jason's right to dominate the class. Though Ms. Copeland might have felt as though she was being harsh and inflexible in insisting that Jason sit down and then *describing* Jason's dominating and homophobic behavior, she had to balance his energy with her own to make way for potential space.

And "balance" is a key word. For while Ms. Copeland sensed that the Third would remain collapsed if she stayed silent, she also understood that dominating Jason in turn (by yelling at or humiliating him or sending him to the office) would have the same damaging effect. In other words, she intuited that being an overly accommodating not-good-enough teacher or a co-opting not-good-enough teacher would be equally harmful. She chose to be *great enough* by showing up and standing her ground: seeing Jason, *guessing* at his feelings, unapologetically *setting limits* on his behavior, and *describing* his and his classmates' actions, all in order to restore potential space and the possibility for a meaningful discussion in a shared, third reality.

MORE BLACK BELT MOVES

The follow-up to this story could go as follows: Once all the freewriting was completed, Ms. Copeland could ask students to share their responses. In the interest of *self-disclosure*, she could read all or part of her own. Rather than analyze or evaluate each contribution, Ms. Copeland could ask students what words or phrases from each piece stood out to them, what each piece made them feel, what it revealed to them, how it changed the way they saw bullies and the bullied. In this way she would be cultivating empathy, an extremely important life skill. In addition, having students represent their thoughts and feelings while respecting those of others would reinforce emotional boundaries, foster intellectual discipline, and contribute directly to the emergence of the Third.

A Thought Experiment

Despite the lack of a lockstep plan, Ms. Copeland and her students had managed to address her question about the impact of bullying. This could be seen as a stroke of luck. It could also be seen as a direct result of good instructional design. The open-ended questions Ms. Copeland asked, the authentic

thinking she and her students did, and the accurate intervention
Ms. Copeland enacted when Jason took over allowed the most
important issues about bullying to emerge in the discussion.
Ms. Copeland could now move on to the final phase of her
lesson plan where students would apply their thinking about
bullying to a thought experiment.

"Let's imagine," she could say, "that a cat and a dog
move in together — their family adopts them at the same time.
This cat, named Mink, and the dog, named Harvey, HATE
each other. Mink attacks Harvey's face, often leaving the nails
of her claws in his nose. And Harvey attacks Mink, trying to
bite (and, he hopes, eat) her. Are you with me so far?

"The family, who love both Harvey and Mink, cannot
stand how they fight. So they give the animals an ultimatum:
Figure out how to coexist peacefully or you will have to move
out. Harvey and Mink also love their family and do not want to
leave. So they decide to try to do what their family members
want them to do: figure out how to live together in peace.

"What do you think Mink and Harvey would have to do
to accomplish this? What do you think they would discover
about each other?"

At this point Ms. Copeland could have the students talk
to each other in pairs, write independently, or continue with the
full-group discussion. She could ask the students to think about
the story and her questions privately until the next day, when
they would continue the discussion. However she structured it,
she would need to give the students time in class to *play* with
the thought experiment by trying out different ideas,
responding to each other, following a thought along to its
logical conclusion, applying their thinking to human bullying,
and so on.

A Plan

By the end of the discussion, students would most
likely have a very different sense not just of how homophobia
and the construction of "difference" work but of how hate and
fear in general work. They would have contemplated
alternatives to the extremes of bullying and domination. And
they would be in a strong position to make a *plan* that would
guide them in handling future intolerance in the classroom and
the school.

These conversations would take time; they would push other priorities aside and force Ms. Copeland to scramble to catch up with the regular curriculum later. But the conversation would be invaluable for a number of reasons. It would support students in engaging honestly and bravely with ideas and with each other. It would promote a classroom environment in which complex thinking could be done in the future. It would address actual curricular standards. Thinking within the constraints of fair and considerate ground rules, answering authentic open-ended questions, and playing with a thought experiment for the purpose of deep understanding would allow students to inhabit potential space and encourage the emergence of the Third.

Importantly, reviving the Third in this way would open up space for Raphael to be himself. Whether Ms. Copeland suspected Raphael was gay or not, she might have changed his life with this one brave move. No vicious fight would have been necessary at recess. Raphael would still have had much to work on internally, and homophobia would not stop in his life just because of this classroom discussion. But the experience of being able to exist in a safe space *as he was*, even while keeping his sexuality secret, could have planted a crucial seed of self-acceptance inside him. This is a type of learning that teachers and schools should strive for.

FOOD FOR THOUGHT

Ms. Copeland's story could have featured any number of "others" — people of races, ethnicities, or cultures that are different from a school's majority population; people with learning disabilities, physical disabilities, or mental illness; people whose first language is not English; people from different socioeconomic groups; people of different religions and family norms; people of different sizes or builds. Students from any of these groups can be misunderstood, overlooked, and bullied in schools.

While it is certainly important that teachers inform themselves about the various cultures represented in their classrooms, the notion of the Third emphasizes the unique character of interacting parties. Rather than presuming to know about other cultures or inviting individuals to act as cultural representatives, teachers can cultivate the Third by getting to know their students as multifaceted people.

Asking the sole member of a group — say, the only Muslim student in the class — to represent the entire group, for instance, ignores that student's other identities. While such a move might appear to support the Third by opening up space for the Muslim perspective, it actually forces the student into a one-dimensional box where the student's only identity is a religious one. The potential space all students need is one in which they can explore multiple identities and, importantly, move through the stages of identity development at their own pace.

And identity development happens along many dimensions. Deciding ahead of time that a student with a learning disability is also cognitively deficient diminishes him. Pinpointing a student as a chronic troublemaker almost guarantees that she will fulfill the prophecy by being a troublemaker. Putting a student on a pedestal — insisting, for example, that she is a precocious writer or that she is a remarkable harpsichord player — can limit the student's sense of her options, of her right to sometimes hate writing or to prefer watching a movie to practicing her instrument. Keeping space open for people to be members of many groups as well as unique individuals allows all students room to be themselves and to develop freely.

Forced Compliance

Raphael's story is one of *forced compliance*. Forced compliance happens whenever one person or party wins a power struggle and shuts down the Third at the expense of another. Teachers, by virtue of their positions of power, are always poised to eclipse the Third, but as the above two stories show, students can do it, too.

To revive the Third by opening up the potential space in which learning, growth, and change can occur, teachers and students must hold on to their beliefs and identities. They must *show up*. And they must respect the right of others to show up possessing different beliefs and identities. Diehard conservatives, for example, must make room for progressive views just as sworn evolutionists must allow for creationists in their classrooms. The point of education is not to colonize, or impose one's own views on others, but to cultivate growth in students.

This is not to say that teachers must approve of all perspectives and abandon their own values. Far from it. What teachers need to do is, first, attend to their own prejudices and notice their students'. Second, they need to accept the perhaps unwelcome fact that they actually have no control over who their students are or who they become. Teachers have *influence*, but they do not have control.

And with all this in mind, teachers need to hold open the space in which differences can be stated and examined, in which relationships can thrive, and in which the Third, the unpredictable, uncontrollable, and often remarkable cocreated third reality, can flourish. In this potential space students can be themselves, play with being someone else, make creative accommodations, and, ideally, experience epiphanies that mark lasting learning.

Voluntary Compliance

But forced compliance need not give all compliance a bad name. *Voluntary compliance* is, of course, an important goal in classrooms and can be quite enriching for students. The discussion of bullying in Ms. Copeland's class, for example, could not have occurred without voluntary compliance from the students. Students who take pride in their seatwork or homework because they perceive its value to themselves are benefiting from voluntary compliance. This type of compliance is actually necessary for the existence of the Third and does no harm. It is a stance that students can take when they feel respected and empowered to be authoritative agents in their own learning.

Definitions

Forced compliance *happens when one person or group shuts down the Third at the expense of another person or group.*

Voluntary compliance *happens when people agree to comply because they perceive cooperation's benefits. This is a goal in classrooms.*

Forced compliance works against the Third. And resistance can be *good* for the Third. So how might a teacher think about responding to resistance so as to nurture its benefits? In the next three stories, we consider very specific answers to this question.

LEARNING TO NOT-LEARN

Ms. Bernstein was a reading specialist who taught third grade. She prided herself on her ability to help students "break the code" and improve their comprehension skills. As a third grade teacher, she was the last resort for many students who had not yet reached grade level in reading, and she had many success stories. It had been a long time since she had encountered a student as stubborn as Danny, though. Try as she might, he simply would not improve.

Ms. Bernstein took to keeping Danny after school so she could help him individually with his reading. He would sit obediently at his desk with a book open in front of him. When Ms. Bernstein worked with him, he would read haltingly, taking an excruciating length of time to get through a sentence. When Ms. Bernstein left him to work on his own, he would look out the window, doodle on a piece of paper, rifle through his desk, or just stare off into space. Reading just was not happening. Ms. Bernstein, feeling intense pressure to get Danny up to grade level, tried every trick in the book with Danny, but he did not give in.

There is clearly no Third in this story. Danny and Ms. Bernstein were like two rocks in a cave, sometimes next to each other, sometimes apart, never actually accomplishing anything. At first glance it appears that Danny was responsible for this impasse. It was his boulderlike resistance to improving his reading skills that blocked Ms. Bernstein from having an impact on him.

Since Ms. Bernstein had tried everything to get Danny to read, we can assume that she had already made her white belt move and considered the possibility that Danny lacked the necessary skills and knowledge to read fluently. When

236

encountering resistance, teachers must consider this possibility first and foremost; they must get creative about figuring out what students lack and taking useful steps to remediate.

What Ms. Bernstein might not have considered was the possibility that Danny, however indirectly, might have been reminding her that learning to read is more than simply acquiring a skill set. It involves *personal change* that for some students means a revision of identity that is simply too threatening to undertake.

What might some "good" reasons be for Danny's resistance, then? One possibility is that Danny feared he *could not* read. He may have sensed the concern his teachers and parents felt about his ability and concluded for himself that he was not smart enough to learn how to read. Distracting himself from reading tasks prevented him from facing this fear directly and allowed him to *project* his anxiety into his teachers.

Another possibility is that Danny could not fathom *being* a reader. The identity may have made no sense to him. He might have come from a family that sought information and entertainment from the television, for example, not from books. Danny might have perceived that reading was unnecessary, as he could get what he needed in other ways.

Being a reader may have put Danny at odds with his family. The kinds of changes that educators take for granted can challenge certain family norms, hierarchies, or expectations and force an unbearable choice upon a student: learn and upset the *status quo* of the family or not-learn and fit in at home. For Danny, then, becoming a reader might have meant taking a first step away from his family, a move he would fight as long as he could.

Another possibility is that Danny was attached to an identity of incompetence. He might have been the "baby" in the family. He might have lived in a family culture in which passivity served him better than activity, where being inept guaranteed a certain measure of attention. Or he might have been accepted and even admired in his family as a daydreamer who was too artistic and ethereal to buckle down to mundane tasks.

In the case of playing the incompetent role, being able and proficient might carry with it responsibilities and expectations that Danny simply did not want to take on. He might also have worried that shifting an identity that his family seemed to count on would upset and disappoint them. If he (unconsciously) perceived himself to be known in terms of rigid categories, he might have been loathe to move outside those categories for fear of suddenly feeling unknown in his own family.

FOOD FOR THOUGHT
Learning can alter students' identities. If a student suspects that learning will change who he is or who others think he is, he might want to avoid it. Unwanted **identity change**, *then, is a good reason for resistance to learning.*

Identity Change
Danny's story beautifully illustrates the relationship between learning and personal change and introduces us to its perils. To become a reader is to alter one's identity, to change forever. For many students this change is so welcome that its cultural significance goes unnoticed. For others the change to literacy — and other changes like it — holds meaning that many teachers, administrators, and policy makers may not immediately grasp.

As mentioned above, learning can alienate a student from his family of origin. Moving into the professional class, for instance, can be extremely disorienting for someone who comes from a working-class background. Gaining skills that one's parents do not possess can invert power structures within a family in ways that no member appreciates.

Becoming an English speaker in a family whose first language is not English, for example, can cause ever-widening, deeply damaging rifts between generations. Resistance from a Native American student, a Black student, or a Chicano student to school curricula often represents resistance to "becoming White," to "selling out" to a culture that dominates and devalues difference (Tatum, 1997). Once again, such resistance can be seen as a way of fighting the shutting down of the Third and, as such, demands understanding and working through.

238

Ms. Bernstein's Emotion Work

What could Ms. Bernstein have done with Danny if she had considered his resistance from the perspective of *identity change*?

BLUE BELT MOVES

Ms. Bernstein's first step could have been to explore the meaning for Danny of making this change, of learning to read and becoming a reader. She could start by *describing*.

"I notice," she could have said to Danny, "that you avoid reading at all costs. Usually you will read for me, but you really don't seem to like reading for yourself. Does that sound right?" She could also *self-disclose*. "You know, I love to read. I mean, I'm a teacher, after all! But my love for reading isn't helping me much right now because I so easily forget why people might *not* like reading. And I know there are some good reasons to not like it."

If Danny did not offer any reasons for disliking reading, Ms. Bernstein could propose some of her own; that is, she could make some *guesses* as to why Danny might not want to read. Depending on the strength of Danny's resistance, Ms. Bernstein might have to wait in silence quite a lot, or she might have to stretch this conversation over several days. If Danny did speak, she would have to *listen* very carefully to his answers, looking for clues to his perception of the change she was asking him to make.

As might be obvious, the issue of *learning to read* can be quite different from the issue of *becoming a reader*. If Danny's answers indicated that learning to read was the issue, then Ms. Bernstein could explore his beliefs about himself. Did he feel too "stupid" to learn this skill? Where did that belief come from? What did "stupid" mean? What type of person *could* learn how to read? What did this type of person have that Danny did not have? If Danny was an avid player of video games or baseball or Chinese checkers, could he tell his teacher how he learned to be good at these games? Could he actually *teach* her how to play one of them? When Ms. Bernstein lost confidence or felt too incompetent to get better at the game he was teaching, what would he recommend she do?

239

If Danny revealed that he was resistant to *becoming a reader*, the exploration would focus on identity change. What did it mean to *become* or *be* a reader? Whom did Danny know who embodied this identity? What was that person like? What had that person gained by being a reader? What had he lost? What did it mean *not* to be a reader? Whom did Danny know who was not a reader? What was that person like? What had that person gained and lost? How did Danny relate (or not) to each of these people?

Whatever approach she took to this exploration, Ms. Bernstein would have to be genuinely curious about Danny's experience and absolutely refuse to judge it. And she would have to think and act on a number of levels all at once.

- She would have to think about relationships: How was Danny pushing her buttons? How were she and her expectations about reading pushing *Danny's* buttons? What shifts could she make to help change the enactments she perceived?

- How was Danny using her? How was she using Danny? How could she make herself available for use that promoted his development? Did he need a twin? A statue on a pedestal? A mirror? Something else? If she couldn't play those roles for Danny, who could?

- What boundaries needed to be in place? What support did she need as a developmental partner for a particularly resistant student?

The purpose of this exploration, which would require dedicated emotion work from Ms. Bernstein, would be to *listen*, to make room for the Third, so that Danny and Ms. Bernstein and reading could all coexist in potential space and respect their uncertain relationships to each other.

Conflict

An element that often permeates uncertain relationships is *conflict*, the contest between one path or choice and another. Danny's conflict seems to be between changing, or saying "yes" to learning, and staying the same, or saying "no."

If Danny were truly conflicted, Ms. Bernstein's questions would probably unearth some contradictions in his answers. At the same time that he might say he is too "stupid"

240

to learn to read ("no" to learning), he might hint that he is not ("yes" to learning). While he might identify strongly with an illiterate father ("no"), he might still yearn to be a reader himself ("yes").

At first such conflicts might appear as juicy openings for supportive cheerleading: "But you're not stupid! See? You even said so yourself. You *can* learn to read!" or "But you can be like your dad in other ways. He would be so proud of you if you learned to do something he cannot!" It is easy to guess that such well-meaning statements, which would jump prematurely to the teacher's solution ("Learn to read!"), would close down the Third and spawn more resistance.

Useful alternatives exist. One way to capitalize on conflict is to flow with the student's resistance, his "no." Ms. Bernstein could say to Danny, "Yes, I hear you. When you feel too stupid to do something, that's the last thing in the world you want to do." Or "Of course! Your father is very important to you, and you hope to be just like him." This approach might grate on Ms. Bernstein, as it would appear to support the very behavior she was attempting to change. But *going with the resistance* would keep the Third open, allowing Danny to be himself without any hint of judgment. And in being himself Danny would have the chance to experience his conflict openly, even arguing with himself as he weighed the pros and cons of each side.

For example, Danny might respond to Ms. Bernstein with "But I'm not *that* stupid. I mean, I *want* to read. I really like it when you read to the class. I just don't know if I can be a *really good* reader." The source of Danny's resistance would now be a little clearer: He might believe that learning to read meant being perfect at it, or being "really good" (and exploring what he meant by this would be Ms. Bernstein's next step).

Or Danny might say, "I don't want to be *just like* my dad. He's a machinist, and I want to be a pilot." Now Ms. Bernstein could follow up on Danny's ambition to be different from his father in this way. "So how would your father feel about your being a pilot when he's a machinist?" she might ask. "Oh!" Danny might respond. "He'd be proud. We both love airplanes!" An exploration of what it takes to become a pilot could follow, and reading, whether of instruments, weather, or manuals, could come up. Without pressing the issue, Ms. Bernstein could let Danny sit with these requirements and the differences between his father and him, perhaps expanding on them, playing with the picture of his own success and his father's proud acceptance of it.

Conflict statements. Another approach would be for Ms. Bernstein to describe the conflict, or *label* it. If she sensed that Danny was on the fence about his intelligence, and she perceived that Danny was ready to wrestle with this contradiction explicitly, she could make a *conflict statement* that captured the "yes" and the "no" of the issue. Conflict statements, by acknowledging both sides of a conflict, invite examination of feelings that appear inconsistent but nonetheless coexist within a student. The resistance that erupts when the two sides of a conflict are not resolved destroys any possibility of the Third. Explicitly acknowledging the two sides can open it up.

"You think of yourself as stupid sometimes, but other times you know you're smart," Ms. Bernstein could offer.

"Yeah!" Danny might exclaim. "Sometimes I even *try* to be stupid. Why would I do that? I'm not stupid! I *am* smart!"

"Well, why *would* you do that? Why would you pretend to be stupid when you're actually smart?" Ms. Bernstein could ask. In this way Ms. Bernstein would be supporting Danny not just in feeling his conflict but in working it out, playing with the ramifications of remaining caught in it.

Labeling conflicts with conflict statements relies on *active listening*, or feeding back to a speaker what the listener heard him or her say. Active listening is an effective way to avoid misunderstanding, as it slows communication down and gives conversation partners a chance to double-check each other's meaning by filtering out inappropriate interpretations.

DEFINITION

*People who engage in **active listening** can avoid misunderstanding by slowing conversations down and* *frequently double-checking each other's intentions and meanings.*

With conflict statements a listener focuses specifically on the conflict she perceives in the speaker, formulating a statement — not a question, not a command — that captures the "yes" and the "no" neutrally. (Of course, it is the neutrality that supports the Third.)

- "You want to grow up and learn to read, but you want to stay little and not take on any big responsibilities."
- "Sometimes you want to be smart, but sometimes you want to be stupid."
- "You want to be like your dad, but you want to be uniquely you."

Making conflict statements is another way of making *guesses* about a student. The power of conflict statements lies in their ability to capture complex resistance in a simple declaration, leaving room for the Third as the student struggles with his own internal forces.

Even if the teacher has guessed wrongly, an inaccurate conflict statement can inspire correction from the student, possibly deepening the teacher's (and the student's) understanding of the real underlying issues. "What do you mean, I 'want to stay little'?" a student might respond to the first conflict statement above. "I don't want to stay little; I just don't want to be big!" This correction could lead to a discussion of options: If a student does not want to stay little *and* does not want to be big, what choices does he have? Since the student's struggle is manifesting anyway in resistance (which is getting the student nowhere), giving the student room to make the struggle explicit through conflict statements can be a relief for student and teacher alike.

DEFINITION
Conflict statements *are statements, not questions, that capture the "yes" and "no" of a conflict neutrally.*
[Credit to M. Stark (1994), *Working with resistance*, Northvale, NJ: Jason Aronson Inc.]

Explicit, contained, supported struggle can also help to actually dissolve the conflict that underlies resistance. Amazingly, sometimes just acknowledging a conflict can resolve it. Contrary to what some teachers might intuitively prefer, leaving conversations dangling, not providing any solution at all, can be helpful for a student who experiences resistance. The tacit act of respecting a student's authority by exploring the resistance but leaving it alone can activate the student's natural drive toward growth and development, a drive he can now follow of his own free will.

Indeed, merely engaging in a supportive, listening, respectful, and actively caring relationship can work miracles for people. As we discussed in chapter two, being seen (and heard) can be validating and intensely relieving. If, through an informed conflict statement, a teacher shows a student that he is seen and accepted, not judged, resistance might become unnecessary.

FOOD FOR THOUGHT
Making conflict statements is a form of **mirroring**.

Going with the Resistance
A powerful if possibly counterintuitive way of defusing power struggles, then, is to *go with the resistance*. One way to do this is to listen actively to what students say about their struggle. *Active listening* calls for deliberate, empathic, nonjudgmental use of others' language to encourage reflection and elaboration. Another way to go with the resistance is to label a student's apparent struggle by making a *conflict statement*. The next story, which should be familiar, as it appeared in chapter one, illustrates a few more ways to go with the resistance.

OPPOSITIONAL TEACHING
Mr. Apkin, a teacher educator in a liberal arts college, was sitting in a small group of preservice teachers. He had broken his practicum seminar up into these small groups to give the students more time to talk to each other about their student teaching experiences. He happened to join a group that included Sean, an opinionated student who described his learning style as "oppositional." Mr. Apkin's approach to Sean tended to be tolerant even when the

student dominated large-group discussions, though he (and the other students in the seminar) found Sean's monopolization irritating and sometimes alarming.

In the small group Sean was talking about his experience in a public high school classroom when he addressed Mr. Apkin directly. "Where do you stand on private versus public schooling?" he asked solicitously. Mr. Apkin immediately launched into an answer to Sean's question. No sooner had he expressed an opinion than Sean opposed it. Mr. Apkin heatedly argued with Sean, continuing even when he perceived that the other students in the room had grown uncomfortable. When the time came to reconvene the larger class in the seminar room, Mr. Apkin was physically shaking with anger and frustration.

As a self-styled "oppositional learner," Sean was, by definition, resistant in the classroom. He seemed almost *allergic* to potential space. If Mr. Apkin's guess about Sean was correct — that Sean, like Mr. Apkin, had to fight for the right to his own opinion when he was growing up — then it makes sense that Sean would be enacting a developmental need with Mr. Apkin, prodding him to make room for Sean to grow up into an independent agent.

Like Danny, Sean might be terrified of taking on this new identity, one of intellectual independence and openness, for it would require a wholesale revamping of his most fundamental relationships and his oppositional worldview. It appears that conflicts abounded in Sean. Because his conflicts were mostly unconscious and difficult to sort out under any circumstances, Sean was stuck in opposition, a safe stance for him but one that prevented any learning or change.

Sean's internal conflicts revealed themselves in external behaviors that sowed conflict throughout the class. While doing his emotion work, then, Mr. Apkin could wonder about the *conflicts* inside Sean that might have been feeding the power struggles Sean seemed to provoke wherever he went.

One way Mr. Apkin could acknowledge Sean's conflict would be to label it. He could try a *conflict statement*: "You are very smart but seem unwilling to let others around you be smart." This statement would invite Sean to wrestle with his personal conflict: his desire for intellectual recognition coupled with his need to take out all competition. By framing it in positive terms — highlighting Sean's intelligence as well as that of his peers — Mr. Apkin could encourage honesty, even self-revelation, in Sean.

"What?" Sean might respond. "I'm not smart." Or he might say, "I don't care if anybody else is smart. I just can't stand it when they're wrong." In the first instance Sean would be revealing his true suspicion that he did not merit the recognition he craved, thus confirming that his blustery opposition masked painful insecurity. Mr. Apkin's work would then revolve around helping Sean to construct a more accurate appraisal of his intelligence, one that better matched others' reality and relied less urgently on manipulation and discord.

In the second instance Sean would unintentionally open up a valuable conversation about the role "being wrong" might play in learning. Another conflict statement could be in order: "You really want to be a good teacher, but you have a hard time letting other people be wrong." A declaration like this one would move beyond Sean's personal conflict to his professional conflict — his desire to help people learn versus his refusal to yield them the space in which to do it.

Siding with the resister. As Ms. Bernstein did above, Mr. Apkin could also *listen* actively. This could happen in a number of ways. One approach would be to use Sean's own words to describe his difficulty. For instance, if Sean elaborated on Mr. Apkin's confession about his own father with "Yeah, my dad thought he was the only one with a brain in the family," Mr. Apkin might say, "It must be difficult having to constantly remind people that you, too, have a very fine brain." Such a statement would convey sympathy and understanding and possibly encourage further self-revelation and introspection on Sean's part.

This approach could be called "siding with Sean," an approach that opens the Third by giving Sean space to reflect and represent himself honestly. *Siding with the resister* is the same as joining with him, consciously looking at the world through his eyes to better understand his perspective. Just as joining with someone can shift an enactment, siding with the resister can defuse a power struggle.

Going with the purpose. A second way of going with the resistance would be to look beneath the *content* of Sean's comments to respond to the *purpose* of his comments. This approach takes the valuable step of looking for "good" reasons for student behavior a bit further.

Once Mr. Apkin thought he might have a handle on why Sean opposed everyone in class — his fear of intellectual domination and the underlying belief that he was not smart, for example — Mr. Apkin could *go with* Sean's need to be recognized and affirmed as an intelligent individual. "What an interesting criticism, Sean," Mr. Apkin might say in seminar. "No one else has thought of that. Let's see what kind of case we can make together in support of your opinion." The content of Sean's opinion would matter less than that the class rallied around it and explored it open-mindedly, affirming Sean's right to have it in the first place.

This method, what we might call *going with the purpose*, keeps the Third open by ignoring the distraction of content and heading for the heart of the matter: Sean's need. The assumption underlying this approach to going with the resistance is that attending to needs rather than to the defenses that mask them is an efficient way of interacting. When needs are met, whether they are conscious or not, resistance is no longer necessary.

In Sean's case going with the purpose could give Sean an ego boost and a much-needed break from fighting. And in all honesty it could present his classmates with a perspective they had not thought of before as well as a process they could facilitate in their own classrooms.

Another way to go with the resistance is to **go with the purpose**, *which means looking beneath the content — what the resister* says *— and responding to the underlying* **need**, *or why the resister said it.*

Becoming the resister. A third way of going with the resistance would be to *become the resister*, to play the resister's role for him. The plan that Mr. Apkin came up with after his skirmish with Sean in the small group is a good example of this approach.

As Mr. Apkin told Sean, he himself had had to "fight for the right to have my own ideas and opinions" when he was a boy. Mr. Apkin readily identified himself as occasionally oppositional and apologized for the defensiveness he displayed when Sean questioned him in the small group. In other words, Mr. Apkin *became* Sean by acknowledging his own tendency to argue and oppose.

But Mr. Apkin did not stop there. He informed Sean that he was going to change: From then on he would limit his contributions in seminar to comments that explored and expanded on students' ideas rather than immediately critiquing or discounting them. And he was going to ask the class, including Sean, to help him.

By taking on Sean's oppositional role, Mr. Apkin relieved Sean of that burden (which included immense disapproval from his peers). By committing to practicing a different type of behavior, Mr. Apkin not only genuinely challenged himself to lead class differently but also provided an explicit model for Sean's classroom interactions. The method of *becoming the resister*, then, is another way of going with the resistance and keeping the Third open.

Becoming the resister *is another form of going with the resistance. It involves taking on the resister's role for him and modeling alternative ways to act.*

Playing the victim role. Yet a fourth way of going with the resistance is to *play the victim role.* A story can best illustrate this approach.

TAKING THE HIT

Zack was the least popular student in all of Ms. Devereaux's eleventh grade social studies classes. He never missed an opportunity to make fun of someone; he was like a shark cruising the classroom, sniffing out weakness and striking without mercy. Unlike many instances of bullying, Zack's abuse took place in full view of his teachers. It seemed that he expected his teachers to side with him against his contemptible classmates.

One day Ms. Devereaux handed back drafts of outlines students had written in preparation for a research paper. She had made comments on these drafts and circled words that were misspelled. Zack caught sight of all the circled words on his neighbor's paper and immediately attacked. "What a retard!" he exclaimed. "You suck at spelling! You must be so stupid." When the student's eyes filled with tears, Zack cried, "Aw, wittle baby's feelings are hurt! Doesn't want to be so stupid, but she just can't help it. Poor wittle baby!"

[Credit for the story and the approach to resistance to Kirman, W.J. (1977). *Modern psychoanalysis in the schools.* Dubuque, IA: Kendall/Hunt Publishing Co.]

As we saw in the stories about Jason and Raphael, bullies are experts at crushing the Third. Their effectiveness actually depends on it: When bullies go on the attack, they demolish their victims, reducing them to objects with no rights or existence beyond what the bullies allow. It makes sense, actually: Bullying requires objectifying, or turning people into things. *Projection* is easiest when one can *use* a victim as a *screen* or a *jar* for one's own terrible emotions, as we noted in chapter two.

Of course, Zack was no exception. In this story he appears to have been projecting his self-loathing (which he undoubtedly learned from someone else) onto his neighboring student. As with Raphael above, the viciousness of Zack's attack suggested the degree of self-hatred he must have felt. The student's tears indicated her ability to identify with Zack's accusations. Her evident susceptibility to Zack's cruelty brought on even more of it as Zack berated her for showing weakness that, we might guess, he could not stand in himself. Through *projective identification*, Zack and his neighbor unconsciously conspired to protect Zack from his unbearable feelings. But the emotional cost for everyone in the classroom was high.

While most would agree that bullying is a terrible social crime and must be dealt with in school, it might not be clear how Zack's bullying constitutes resistance to *learning*. Once again, when the Third is squashed, academic learning cannot take place. Relational learning can, of course: Zack's role as sadistic dominator and his classmates' roles as passive objects are reinforced. This type of learning is profound and, in addition to influencing future relationships for all concerned, can have a negative impact on the classroom relationships upon which academic learning is based.

Ms. Devereaux's Emotion Work

So how might *playing the victim role* help Ms. Devereaux neutralize Zack's influence in her classroom? The idea is that, by becoming the focus of Zack's assault, Ms. Devereaux could both draw his energy away from his innocent classmates and channel it into a healthy and corrective interaction with herself. Note that the choice to take on this role would best be made after careful *emotion work* and thoughtful *anticipation* of how and when to play the role — that is, *whether* and *how* to be *used* by Zack.

BLACK BELT MOVES

"Wow, Zack," Ms. Devereaux could say, "you obviously have no use for bad spellers. I have to make a confession here: I myself am a terrible speller. Always have been. I guess that means you have no use for me."

Chances are that Zack's response would not be particularly compassionate. He might say, for instance, "Whoa — how can you be a teacher if you're so stupid?" At this point Ms. Devereaux would be facing a fork in the road: Should she gently disabuse Zack of his misconceptions of what it means to be a teacher and address his blatant disrespect? Or should she continue *playing the victim role*? Both forks have benefits.

Of course, addressing disrespect could involve *describing* — "Zack, you just called me stupid" — *self-disclosure* — "which could be extremely hurtful to me" — and humor — "if I weren't such a superhero." Following up with a *plan* — "How about you rephrase your question to avoid any insulting words?" — and working with Zack to help him think through what might be a difficult assignment for him would help with the disrespect. Discussing what it means to be a teacher, who is necessarily imperfect, could also be beneficial.

Taking the second fork would offer different benefits. The value of playing the victim role would be in embodying for Zack his own insecurities and showing him how someone might survive and even thrive in spite of them.

"It sure is a handicap," Ms. Devereaux could say as she *went with* Zack's resistance. "I do wish I could spell well. I feel this is a real weakness, and it's hard for me to let people see it. What do you suppose would happen if the administration knew I was such a poor speller? Would they hurt me?"

"They might fire you," Zack might respond. "They don't want stupid people teaching here."

"Yes," Ms. Devereaux could respond. "And that makes me feel like an outsider. Really vulnerable. These are hard feelings. Well, you know my secret now, Zack. What do you recommend I do about it?" With Zack's help Ms. Devereaux could lead a brainstorming session on how to compensate for being a poor speller. And she could enlist Zack as her own personal spelling aide (not as an aide for his classmates yet), asking him to correct her when she misspelled a word on the board or in a worksheet. As she would with any student who lacked required skills, Ms. Devereaux would probably have to work with Zack on gentle ways to correct her, lessons in common interactional etiquette that he could certainly use.

This technique of *playing the victim role* can require some playacting. No teacher is going to possess every weakness the bullies in her class choose to attack. But they can pretend. Or, if pretending won't work (if Ms. Devereaux, for example, had already distinguished herself as an excellent speller), then introducing a thought experiment using a different victim – John F. Kennedy, say, or Albert Einstein or Jane Austen, all notoriously bad spellers – could suffice. "What," Ms. Devereaux could ask, "would you do about a President (or scientist or author) who couldn't spell? Would advice would you give him?"

Again, the *content* of the bully's accusation matters less than the *purpose* of it, and playing the victim role addresses the purpose, which is the bully's need to disown his own insecurities. Zack's insecurities probably had little or nothing to do with spelling. They most likely had to do, as Ms. Devereaux guessed, with his fear of weakness, vulnerability, and imperfection as well as his sense that he might not fit in, that he was an "outsider."

By playing the victim role, Ms. Devereaux was able to uncover these fears for Zack. She labeled some of them with the words "weakness," "hurt," "outsider," "vulnerable," "hard feelings," and "secret." She showed him that such terrible experiences as being uncertain, incapable, and rejected can, in fact, be borne; that people with these experiences are not alone; and that help is available. In this way she offered herself as a model for Zack of tolerating difficult feelings.

So what, exactly, did Ms. Devereaux do when she played the victim role? First, and very importantly, she committed to taking on Zack's cruelty, to taking the hit, as it were, for his other potential victims. She decided to be a model for Zack so she could show him what it was like to be strong amidst one's inadequacies.

Second, she *listened* to Zack's attack. She did not just hear what Zack said to his neighbor — the *content* — but she also listened for the intent behind the comments, the *purpose* the comments were serving for Zack. Playing the victim role, then, can include going with the purpose and other techniques for dissolving resistance.

Third, based on what she heard with her gut, Ms. Devereaux sensed the *good reasons* for Zack's attack and made some *guesses* as to what types of feelings Zack was disowning. Pouncing on spelling mistakes implied that he feared imperfection and what he considered stupidity; ridiculing tears implied that he hated vulnerability and weakness; accusing his neighbor suggested that he preferred to alienate others than to be rejected himself, that he would rather hurt than be hurt. It is important that Ms. Devereaux used explicit labels for these feelings, as this kind of emotional parsing can help reduce overwhelming, confusing emotion of the sort Zack probably felt into graspable, more manageable elements.

Obviously, Ms. Devereaux made these guesses through *self-disclosure*, playing the role of a poor speller. And she came up with a *plan* aimed at empowering both spellers and nonspellers and specifically Zack to begin dealing more maturely with a certain form of "weakness" in his teacher (and, by extension, his peers and himself).

DEFINITION
Playing the victim role *means stepping in to become the object of a student's attacks. By playing the victim teachers can, first, protect innocent students and, second, model for the attacker ways to handle unbearable feelings.*

This one instance of playing the victim role would probably not turn Zack around. Ms. Devereaux would most likely have to play this role repeatedly, taking on many different types of weakness, before Zack could begin to relax into his feelings. In many instances going with the resistance requires a long-term commitment. It would take time for Zack to develop enough inner strength to abide his own difficult feelings without projecting them onto others. Ms. Devereaux's ability to show him, consistently, what surviving weakness looked like would be key to this development.

There is danger with this technique. Because *playing the victim role* in effect lures the resister, inviting him to exert his power and squash the Third, the teacher who chooses this approach needs to commit clearly to staying in the victim role. Ms. Devereaux would have to keep potential space open by expressing the feelings Zack could not and modeling for him how he could be were he internally strong enough.

253

With bullies these disowned feelings can be very strong indeed; Ms. Devereaux would have to be prepared to feel horrible, precisely how Zack felt most of the time. And she would have to expect that Zack would sense and seize upon her own insecurities, since that is another talent bullies tend to possess.

The difficult work of playing the victim role is resisting the numerous opportunities to reverse the roles and bash the bully, to take revenge on a student who inflicts hurt and to squash the Third oneself. The capacity to detach, observe, and let compassion flow is crucial. And allowing oneself to be *used*, first as an object for projection and then, repeatedly, as a mirror, would create the space in which the bully could play out and witness different ways of being that he could eventually internalize for good.

The Importance of Support
It follows that, to model inner strength, a teacher must *have* inner strength. And in those inevitable moments when inner strength wavers, the teacher must know she has the necessary professional and collegial support to renew her resolve. No teacher should *go with the resistance* alone, as it can be difficult and confusing work. It is easy to get mired in students' defenses and resistances, to lose track of one's goals, to be flooded with unwelcome feelings, when embedded in a complicated classroom relationship. Blind spots exist in all relationships and by definition are impossible to illuminate without outside help.

So outside help is essential for teachers. Such help can be informal, as in teacher lounge chats, or formal, as discussed in the next chapter. The crucial point here is that teachers need support not just to deal with the demands of developing schoolchildren but to assist their own growth and development.

One last word about resistance: It can arise in all instances of change. Even when the change is for the better — when, for example, Mr. Apkin guides the class to support and explore one of Sean's oppositional claims — such change can feel risky. Working collaboratively with peers, rewarding as it might be, could feel unfamiliar enough to prompt Sean to resist yet more vehemently. Or his classmates, despite their complaints about Sean's domination of the class, could resist efforts to free Sean from the scapegoat role in the group. Getting what one wants, paradoxically enough, can be disorienting if one has no idea what to do with it or feels guilty about having it. Just as psychic structures take time to contort, so they take time to straighten out even when the adjustment feels better.

KEEP IN MIND
Change is always risky, even change for the better. Teachers need to be alert to the good possibility that students will insist they **change back** *to the old ways of interacting, unpleasant as those ways might have been.*
[Credit for "Change back!" to H. Lerner (1989), *The dance of intimacy: A woman's guide to courageous acts of change in key relationships*, New York: Harper & Row.]

Working with Resistance
But as I have said before, change can also happen instantaneously. Power struggles can melt when the resister's needs have been met and the reason for the struggle has disappeared. The next story illustrates how this can look and feel.

FIGHTING FOR THE THIRD
Shawna had just finished a presentation at a professional conference. As usual, several people stayed afterward to discuss aspects of her talk. The last person, who introduced himself as Victor, began immediately to take issue with the argument Shawna had made in her presentation. Citing various somewhat obscure theoreticians, he proposed alternative terms that Shawna should have used and extended her argument in directions she had been unable to explore in her talk.

Shawna was taken aback by Victor's attack. Somehow, she was able to maintain a calm exterior, but inside she felt electrocuted. Having her ideas and, by extension, her intelligence questioned so ruthlessly made her feel shaky, utterly uncertain, and, at bottom, afraid.

As Victor continued his critique, Shawna attended to her sensations, wondering about them, wondering about Victor. Suddenly, Shawna realized two things. First, she did not disagree with Victor, and second, her feelings offered information about how Victor might be feeling: threatened and insecure.

Realizing that she agreed with Victor and that he was probably feeling insecure instantly shifted Shawna's perception of the situation. Because he felt uncertain and threatened, he was projecting those feelings into Shawna. In fact, Shawna realized, Victor was actually accusing Shawna of not being him, of not using his lingo and not making his argument. This constituted a major boundary breach, one she could easily fix.

"Why didn't you raise your hand and say all this during my talk?" she asked him. "You would have given me the opportunity to agree with you and to make sure your points were underlined."

"Well," Victor sighed, "I'm really uncomfortable speaking at conferences. Also, I have a hard time talking about these ideas — I tend to get way too abstract and esoteric." With this confession Victor's manner changed dramatically. He complimented Shawna on her ideas, her presentational style, and her impressive openness to criticism. The two of them began comparing their takes on Shawna's topic, engaging in a constructive discussion.

Shawna's Emotion Work

The *emotion work* Shawna was able to do in the face of Victor's scathing and destabilizing attack was impressive.

YELLOW BELT MOVES

She became *aware* of her feelings, *described* them to herself, and, noting their forcefulness, realized she was in the middle of an enactment. *Guessing* that her own feelings gave her valuable information about how Victor was feeling allowed Shawna to detach from the power struggle and, perhaps, feel some compassion for him.

In fact, Victor's projection of his anxieties into Shawna was a major boundary violation. Attacking her for not being him was a masterful blending of his circle with hers, a fusion that erased Shawna and established Victor as dominant.

Clearly, boundary violations of this sort collapse potential space and rule out any chance of the Third.

BLUE BELT MOVE

But Shawna's emotion work allowed her to make a key move: She *went with* Victor's resistance by *siding with the resister*. At the same time that she *joined with* Victor by moving over and looking at the world from his perspective, she *showed up* and established boundaries between the two of them.

Shawna's move reopened potential space in an instant. By asking Victor why he hadn't spoken up during her talk, she placed responsibility for his thoughts and his silence squarely on his shoulders, where it belonged. When she said, "You would have given me the opportunity to agree with you and to make sure your points were underlined," she literally described the alliance she and Victor could have forged had *he* been willing to show up during her talk. And by acknowledging the validity of Victor's ideas, she *mirrored* him in a way that he apparently needed. All this was possible because Shawna established boundaries.

And Victor responded immediately. Shawna's acknowledgment of his worth permitted him to retreat to his own circle and represent himself honestly. Now he could show up and share his vulnerability. And having received the reflection he needed, he could admit his admiration of Shawna's talk. Thanks to the emotion work she did *in the heat of the moment*, Shawna was able to turn a shockingly destructive interaction into one in which both she and Victor could bask in the Third.

In short, $1 + 1 = 3$.

WRAP-UP

As Shawna illustrates, teachers need not teach to the Third. Doing emotion work on enactments, on insults and compliments, on boundary crossings, and on instances of resistance naturally opens and strengthens potential space. As that space is protected through attuned relating, the Third can emerge.

But make no mistake: Opening potential space and protecting the Third require effort. They demand understanding of relational forces and commitment to doing solid emotion work. They also rest on the ability to design robust instruction or to organize learning activities that foster respectful, playful, creative interactions among students and with ideas. I cannot blame any teacher for turning away from such a seemingly gargantuan challenge.

On the other hand, forced compliance and resistance flourish in classrooms for innumerable good reasons. Teachers can certainly choose to butt heads endlessly with resistant students, but there lies a path to burnout. What to do? An answer is to experiment with the Third. Denying its relevance is an option, but embracing it can make teaching — and learning — one of the most exciting and rewarding activities imaginable.

CHAPTER ANSWERS

We should now be able to answer the questions from the beginning of this chapter:

- *What is the Third?*
- *Why does it matter?*

The Third is the shared "third" reality that can emerge out of interactions that include healthy connections, generous mirroring, and strong boundaries – that is, interactions that can happen in an adequate holding environment, one that sponsors potential space. While the holding environment is the context *within which teacher and students interact and potential space is the* type *of context (a healthy, mutually respectful one), the Third is the* experience *that can emerge when the conditions are right.*

The Third matters because it is the experience of creativity, of thinking and making meaning, of forging new intellectual and emotional connections. As such, it is the whole point of education. It is the end that the means of emotion work aims at. But because the Third is emergent and what happens in it is completely out of anyone's direct control, it is the beginning of the thrilling if messy process of desirable academic learning.

KEEP IN MIND

- ***The Third** is a shared, third reality that emerges from interactions that are respectful yet firmly bounded. As*

- *the name implies, the Third requires two or more parties to show up and stand their ground respectfully.*
- *An **adequate holding environment** is one that is structured to provide **potential space** out of which the Third can emerge.*
- ***Potential space** is characterized by healthy boundaries and respectful interactions that support creativity and growth.*
- ***Power struggles**, or attempts by one party to dominate another, destroy potential space and squash any hope for the Third.*
- ***Compliance** can be voluntary or forced. **Voluntary compliance** happens when students willingly participate in curricular activities because they perceive such participation to be beneficial. **Forced compliance**, or the compulsion to give in to another's domination, forecloses on growth and development.*
- ***Resistance** is a gift to teachers, as it is evidence that students are willing to fight for potential space and the Third.*
- *Setting relevant **limits** can foster the Third. Setting unreasonable limits can squash the Third.*
- ***Responses to student resistance** include owning one's contribution and **repairing**; **listening** and being patient and consistent; contemplating students' **identity change** and development; labeling the conflict by making a **conflict statement**; and **going with the resistance**.*
- ***Conflict statements** capture the pros and cons of learning. They acknowledge a student's difficulty without judgment and make it available for analysis and discussion.*
- ***Going with the resistance** includes **siding with the resister**, **going with the purpose**, **becoming the resister**, and **playing the victim role**.*
- *Emotion work in general and going with the resistance specifically are demanding and draining. It is essential that teachers who do this work find **personal and professional support** so they can keep perspective and continue their own growth and learning.*

CHAPTER FIVE

KNOW YOURSELF: RIGOROUS REFLECTION AND SUPERVISION

Teachers need to know themselves. They need to know their insecurities, their relational patterns, and their moment-to-moment feelings. They need to know their psychic structures, how they tend to fit with people and ideas in moments of comfort and in moments of stress. In knowing all this, they are in a better position to know their students and their subject matter.

In psychodynamic language "knowing yourself" means noticing your emotions, which in turn offers hints about classroom dynamics. That is, knowing yourself provides insight into

- how others are feeling;
- what enactments are taking place;
- how you are being used;
- what boundaries are being crossed by whom;
- how to defuse power struggles;
- when the Third is alive and well.

Just as the teacher is the hub and heart of the classroom, so are the teacher's self-awareness and self-understanding the hub and heart of her teaching. The more centered and solid a teacher is in her self-knowledge, the healthier and more effective her classroom can be.

As the previous chapters have shown, though, knowing yourself can take great effort and discipline. The simple act of slowing down and looking around in the midst of chaos can feel impossible. Becoming self-aware, describing a situation, looking for good reasons for one's own and others' behavior, making guesses, self-disclosing, listening, and planning — basic skills of rigorous reflection — are easier said than done. How can a teacher develop these skills in the first place?

And even if she does develop these skills, how can she possibly apply them as consistently as she needs to? Whom can she consult for clarity? Where can she find support for and affirmation of the difficult emotion work such reflection demands? In sum, where can she find the type of holding environment she needs just as urgently as her students do?

CHAPTER QUESTIONS

- *How can a teacher develop the skills of emotion work?*
- *Where can teachers find the type of holding environment they need just as urgently as their students do?*

There are two basic answers to these questions: *practice* and *support*. Developing the reflective — actually, introspective — skills teachers need requires ongoing practice in the classroom, in the staff room, in the supermarket, at home. Ways to practice rigorous reflection are discussed below.

And given that few teachers can count on their school administrators or colleagues to provide a consistent, reliable holding environment for them, teachers need supremely safe places to go for support, affirmation, and confidential discussion of the feelings and actions that constitute their daily experience of teaching; that is, they need supportive *supervision*.

As explicated below, the supervision teachers need to make sense of emotional and relational data is not evaluative. It is accepting and nonjudgmental; utterly confidential; and aimed at illumination, understanding, support, and experimentation. It is psychodynamically oriented, meaning it looks for the prongs and outlets that influence a teacher's daily experiences in the classroom. It is specific to each teacher, each class, each day, and each moment. Psychodynamically oriented, nonevaluative, supportive supervision does not work toward foregone conclusions but remains open to possibilities.

The supervisor's job is to hold each teacher — her terrible emotions, her unpardonable thoughts, her shameful mistakes — just as teachers must hold their students. The bottom line is that all caregivers, if they are to continue to care for others, *must* be cared for themselves. As the airlines put it, "In the event of loss of cabin pressure, please put oxygen

masks on yourselves before putting them on your children."
Psychodynamically oriented supervision is the oxygen mask
teachers need and deserve so they can adequately care for —
that is, teach — their students.

PRACTICING RIGOROUS REFLECTION

It is inevitable that teachers will make mistakes with their
students and other people they work with. Some teachers will
yell; some will make incorrect accusations; some will make
inadvertently racist comments; some will neglect students who
need help; some will take revenge; all will, at one time or
another, give the wrong answer or not know something they
think they should know. The list of possible blunders, as all
teachers can attest, is endless. Making mistakes, then, cannot
be the primary focus of concern. What teachers can focus on to
great effect is *repairing*, or revisiting mistakes when necessary
and attempting to make them right.

The reparative steps the teachers in this book took with
their students happened, for the most part, after the mistakes
occurred; that is, the teachers reflected *on* their actions after the
fact and figured out what to do when they returned to the
classroom. And importantly, the steps were aimed at repairing
relationships, not at correcting discrete errors. For example,
while Mr. Apkin apologized for arguing with Sean — his error
— the bulk of their talk was meant to bring their relationship
into balance so Sean could learn and grow as a student teacher.

We have seen numerous examples of the power of
reflecting-*on*-action. But the skills used by the teachers in this
book also work *in the heat of the moment*. Reflecting-*in*-action
is therefore a worthwhile goal for teachers as well. To be able
to defuse difficult situations as they are unfolding can help
teachers and students avoid the burdens of unresolved negative
emotion. And as we saw with Shawna and Victor in chapter
four, it can have a remarkable, almost magical, impact on the
people involved, emotionally, relationally, and cognitively.

DEFINITIONS
Reflecting-*on*-action *happens when emotion work is done
after the fact.* **Reflecting-*in*-action** *happens when emotion
work is done in the heat of the moment. Both are extremely
valuable.*

[Credit to D. A. Schön (1983), *The reflective practitioner*, New York: Basic Books.]

    So the skills of emotion work that the teachers in this book have used are effective both in the heat of the moment and after the fact. The methods I suggest below facilitate both types of rigorous reflecting. They start with the fundamental skill of *practicing awareness.*

Practicing Awareness

Practicing awareness happens in two directions, outward and inward. Practicing outward awareness means noticing what is going on in the external environment. As many of the stories in this book have shown, being able to slow down and describe to oneself what one is seeing can make a big difference in how a teacher behaves and in the quality of the data she is able to gather about her students.

KEEP IN MIND

Practicing awareness happens in two directions, outward and inward. Practicing inward awareness is also known as **introspection** *and* **practicing self-awareness.**

    To practice outward awareness teachers must develop powerful brakes. They must become good at stopping themselves from reacting instantly to buy time to look around. How can teachers develop good brakes that work in the heat of the moment? By doing it: by stopping themselves frequently throughout every teaching day with an internal command — "Whoa!" or "Take a moment" or "Try stepping back now" — that can eventually become automatic.

    Teachers can also *plan* "brakes/breaks"; that is, they can build personal time-outs into their lessons that allow them to step back and observe their students in action. This approach, because it is deliberate, can be much easier than relying on applying brakes in the heat of the moment. It can also lead to more student-centered instructional design.

Introspection

Practicing inward awareness has another name: introspection. Introspection is, of course, the art of looking inward, of seeing internally, of illuminating subjective experience. While this art was once prized in the social sciences, it was eventually shunned as psychologists and others began modeling their disciplines on the "hard" sciences, such as physics and biology, which rely on such quantitative characteristics as replicability and generalizability.

A central assumption of these "hard" sciences is that the reality they are probing is a shared, objective phenomenon, one everyone can agree on. An assumption of introspection, one that better matches the truth about personal experience, is that subjective reality is not absolute. It is perceived through individual lenses that are ground over time by repeated interactions and experiences. In the psychodynamic terms of this book, subjective reality depends on psychic structures and the related ways one perceives and interprets the world.

It is subjective reality that drives our actions. Even when "objective" reality, such as three feet of snow on the ground and temperatures in the single digits, implies the need for snow pants, there are still some folks whose subjective reality impels them to wear shorts when they shovel their driveways. And as we have seen, subjective realities can combine into a coconstructed "third" reality that, while shared, is not necessarily replicable (consistently repeatable) or generalizable (applicable to everyone), as the hard sciences would have it.

Given the multitude of subjective realities that make up one classroom, it goes without saying that classroom reality is exceedingly complex. While there are objective elements to classroom reality, every teacher and student places his own spin on what happens there. It is impossible for any one person to know how everyone else experiences each classroom event. Because the only reference point teachers have for making sense of this complex reality is their own internal experience, practicing inward awareness, or *self-awareness*, is essential.

As stated in chapter one, self-awareness can reveal valuable information about oneself (the teacher), about students' preferred relational styles, and about students' emotions. The ability to notice and use this information to adjust one's own behaviors and to influence others' behavior requires effort. Specifically, this ability rests on a willingness to recognize and dwell in feelings, to welcome them, to let oneself experience them despite the discomfort.

This is where self-awareness practices come in. Three recommended practices are *making the turn, meditating on emotions*, and *journaling*.

Making the Turn

Making the turn is the basic move that marks a shift in attention from the outside to the inside. It is used in any self-awareness practice, including meditating on emotions and journaling.

For some people this move is easy to make: One just tells oneself to look inside, to attend to one's body or feelings. For others making the turn is difficult. In an attempt to formalize the move and encourage both its practice and study, three investigators (a philosopher, Natalie Depraz; a cognitive neuroscientist, Francisco Varela; and a research psychologist, Pierre Vermersch) have broken it down into the following "basic cycle":

- Suspending the "natural attitude"
- Redirecting attention from the external to the internal
- Letting go and accepting what comes

The *"natural attitude"* is the powerful assumption that what one perceives is what is true. For example, if I perceive a student's resistance to be disrespectful, then it isn't informative or justified or courageous or even interesting. It is just disrespectful. End of story. Suspending this "natural attitude" means dropping the assumption that one knows what is going on. It means deliberately embracing a stance of not-knowing.

Here is a description of the next two stages, *redirecting* and *letting go*:

> The last two phases, redirection of attention and acceptance of what comes back . . . correspond to two fundamental changes in what you do cognitively. First you change the *direction* of attention, which tunes out the spectacle of the world, so you can return to the interior world. . . . Now let us not fool ourselves: it is sometimes really quite difficult to turn away from your usual cognitive activity, which is most often locked in

to the world around us. But do not worry: it can be done.

Second, you have to change from voluntarily turning your attention from the exterior to the interior, to simply accepting and listening. In other words, in moving from [redirection to letting go], you go from "looking for something" to "letting something come to you," to "letting something be revealed." What is difficult here is that you have to get through an *empty time*, a time of silence, and not grab onto whatever data is immediately available, for that's already been rendered conscious, and what you're after is what is still unconscious at the start. (Depraz, Varela, & Vermersch, p. 31)

There are many valuable nuggets in this description. One is the notion of "tuning out" the world around one. While a complete "whiteout" of one's surroundings is not always necessary, especially for people who are good at making the turn, it can be useful. This is why reflecting-*on*-action is generally easier than reflecting-*in*-action: It is easier and safer to "tune out the spectacle of the world" in the privacy of one's own company (or that of a supervisor) than in the public arena of the classroom.

A second nugget is the characterization of our awareness as being "locked in to the world around us." Sound like the way psychic structure works, with its prongs and outlets? That is no coincidence. These authors assume, as this book does, that people "fit" emotionally and cognitively with each other and their surroundings and that these fits, being snug and comfortable, or "locked in," can be difficult to dislodge.

Another nugget is the description of the required attitude toward one's internal experience. Making the turn, or practicing self-awareness, does not just involve looking inward; it requires a "not-knowing," receptive stance. It hinges on a conscious letting go, a release of control, an embrace of stillness. It is this attitude that makes the practice of self-awareness so fertile.

A final, related nugget is the acknowledgment that not-knowing, "letting something be revealed," is by definition

267

generally preceded by an "*empty time*" when the mind is necessarily blank. While most people are impelled to fill that void, which can cause immense anxiety, with assumptions and conclusions — with *knowing* — these authors encourage us to wait, to be patient with what is "unconscious at the start."

DEFINITION

The **not-knowing stance** *happens when you suspend judgment and decide to be receptive, to see and hear others and listen to yourself. It can feel unnerving, as not-knowing generally means releasing control and "letting something be revealed."*

While *making the turn* is an essential element in meditating on emotions and in journaling, it is also useful in isolation; that is, once a teacher has figured out how to function in the world while simultaneously placing it in the background of her consciousness, she can make the turn at will — in the middle of class, while walking down the hall, during a conversation with a colleague. Making the turn, going still for even just a moment, can be immensely beneficial all by itself.

Meditating on Emotions

The habit of making the turn at will is called "mindfulness." Mindfulness is the bull's-eye of self-awareness practice.

The standard approach to practicing mindfulness is meditation, where a person concentrates on one thing, such as the breath or a mantra; watches the attention wander; and gently brings the attention back to the breath or the mantra. Repeatedly doing this simple yet very difficult act develops the muscles of self-awareness. It also reveals the thought and feeling content that tends to distract one as well as the sheer force of one's unconscious desire to be distracted.

There are many ways to meditate, or to formally practice mindfulness. They all share the same basic goal: paying nonjudgmental attention to internal states and thus developing awareness both of the feel of those states and of their fleeting nature. Just as physicists keep finding less and less tangible components of material reality, meditation can show how temporary and vaporous moment-to-moment experience of subjective reality is. What is good about this discovery about reality is that, through meditation, one can achieve a state of stillness and acceptance that is fundamentally grounding. It can also invoke a feeling of spiritual oneness that helps put beliefs about the individual self in wise perspective.

But while emotional states are surely fleeting, they are nonetheless extremely informative. The version of formal mindfulness practice recommended for teachers here, then, has them focus on their emotions. Rather than gently calling oneself back to the breath or the chant when one's attention wanders, teacher meditators can call themselves back to their feelings.

One way to call oneself back to feelings is to label the current experience, to name the emotion: "anxiety," "anger." Another way is to center one's attention on the perceived physical location of the emotion: the chest, the abdomen. Staying with a difficult emotion over time allows the emotion to morph and, perhaps, "speak" to the teacher of the core issue from which the emotion stems.

KEEP IN MIND
Practicing self-awareness *can be done through mindfulness practice. Whereas the purest form of mindfulness practice is meditation, the form advocated here is a variation that asks teachers to focus on their emotions. This focus can allow emotions' meanings to emerge, or "speak."*

The following story illustrates how meditating on emotions can help reveal their meanings and the psychic structures underlying them.

FEAR IS SAFE
Rashid, a middle school teacher, was nervous when he was summoned to his principal's office after school one day, but he was an absolute wreck by the time he left. In their meeting the principal informed him that a parent had complained about a statement Rashid had made in class about an upcoming town election. The parent, who actually sat on the local school board, had accused Rashid of proselytizing. The principal, who was obviously interested in preserving his own relationship with the board member, warned Rashid that he was now on probation.

Rashid's response to his principal's threat was not to defend himself by presenting his own perspective on the incident and not to call his union representative for help. His response was panic. Because he often felt panicked and helpless, Rashid had developed the habit of sitting in meditation when this feeling overtook him.

As he was meditating at home, he focused his attention on his belly, noticing it rise and fall with every breath. It wasn't long before the feeling of panic arose. Rashid felt the urge to stand up and walk away. He found himself reviewing the meeting with the principal over and over in his mind. He also obsessed on the moment of the supposed offense, berating himself for saying what he did.

Whenever he noticed his mind darting off, he brought his attention back to his belly, which allowed him to feel his panic. Uncomfortable as this was, the panic quickly began clarifying into a number of different feelings, which Rashid labeled as he became aware of them: "self-doubt", "self-loathing," and, ultimately, great "fear" of being judged and abandoned. Paying close attention to the panic and labeling the component emotions helped the panic to change.

He focused on the feeling of fear, allowing it to fill his belly. Over time the fear changed into a feeling of safety and security. He pictured himself tucked into the center of a large black cushion, where he was held closely and hidden from danger. With this image and this feeling came a sense of self-acceptance and peace. He sat with this feeling for quite a while until he was ready to focus once again on his belly, rising and falling. Eventually, he opened his eyes and got up. The first thing he did was devise a plan for addressing the parent's accusation and the principal's threat.

It is important to note that Rashid's process was not intellectual. He did not devise a plan *first*; he was able to think clearly and calmly only after he had attended to his panic. In fact, his intellect proved to be a prodigious distraction. Obsessing on the meeting and the original political comment sent him deeper into his anxiety. It was only through retreating from his intellect, digging underneath the content of his mind, that Rashid was able to get to the fundamental problem: his fear of abandonment.

Rashid's feelings could have changed in any number of ways. He might have conjured the memory of a formative experience in which he was accused of a minor offense and shamed for it. Recognizing that the current situation was a repetition of that earlier experience could have put his interaction with the principal in perspective, reducing its importance and moderating Rashid's overwhelmed response. Rashid's self-loathing might have transformed into compassion for himself. The engulfing black cushion seemed to be evidence that, at least in this case, Rashid's fear was self-protective and pointed to his present need for comfort and self-forgiveness, which he was able to provide for himself.

As this story shows, the power of mindfulness, of focusing unblinkingly on difficult emotions, can lead one to the core of a problematic experience. It can expose psychic structure. Along the way the emotions' meanings, the messages they are sending, can also become clear. Following them down — from panic to fear to protective calm, for example — can demonstrate that there is more to emotions than initially meets the eye.

There is method to emotional madness, in other words. While intellectual problem solving often gets us out of tricky situations, there are times when emotions take over and make rational action impossible. Contrary to popular bias, irrationality — that is, being overtaken by emotion — is not necessarily a sign of weakness. It suggests that another powerful source of information, our emotions, must be attended to, listened to, learned from. *Meditating on emotions* is an excellent way to do this.

Journaling

Writing is another way to focus on and learn from emotions. *Journaling* can serve as daily grounding, as when one keeps a diary; it can ease one through a difficult process, emphasizing the flow of events over isolated experiences; it can provide much-needed perspective; it can even heal. As with free association, the famed approach Freud took to psychoanalysis, writing can release the unconscious and simultaneously organize its contents in unexpected and illuminating ways. So at the same time that writing allows one to vent, it can foster understanding.

Valuable as journaling can be, not all versions specifically facilitate self-awareness. Though describing and storytelling, self-talking, and other uses of journals are undoubtedly helpful, teachers who want to cultivate self-awareness must structure their writing to focus on emotions. A good way to do this is to, first, zero in on an actual experience that still echoes emotionally inside the teacher and, second, come up with questions that aim at the emotional core of the disturbing experience. The next story, an entry in the journal of a teacher educator about a difficult meeting she had with her student teacher, Leon, and his Master Teacher, Ms. Juarez, offers an example of how a teacher might structure such exploration.

A MOMENT THAT MATTERS

What is the moment? (Description)
I met with Leon today for the first time this semester, five weeks in. I have not yet observed Leon, despite the requirement that he arrange for an observation within the first three weeks of his student teaching placement. At our meeting Leon told me he was overwhelmed with work and thinking of quitting the program. When I asked for specifics, he said he felt he couldn't tackle the unit plan assignment I had given him; I was demanding too much.

At this point Ms. Juarez came into the room, and though she looked as if she knew this was a sensitive meeting (giving me the feeling that she and Leon had discussed it ahead of time), she sat down with us. As Leon and I talked, she nodded whenever Leon made a complaint (the workload is too much, he "just wants to teach," I need to communicate better with him) and pursed her lips when I spoke. I explained that, while the workload was intense, it was manageable; that teaching well requires understanding and effective application of the concepts the workload is meant to instill; and that it is Leon's job to communicate with me about his student teaching placement, not the other way around. By now Leon had stopped speaking and the conversation was taking place between me and Ms. Juarez. She set up two observation dates and times for this week and next, and I left.

Why does this moment matter? *(Practical and emotional significance)*
This moment matters because I felt so terrible during and after the meeting. I was stunned by the tension at the meeting. My impression was that Ms. Juarez was angry with me; whatever her feelings, she took over the conversation, running interference for Leon, attempting to blame me (it seemed) for Leon's overwhelmedness (it's the workload) and for the poor communication around observations (it's my responsibility). The moment matters because I felt upset and shocked after the meeting, even betrayed (I had thought Leon, Ms. Juarez, and I had a friendly relationship). I felt set up to be the bogeyman for a student who won't take responsibility for his own life.

What was going on with me in this moment? *(Self-awareness)*
I was stunned. I felt attacked, even ambushed. The fact that Ms. Juarez seemed to know that Leon had some important complaints about me suggested that they had already talked about me and decided that I was to blame for all of Leon's discomfort. So I felt paranoid and alone. I also felt actively excluded and scapegoated; I felt sucked into a one-way reality where I was painted as the bogeyman and had no voice or authority to define myself or the situation that the three of us were sharing. That feeling of being a bogeyman came from my sense that Ms. Juarez was protecting Leon from me. Am I that monstrous? Apparently, I am to blame for everything; I am despicable; I am demanding and (paradoxically) uncommunicative. I'm just too much! And other people have the right to slack off in the face of my intensity. Wow — this is a very

273

familiar set of beliefs. I've had them for as long as I can remember:

- *I am responsible for other people's suffering.*
- *I'm too much, too tough, too demanding, too bitchy.*
- *I'm a monster.*

The anger I felt from Leon and Ms. Juarez was — is — matched by my own feelings of disgust and impatience with myself, feelings I started having as an impotent little girl. This was and still is an unbearable feeling.

What do I need? *(Self-care)*

- *I need, first of all, to let myself off the hook for being human, for feeling vulnerable and despised, for wanting to feel loved, for contributing to Leon's suffering, and for not always knowing what to do in difficult moments like this one.*
- *I need to acknowledge that my reality is just as legitimate as Leon's or Ms. Juarez's.*
- *I need to listen to the content of their complaints and seriously consider what I can change to help Leon succeed.*
- *But I also need to attend to the purpose of Leon's complaints, the subtext or emotional messages he's sending me: Save me! Make this easier for me! Relieve me from the pain of learning! And from Ms. Juarez: Continue to be the bogeyman so I can be the beloved savior (enabler)! I need to set boundaries: to separate my responsibility from theirs and let them have their responsibility (and feelings). I need to figure out what I can and am willing to do and leave the rest to them.*
- *I need to be with friends right now who can empathize with me, deepen my understanding of this situation, help me devise a plan, and support me in executing it.*

The important work this teacher did, aside from letting her difficult feelings flow onto the paper, was to establish boundaries. At the same time that she identified old feelings and beliefs that this situation activated in her, she also recognized that Leon and Ms. Juarez were enacting their own patterns. Committing to doing necessary emotion work within her own circle — that is, owning her contributions to Leon's suffering and thinking of ways to change that would help him — but also refusing to take responsibility for the work Leon and Ms. Juarez had to do within their circles was crucial. Her main need, in other words, was to establish clarity in this complicated triangular relationship. Seeking supportive friends that could help her work out a plan of action was another important outcome.

KEEP IN MIND

Journaling, *or writing about emotions and experiences in a structured format, is another way to practice self-awareness.*

There is no way that journaling will help develop self-awareness if the writing gets in the way of the feeling. Beautiful, concise writing can certainly capture emotions, but it can also fabricate or cover up feelings. The key to journaling, as it is with mindfulness practice, is to stay with the feelings. They will lead the way.

In fact, staying with the feelings *is* practicing self-awareness. *Meditating on emotions* and *journaling* are just two ways to develop the skill. There are many more, as diverse as the individuals practicing them. Teachers are encouraged to experiment with self-awareness to come up with their own methods for strengthening and utilizing this crucial muscle.

The introspective step in emotion work, while extremely important, is also specialized; that is, it does not necessarily come naturally. Making the turn inward and, importantly, keeping one's attention there demands will, effort, and commitment. And practice. And support.

Even the most dedicatedly aware teachers will sometimes fail to make the turn, whether inward or outward. As always, self-blame will never help. Curiosity and persistence, the very qualities we might wish from our students, bolster this essential first step of emotion work.

Describing

Simple as it sounds, describing can take a great deal of discipline. It requires the removal of judgmental lenses we do not even know we wear. The goal of describing is to strip out judgment and bias, which often reveal damaging internal expectations that simply do not match reality, and get down to the bare, unassailable facts. Because our perceptions of "truth" are inescapably colored by our unconscious biases (our psychic structures), the project of discerning the facts can be painstaking. But it is essential if useful emotion work is to be done.

A particular version of bias, one that is highly influential and often difficult to perceive, is the *assumption*. What is tricky about assumptions is that they are a natural consequence of sifting through and organizing information; that is, they are the result of drawing conclusions based on inferences and syntheses that have taken place pretty much unconsciously. Stripping assumptions out of observations is important, and careful describing can do that.

Imagine, for example, if Ms. Bernstein had stopped to consider her assumptions about Danny, the reluctant reader in chapter four. In addition to describing for herself Danny's behaviors, she could chisel away at her assumptions about Danny and about learning to read in general. Such internal investigation might have led Ms. Bernstein to realize she assumed Danny *wanted* to learn to read. Replacing this assumption with accurate data would mean asking Danny, "Do you want to learn to read?" The ensuing conversation could be very illuminating for teacher and student.

KEEP IN MIND

Describing *is a discipline that requires one to strip away bias and judgment and to take stock of one's hidden assumptions. This skill is, then, much harder than it might seem.*

To practice describing, then, means to pay attention to evidence of bias, including assumptions, and to constantly remind oneself to provide "just the facts, ma'am." This can be done alone by describing an object or experience in writing, then reviewing the description with an eye for evaluative words or phrases. Two or more people can practice by describing an object or shared experience and comparing and critiquing the descriptions.

Here is one such description from the point of view of someone observing a children's choir rehearsal:

The choir director stood in front of the <u>restless</u> group of children and tried <u>in vain</u> to quiet them down. While the children talked to each other, the director <u>flapped</u> her hands, shushed loudly, and eventually began to yell <u>in frustration</u>. Some students looked at her <u>fearfully</u> and stopped talking, but others <u>just</u> talked more loudly. It was <u>futile</u>.

The underlined words imply assumptions on the part of the writer about what the students or choir director were feeling. Words like "restless," "in vain," "flapped," "in frustration," "fearfully," "just," and "futile" imply the writer's interpretations. A more effective description would include the data the writer picked up on that led to these interpretations. The revision might read as follows:

The choir director stood in front of a group of children who were talking to each other with their backs turned to her. Some children skipped between groups. Few children were actually looking at her.

The choir director tried to quiet the children down. She waved her hands rapidly, shushed loudly, and eventually began to yell, "All right! All right! I need QUIET!" Some children turned toward her, heads down and bodies still, and stopped talking. Others continued to talk, and the decibel level in the room seemed to rise. The choir director dropped her hands, sighed, and walked over to the piano to talk to the accompanist.

Stripping out evaluative words might lead this observer to wonder about her assumptions. She assumed the choir director was frustrated and helpless. What if that was inaccurate? How else might the choir director have been feeling? Perhaps she was unusually anxious and was rushing the singers through a timeworn ritual of talking with each other before settling into singing. Perhaps what she really wanted to be doing was talking with the accompanist. Of course, the only way to be sure would be to ask the choir director directly. Describing and looking for assumptions would make the need for such inquiry obvious.

Revising descriptions by deleting the evaluative words and phrases and adding purely descriptive language could seem tedious. But practicing the skill of effective description requires this kind of attention to detail, to just the facts. The best way to gather emotional and relational data is to detach; observe; put into words, either written or verbal, what one notices; and uncover assumptions. The accuracy of this step increases the chances of accuracy in the subsequent steps.

Looking for Good Reasons

Looking for good reasons requires a strong belief that there *are* good reasons for all actions and behaviors. This belief follows from the viewpoint taken in this book. If psychic structure determines behavior, then working to reveal psychic structure, one's own and others', can expose the roots of emotions, relationships, and behaviors.

Keep in Mind

Looking for good reasons *rests on the belief that there* are *good reasons for all emotions and behaviors, a belief that is central to the psychodynamic perspective.*

The search for good reasons is aided by genuine curiosity. Curiosity implies engrossment, but it also requires a certain detachment from the phenomenon under scrutiny, a certain distance. If one is curious about oneself — Why am I feeling the way I am right now? — one must be able to step back and ponder the subjective objectively. When it comes to wondering about a student, the teacher must detach from the self *and* from the student, lifting out of self-absorption and focusing curious attention on the other.

The suggestion to lift out of self-absorption and focus on another might sound contradictory. After all, didn't you just read that dwelling in one's feelings is a crucial step in emotion work? Obviously, the process of making sense of classroom dynamics requires many moves, from internal (yellow belt) to external (blue and black belts) back to internal as necessary. In this way emotion work is "muscular," requiring emotional suppleness, flexibility, and endurance.

FOOD FOR THOUGHT

It is difficult to feel curious about others when you yourself have unexpressed emotions and thoughts. Another way of saying this is that it can be difficult to be generous with others if you are not treated generously yourself. Seeking generous others who can listen and validate empathically (as in supervision) can be prerequisite to feeling genuinely curious. [Credit to D. Stone, B. Patton, & S. Heen (1999), *Difficult conversations: How to discuss what matters most*, New York: Penguin Books.]

Looking for good reasons also demands knowledge of psychodynamic forces. It involves finding possible answers to specific questions:

- Why does this enactment work for the student?
- What defense(s) might the student be utilizing?
- How is the student using me? How does he *need* to use me?
- What boundary violation have I or the student committed?
- What limit(s) does the student need? What limit(s) do I need?
- Why and what is this student resisting?
- What conflict might the student be gripped by?
- What role am *I* playing in all of this?

Any time a teacher asks herself one of the above questions, she is *reframing*; that is, she is abandoning old assumptions — "It's his fault!" "She's a troublemaker!" "I'll never reach this kid!" — and exploring different possibilities. Each of the questions above is a frame; it highlights some explanations and blocks out others. When looking for good reasons, considering a number of frames can help bring students and teacher into a refreshing new focus. When the explanation inspired by a particular frame resonates, it's time to start making guesses.

279

Reframing means looking at a situation through different lenses in order to see it more fully and, hence, more clearly. This book offers a number of different frames, or lenses, for teachers to use in their classrooms, including the frames of psychic structure and fitting together, using people as emotional or developmental objects, and boundary violations.

Reading books about psychodynamics can build up the type of knowledge teachers need to reframe. Simply scanning for the psychodynamic forces at work, seeing students and classrooms as fascinating webs of relationships and emotional energy, can strengthen a teacher's ability to look for and find good reasons.

An open-minded, nonjudgmental attitude is crucial to looking for good reasons and to doing emotion work generally. Psychotherapist Carl Rogers calls this attitude "unconditional positive regard," which he defines as "a warm caring for the client [or student] — a caring which is not possessive, which demands no personal gratification. It is an atmosphere which simply demonstrates 'I care'; not 'I care for you *if* you behave thus and so'" (p. 283). This is precisely the "atmosphere" from which to look for good reasons, as it avoids judgment, rejects control, and makes one available for use as a developmental partner.

DEFINITION
Unconditional positive regard *is an open-minded, nonjudgmental, well-bounded, caring stance or attitude that honors another's right to be herself. It is the stance that is most conducive to looking for good reasons.*
[Credit to C. R. Rogers (1961), *On becoming a person: A therapist's view of psychotherapy*, Boston: Houghton Mifflin.]

Importantly, unconditional positive regard depends on a solid respect for boundaries. As Rogers says,

It involves an acceptance of and a caring for the client [or student] as a *separate* person, with permission for him to have his own feelings and experiences, and to find his own meanings in them. To the degree that the therapist [or teacher] can provide this safety-creating climate of unconditional positive regard, significant learning is likely to take place. (pp. 283–284)

Note how these conditions, where boundaries mandate respect for everyone's circles and make room for teacher and students to show up, set the stage for the emergence of the Third. Thus, looking for good reasons with genuine curiosity, open-mindedness, and nonjudgment link directly to "significant learning."

Guessing

Guessing is the culmination of all the emotion work just discussed. It is the moment when a teacher gets to formulate an informed hypothesis for herself and, if she chooses, to share that hypothesis with her student. As with any hypothesis, the teacher must be open to contradiction, recognizing that any information, whether it confirms or disconfirms her hypothesis, is valuable.

Through guessing, teacher and student work together to approach understanding of the situation at hand. This process can be fitful, requiring a number of increasingly refined guesses, or epiphanous. That is, if a guess is wrong, or if a student needs time to recognize the truth of a guess, this step can require patience and persistence and can take time. If a guess is right on and resonates instantly, then the positive effect can be immediate.

KEEP IN MIND

Guessing *is the same as interpreting, or putting data together into a possible explanation. The key word here is "possible," for just as guesses emerge from a position of not knowing, so they must be made in the same humble spirit. Guesses must remain open-ended until confirmed; they cannot be helpful if they are treated as certainties.*

As we have seen, guesses tend to be statements, not questions. The difference is that questions demand immediate answers — and those answers sometimes address entirely different questions. For example, if Ms. Foster, in response to Manny's maddeningly slow preparations for recess in chapter one, had asked, "Manny, are you angry at me because I put you in time-out?" Manny might have translated it into any one of the following questions:

- "Are you one of those bad people who feel angry?"
- "Are you feeling sorry for yourself because I put you in time-out?"
- "Are you stupid?"
- "Are you willing to put yourself in danger by admitting you have unforgivably strong negative feelings for me?"

For Manny, these questions would not be conscious. But his answer, almost inevitably "NO," would ensure safety first, not emotional accuracy.

Statements, in contrast, float an idea. No one is necessarily in charge. No one is forced to respond. No judgment is implied. The answer mode can be verbal or physical; that is, answers can come through words, through action (sudden or delayed cooperation, for instance), or simply through a strong feeling of connection, of mutual understanding. Importantly, statements tend to keep the Third open. They are flares shot into the dark by one person for the consideration of another person. And ideally, they give a teacher important information to listen to.

Self-Disclosing

Self-disclosing means describing truths about oneself. But because teachers are developmental partners and hence objects for students' use, the truths that are revealed, even though they're about the teacher, must serve the *students'* best interests. When teachers are doing emotion work, they must consider what they want to disclose as well as how they want to disclose it. A key word to keep in mind with self-disclosure, then, is appropriateness.

An approach to description in general and to self-disclosure specifically is to make "I statements," statements that begin with "I" and devote themselves to honest descriptions of one's own internal experience. "I feel frustrated when I can't help you feel better" is a fair I statement. It carries absolutely no blame and exposes, quite simply, the truth about the speaker's experience. "I feel that you are a brat" is not an I statement even though it begins with "I." Rather, this statement qualifies as "fighting words": It is baldly aggressive; it invites defensiveness and argument; and it reveals absolutely nothing about the speaker.

Making accurate and effective **I statements** *is an art that is well worth cultivating, as it can turn a counterproductive argument into an honest sharing of perspectives that in turn can lead to mutual understanding.*

The point of I statements is to present the only knowledge the speaker can lay absolute claim to: her own experience. And I statements make defensiveness, the bane of mutual understanding, unnecessary.

A good way to distinguish between good and bad I statements is to imagine rejoinders:

I statement	Rejoinder
"I think you're a control freak."	"I AM NOT!"
"I'm angry because you make me crazy."	"I DO NOT!"
"It hurts my feelings when you disagree with me."	"TOO BAD!"

Obviously, if it is possible to imagine a defensive rejoinder, the I statement (or, in the last statement, the "my" statement) is a "you statement" in sheep's clothing. And you statements, no matter how well disguised, are always accusations. It goes without saying that an accusation does not qualify as *self*-disclosure.

The beauty of I statements is that they are unassailable. Even the most determined opponent cannot legitimately argue with a description of another person's subjective experience. To say "You do not!" to the confession "I feel frustrated when I can't help you feel better" would be just plain silly.

The danger of I statements is that they are honest and expose the speaker's vulnerability. If one's interactional partner is untrustworthy, unkind, or unaccustomed to this type of honesty, such self-revelation is risky and therefore takes courage. Self-disclosure takes discipline even in the best of circumstances. Fortunately, with time one learns that making I statements is both effective and relieving. It deescalates conflict and, because I statements are necessarily nonjudgmental, makes way for negotiation.

I Statement	Rejoinder	Negotiation
"I felt frustrated during the math activity because it seemed as though I was confusing everybody."	"I felt frustrated, too, because I *was* confused!"	"How can we work together to reduce confusion?"
"I am feeling nervous about the decibel level in this room."	"We're not."	"How can we work together so you can keep getting your work done and I can keep my anxiety down?"
"I'm feeling a little panicked that your project isn't finished."	"So am I."	"What can we do to rid you (and me) of panic?"

Appropriate self-disclosure coupled with careful listening reinforces boundaries and therefore allows the Third, and possible solutions, to flourish. At the very least, self-disclosure models for students the importance (and methods) of taking responsibility for oneself; the survivability of vulnerability; and the potential for negotiation even with people, such as teachers, who are in positions of power.

Listening
Simple as it sounds, listening can be extremely difficult, as it can mean hearing things one may not like. To listen without judgment, without planning a response, without defensiveness, and *with* deliberate consciousness and a commitment to understanding requires committed discipline. But it is essential if effective emotion work is to be done.

Listening with a wondering attitude and with unconditional positive regard — that is, suspending evaluation and committing to caring and understanding — not only yields valuable information but can shift interpersonal dynamics instantaneously. The key is to put a brake on one's reactions and to listen actively:

- Slow the communication down by pausing, speaking slowly, and taking the time to think.
- Notice intonations and body language.
- Attend to one's internal responses.
- Ask clarifying, not intrusive or accusing, questions.
- Gauge understanding by feeding back what one has heard.
- Accept both what a person is saying but also what he seems to be feeling.
- Note what is *not* being said.

When effective listening allows a teacher to join with her student, as Shawna did with the insecure and attacking Victor in chapter four, she can pick up on the student's fundamental messages about himself and his preferred methods for managing his feelings. The understanding that can come from listening carefully can open potential space, where teacher and student can show up without fear or shame. The transformation, as Victor showed us, can be nothing short of miraculous.

The internal "brake" that aids in practicing awareness can be valuable to listening as well. Consciously stopping oneself from planning one's next comment and focusing receptively on the student's words and manner does not happen automatically for many people. Again, practicing self-restraint with such mantras as "Stop and listen" or "Let go and attend" or "Be here now" is mandatory if one is to listen effectively.

Planning

Emotion work can be cathartic. Working through fear, insecurity, anger, and other negative emotions toward compassion and understanding can be thoroughly relieving. Emotion work, then, can be an end in itself. An obvious last step in the process for teachers, though, is planning, or making deliberate decisions about how to fold newfound insight back into one's actions in the classroom.

Planning is crucial. It increases the likelihood of remaining rational and avoiding complete loss of perspective in the moment. When a person has tipped into cognitive and emotional chaos, he is out of control and cannot be expected to reassert self-control instantaneously. While anticipating, preparing, and planning cannot ensure that a teacher or student will always maintain self-control, these actions raise the chances markedly.

The planning illustrated in this book has focused on social relationships: on interrupting enactments, usurious behaviors, boundary violations, and power struggles between teachers and students. Interestingly, most of these plans, while socially motivated, are curricular. For example, asking a student to be an educational consultant (as Ms. Foster did when she asked Manny if she could check in with him during math time), having an involved discussion about an important concept (as Ms. Copeland did after the homophobic incident in the school hallway), or providing structure for a needy student (as Dr. Digilio did for his anxious student Jackie) are all curricular decisions. They strengthen interpersonal bonds, but they also count as effective instruction aimed at academic learning.

Thinking about curriculum through the psychodynamic lens — that is, planning instruction that allows for healthy interactions with peers and subject matter — is one way of managing enactments, compliments and insults, boundary violations, and power struggles in the classroom. Of course, thinking about relationships between people can result in similar outcomes. The end result, then, of emotion work is self-knowledge, yes; understanding of students, yes; but, ultimately, it is well-crafted instruction that makes a difference in students' learning.

KEEP IN MIND
Planning is helpful in the social realm as well as in the academic realm. It can be helpful to anticipate emotional responses and pushback, one's own and others'. And it can be helpful to prepare lessons that encourage students to fit well with the teacher, with other students, and with the subject matter. Basing one's preparations on emotion work makes success much more likely.

As has been stated many times, emotion work is not easy. It requires discipline and commitment, and it requires courage, for the feelings that emotion work focuses on and in some cases releases can be unpleasant. Why, then, would any teacher do emotion work?

A simple answer is that many teachers do it already, if in a haphazard way. As Karen Madison demonstrated on the very first page of this book, teachers can expend a great deal of energy and effort thinking about their classroom experiences. Were Karen to have attended to a particular feeling and interaction, described it, looked for good reasons for both her own and her students' behaviors, made some guesses about the interaction, and devised a plan based on those guesses that she could bring into the classroom the next day, she might have pulled into her driveway feeling relieved, even excited, rather than exhausted and anxious. Emotion work would have focused Karen and turned her nervous energy into a feasible plan.

Emotion work, in other words, need not be yet another add-on for teachers, one more thing for them to master and execute. What it should be is a means of channeling teachers' emotional energy into productive thinking that is both personally relieving and instructionally effective.

And teachers could use some help developing the skills of emotion work and applying them to everyday life. That's where psychodynamically oriented, nonevaluative, supportive supervision comes in.

RECEIVING SUPPORTIVE SUPERVISION
What is psychodynamically oriented, nonevaluative supervision? It is formal support from a professional who is qualified to see interpersonal dynamics and provide a reliable holding environment in which teachers can do their own developing. It is a place where the holding that teachers need to do in classrooms can be modeled. Supervision is similar to being in a classroom in that teachers are thinking, learning, and acting out together, but it is starkly different in that there are no grades, no evaluation, and no students, parents, or administrators watching.

Teacher supervision is, simply put, a place where teachers can vent productively because they will be guided in doing emotion work. And they will not be judged for it.

Why Supervision?

There are many good reasons teachers need psychodynamically oriented, nonevaluative, supportive supervision. One is that teachers, like all other people, naturally fit together with students in ways that are difficult to perceive. As active participants in enactments, teachers necessarily develop blind spots that block them from seeing certain behaviors and their antecedents, both in themselves and in others. These blind spots simply cannot be illuminated without the help of an outside observer. Supervision can provide this illumination.

A second reason is that, once again, emotion work can be difficult. Teachers, like all others working toward understanding, can use instruction and support through the process. And they need not be alone in experiencing and surviving the emotional hits they inevitably suffer at school. Psychodynamically oriented supervision provides the conceptual lenses teachers need to see enactments clearly; it guides teachers in utilizing the lenses; and it provides empathic encouragement along the way.

Supervision is not just a site for emotion work aimed at solving problems in the classroom. It is also a means of surviving emotional pushback. As has been mentioned, students can resist teachers' benevolent changes just as energetically as they can resist the original unhelpful practices. It can take some persistence to convince students they deserve what they need.

A potentially more dangerous form of pushback is a teacher's own resistance to personal change. Psychic structures, the old, familiar, often maladaptive ways of responding to the world, were formed over time as extremely effective means of self-protection. Shifting out of these habits can release the fears and insecurities the structures were created to avoid. Teachers who try new behaviors might experience nagging doubts, vague expectations of doom, and other unpleasant emotions that tempt them to retreat from their own growth. Supervision is a reliable place to explore all forms of pushback to gain the strength and perspective required to forge ahead.

A final reason teachers need psychodynamically oriented supervision is that, ideally, teachers, like their students, are developing emotionally and cognitively. Consequently, teachers, too, need a holding environment in which they can grow. Sadly, not all schools qualify as healthy holding environments, so teachers need to look elsewhere for the specifically emotional support they need. Psychodynamically oriented supervision can be such a place.

Individual and Group Supervision

There are at least two forms of teacher supervision: individual and group. *Individual supervision* takes place between one teacher and one supervisor. *Group supervision* takes place, obviously, in a group: a group of teachers with a facilitator, the supervisor.

DEFINITION

Psychodynamically oriented, nonevaluative **supervision** *is formal, professional support of teachers' emotion work. It can happen individually or in a group.*

Whether supervision is individual or group, certain principles always apply:

- The emotion work teachers do is completely confidential.
- The supervision is meant to facilitate working through the steps of rigorous reflection about classroom events and experiences, not to uncover teachers' deep, dark secrets.
- The supervision happens in a safe place where comfort and empathy, not judgment, abound.
- The work involves learning about psychodynamics or how emotions and relationships function.
- The ongoing work is devoted to growth: to planning, experimenting, and revising one's understanding of how the classroom functions.

The supervisor's role is to manage and model the reflective process for the teacher(s). This means supervisors must, first and foremost, understand psychodynamic forces and have the capability to see, tolerate, and understand these forces.

They must be comfortable utilizing the skills of emotion work themselves so they can guide teachers confidently.

Supervisors must also possess an understanding of classroom life, not just from an experiential perspective but also from the point of view of instructional design. Without a grasp of the mechanics of teaching, supervisors can easily miss the structural issues at work in any classroom, or the role that curriculum and acts of teaching play in students' and teachers' emotional responses.

The teacher's role in supervision is to embrace emotion work: to practice awareness, to describe accurately to the supervisor and other group members, to look for good reasons for her own and others' actions, to guess, to have the courage to self-disclose, to listen, to work collaboratively on a plan of action, and to support this work in the other group members.

At its most basic, supervision, whether individual or group, helps a teacher figure out what is going on in her classroom by offering perspectives that she is unable to provide for herself. The following three stories illustrate the process of psychodynamically oriented, nonevaluative supervision and its potential impacts.

FROM LAZY TO AFRAID

Maxwell was meeting with his supervisor, Rebecca. He was describing to her a community service project he was trying out for the first time with his eighth graders. The project required students to consult with various town leaders to come up with an issue they could try to remediate as a class. Part of the process was regular group check-ins at which students were supposed to report out on their progress.

"At the last check-in," Maxwell told Rebecca, "the students got, well, vicious."

"What do you mean by 'vicious'?" Rebecca asked.

"Well, they were mean. They were attacking the project, which I hold really dear. After a while it felt as though they were attacking me."

"What was the attack like?"

290

"'This project sucks!' 'What a lame idea.' 'What are we supposed to be learning?' 'I'd rather be doing worksheets than this.'"

"And how did this attack feel to you?"

"It felt — " Maxwell made the turn inward and concentrated. "It   terrible, like I've done something very wrong and cannot fix it. I feel surrounded by a thick, impenetrable wall, and I'm all alone in here. It feels, well, it feels scary. I actually feel frightened."

"Nicely put," said his supervisor. "I'm wondering if the emotions you just described reflect how the students were feeling in that moment. What do you think your students might be afraid of?"

"Wow. I hadn't thought of it that way before. I just thought of them as being lazy and mean. But yeah — they're probably pretty thrown off by this new project that demands so much of them."

He and his supervisor agreed that Maxwell would open the next class with the question, "What are you all afraid of in this project?" and take thorough notes.

Maxwell's Emotion Work

This story shows how individual supervision can work: an individual teacher doing emotion work with an individual supervisor. And, in this seemingly simple interaction, Maxwell did some remarkable emotion work.

YELLOW BELT MOVES

With the support and prompting of his supervisor, Maxwell practiced self-awareness, described, looked for good reasons, made a guess about his students — that they were "thrown off" by and possibly afraid of the service learning project — and made a plan that would give him plenty of information to listen to. Based on what he heard from his class, Maxwell could make another plan, with or without his supervisor's help, to revise the project in such a way that it was more accessible to his students.

What did Maxwell's supervisor do? *Listening* to Maxwell's *description* of his classroom and feelings, she wondered about the *good reasons* for the students' responses at check-in. Their "vicious" comments about a perfectly reasonable, even exciting, but totally unfamiliar project were so exceptional that it was easy for Rebecca to assume that the students were (legitimately) anxious.

Knowing about *projection* — that is, knowing that students can induce in their teachers the emotions the students cannot handle themselves — led Rebecca to *guess* that the feelings Maxwell described in supervision were also the feelings his students were struggling with in class. Because she had already taught Maxwell that his own emotions can mirror his students', all Rebecca had to do to enlighten him in this case was to remind him of this phenomenon and to ask the simple question, "What do you think your *students* might be afraid of?" Maxwell could take it from there.

The learning Maxwell underwent in supervision undoubtedly made a huge difference in his and his students' lives in the classroom. By sharing his disturbing feelings with a nonjudgmental supervisor, Maxwell was able to gain immediate emotional relief; first, through honest self-disclosure and, second, through understanding. In turn Maxwell was able to treat his students with a sense of compassion rather than fear. The expectation is that he was able to hold his students' emotions by hearing them just as Rebecca was able to hold and hear Maxwell. And the whole point of the emotion work would have been curricular revisions that allowed students to fit better with the valuable service learning project.

So supervision can solve immediate classroom problems, as Rebecca and Maxwell did in the above story. Its focus can be on teachers' experiences and the feelings that accompany them. The outcomes can be relieving for the teacher and can lead to better, more finely tuned interactions with the students.

Supervision can also focus on the rich drama unfolding right there in the meeting room. Any interaction, whether one-on-one or in a group, provides ground for enactment, and teacher supervision is no exception. While supervision is not therapy, it is a place where psychic structures can reveal themselves.

Attending to enactments in supervision gives teachers a rare opportunity to work out among themselves, with the help of an astute supervisor, the very same enactments that appear in their classrooms. On top of that they get to witness their supervisor handling these enactments firsthand. Supervision, then, both solves classroom problems and models ways to approach the problems, educating teachers all along the way.

TEACHER RESISTANCE

It was the seventh of a 16-session teacher support group aimed at discussing emotions in the classroom. The group consisted of five teachers — Aimee, Beatrice, Meredith, Roger, and Thomas — and their supervisor, Christina. The teachers' conversation centered on plans for vacation even though break was many weeks away. Eventually feeling frustrated at the superficial level of talk, Christina stepped in.

"I'm going to take a chance here," she said. "There's a phenomenon called 'resistance,' which means that people work against doing something. I've been feeling a little impatient and anxious about this discussion. It feels as though we might be resisting talking about emotions. I'm wondering how people are feeling about this discussion, their possible resistance, and wonder how our experience might help us understand resistance in our classrooms."

One teacher, Thomas, responded immediately. He admitted that he had been feeling irritated himself and was wanting to steer the conversation in the direction of how people felt about their teaching, not about vacation.

Meredith, who was usually quiet during support group sessions, said that her silence meant that she was waiting patiently for the discussion to move in a more useful direction.

Aimee admitted she knew the group was going off track but did not know what to do about it, so she had just gone along with everyone else.

Christina pointed out that students might also play these roles in class, roles that stemmed from legitimate urges but that prevented discussions from moving forward. "What about you, Roger?" Christina asked.

"I thought about saying what you said about resistance," Roger replied, "but a few weeks ago I decided I didn't need to work so hard. I decided I have no agenda for this group. I just like being able to talk to colleagues and can go wherever everybody else wants to go. I don't get why we don't use a talking stick to help organize our discussions; letting discussions happen organically is just sloppy and inefficient and leads to time-wasting conversations like the one we were having about school vacation. It feels like bad teaching to me. But I don't really care what we talk about. If you, Christina, want us to talk about emotions, then you can make sure that happens. That's your job, not mine."

Christina paused as she gathered her thoughts, which were swirling around her sense that Roger was pushing her away, that he was angry. "You know, sometimes students feel angry at their teachers for doing things wrong," she eventually said. "The same can be true in a support group. I'm wondering if any of you is feeling angry?"

Roger was silent.

"I was definitely feeling irritated," Thomas reiterated.

"Maybe because I wasn't moving the group along at the right pace in the right direction," Christina suggested.

"Yes, that sounds accurate," said Thomas.

"What about you, Beatrice?" Christina asked.

"Well, I was one of the people who was sidetracking the group," Beatrice said. "But the truth is I've got a really important issue on my mind."

"Would you have brought it up if you'd been holding a talking stick?" asked Roger. Christina felt a jolt of surprise and uneasiness at this question, which was delivered innocently but felt like a slap to her.

294

"Maybe. I've been thinking about talking about it in this group all day. It's been making it so difficult for me to concentrate; I've really lost my confidence as a teacher." Beatrice's eyes filled with tears.

"So that's the thing we needed to talk about," Christina said. *"Beatrice really needs our help. I'm struck by how effectively we as a group collaborated to distract ourselves from noticing her need — and, by the way, how willing Beatrice was to distract us, too. We can easily imagine our students are just as good at avoiding the hard work of learning at school."* The group focused on Beatrice's issue for the rest of the session.

Like students, teachers want to avoid difficult emotions and situations. Like students, they can muster masterful defenses against exploring and learning. This support group exemplified these tendencies beautifully. Despite her intense distress Beatrice and her colleagues cooperated unconsciously to protect the group from addressing it. By noting this possible resistance and, importantly, asking about it, Christina opened a door that the group was able to pass through into potential space, where they all had the right to their own responses and could work together toward mutual understanding. They were able to overcome their resistance and move into valuable emotion work.

The Group's Emotion Work

Becoming aware of personal resistance was extremely helpful for the teachers. First, it drew their attention to some of the different roles group members can play that add up to avoidance: distracting chatterer, impotent fixer, silent waiter, ignorant accomplice, angry judge. At some level these roles worked for each teacher because playing them allowed the teachers to maintain a disengaged *status quo*. Even Beatrice, who knew she had a pressing issue to discuss, contributed to the construction of this safe, no-emotion zone.

Second, it highlighted the automatic and, for the most part, benevolent nature of these roles. Apart from Beatrice, no other teachers were consciously aware that the group had some difficult emotion work to do together. They simply did what felt right: They fit together to accomplish the conscious task of being friendly and connected and the unconscious task of avoiding Beatrice's distress. They did not do this maliciously; they did it naturally, the way a flock of birds executes swift figure eights in the air or the way students can stall a teacher's announcement of the homework assignment.

Importantly, this group of teachers was able, just as naturally, to focus intently on Beatrice's issue once it was brought to light. The group dynamics did not cease, of course, but the fit that the teachers achieved with one another after they became aware of their resistance allowed them to address Beatrice's problem and everyone's emotions much more effectively.

Finally, becoming aware of personal resistance made the concept of resistance in the classroom concrete. Now, rather than simply *talking about* their students' resistance, the teachers would be able to refer back to their own experience of resistance (and there would undoubtedly be more during the nine remaining weeks of group meetings). They would be better able to relate to and, importantly, understand their students' behaviors because they themselves had enacted them. This is the essence of psychodynamically oriented supervision: understanding one situation through the experience of and deliberate analysis of the same behaviors in another, safer situation.

Formal or Organic?

Note that using a talking stick might have given Beatrice the spotlight she needed to bring up her problem. Rather than schmoozing endlessly, the group would have become focused on her issue directly and efficiently. This was Roger's point, it seems: The absence of any means of organizing and formatting discussions was problematic for him. Despite his strong preference Christina had opted to allow conversations to happen "organically." Why might she have done this?

Few teachers use talking sticks in their classes. It is likely that Christina chose an informal approach to running the group meetings to imitate the teachers' circumstances in their own classrooms. In this way she and the teachers could experience natural group process as it happened.

Messy, unpredictable, and apparently inefficient as this process was, it also offered invaluable opportunities for enactment. By observing the group's process, identifying an enactment, and drawing the teachers' attention to it, Christina accomplished two very important goals: First, of course, she focused the group on the issue they needed to discuss. Second, she focused them on their process.

But this wasn't just any old process. It was *parallel process*; that is, the teachers' behaviors paralleled, or mirrored, their own students' behaviors. Surely all the teachers in this group had witnessed their students chatting amiably at the beginning of class. Surely they had, at least occasionally, been irritated and possibly mystified by this behavior. Noticing and attending to distracting behaviors in themselves could help the teachers better understand the possible reasons their students engaged in these behaviors. And the teachers could change the ways they responded in the future. In psychodynamically oriented supervision, parallel process is a gold nugget.

DEFINITION

Parallel process *happens when one group mirrors the behaviors of another group and gets to analyze the similar dynamics. In supervision, parallel process occurs when (1) teachers act out in the same ways their students do and (2) teachers enact their own relational patterns. Needless to say, parallel process can be eye-opening.*

In the Heat of the Moment

This example of resistance illustrates how groups can collaborate to complete an enactment. This is one reason group supervision can be extremely valuable for teachers: It simulates the classroom as a collective and permits teachers to notice and learn from the similarities. But enactments, of course, also happen in dyads; that is, a teacher can enact with his supervisor the very same behaviors that he enacts with his students or that his students enact with him. This type of enactment is also present in the above story in Roger's disavowed but palpable anger at Christina.

Some brief backstory: The very problem that brought Roger to the support group, the problem he wanted to solve, was his anger in school. As Roger regularly reported to the group, he found that his patience ran out with his students on a daily basis. He was appalled at the rage he could feel and the snide ways he showed it. It was virtually impossible, Roger told his colleagues in the group, to suppress his anger once it had welled up.

Given this background, it should come as no surprise that Roger would eventually become angry in the teacher support group. After all, Roger brought his psychic structure, his ways of fitting with others, everywhere he went. It was just a matter of time before whatever triggered his rage in the classroom would activate it in the teacher support group.

What did Christina do with Roger's evident anger? One thing she did was to *make a guess* that Roger's expressed intent to withdraw from active participation in the group was evidence of simmering anger. She *disclosed* this suspicion by labeling it as a common phenomenon ("feeling angry") and indirectly inviting Roger to own up to it. He did not, but Thomas did.

Christina took the opportunity to suggest a *good reason* for Thomas's irritation (and Roger's anger): her failure to move the group along when they were clearly wasting time. Data she might have relied on to make this guess could have come from some of Roger's comments:

- "I thought about saying what you said about resistance."
- "Letting discussions happen organically is just sloppy and inefficient and leads to time-wasting conversations like the one we were having...."
- "It feels like bad teaching to me."
- "You can make sure that happens. That's your job, not mine."

Apparently, Roger was struggling with an urge to merge with Christina, to do her job and do it *better*. The way he would have done it would have been neat and efficient and would have avoided the messy interactions that most groups, including class groups, engage in when faced with an unpopular or demanding task.

While her guess satisfied Thomas, it did not appease Roger. His anger persisted, as evidenced by his pointed question to Beatrice: "Would you have brought your need up if you'd been holding a talking stick?" Judging by the jolt it caused in her, this question doubled as a further accusation

298

against Christina and her refusal to adopt Roger's preferred approach.

Evidently, Roger was willing neither to discuss his anger nor to let it go. So Christina, true to the group's wishes, moved on. She had done some good emotion work in the heat of the moment. But more emotion work was clearly necessary. Given that Roger's anger would likely surface again, Christina would do well to *anticipate* how to turn future angry interactions into corrective emotional experiences.

The Supervisor's Emotion Work

It is important to note here that Christina *did not know* what was going on inside Roger. Like all other teachers, she had no direct access to her student's experience; the only data she could work with were Roger's words and actions and her internal responses. It is possible that Roger was not angry at all, that Christina was simply reading her own anxiety or anger into his acts. Through emotion work Christina could sort through the emotional and relational data she had collected.

YELLOW BELT MOVES

Her starting point, of course, would be her own emotions during group. Once she had time to reflect in private (ideally, with a supervisor of her own), Christina could *practice self-awareness*. How did she feel when Roger made his short but angry speech to the group? She might remember that she had felt several emotions, including alienation, surprise, and uneasiness. All together, she might admit she had felt vulnerable and afraid that Roger, whom she respected, was deeply disappointed in her.

These emotions might have revealed to Christina important *information about herself*. Surely, as a supervisor of several accomplished teachers, she had a right to feel vulnerable to their judgment and afraid of disappointing them. She owed it to herself and to the teachers in her group to bolster herself against these debilitating feelings. Purposeful self-care, including regular meetings with a psychodynamically oriented supervisor, could help her maintain realistic perspective.

Her emotions could also yield important *information about Roger's emotions*. Perhaps he was feeling vulnerable and afraid in his own right. If so, why might he have felt this way during the group meeting? Fortunately, Roger provided a concrete complaint that Christina could focus on: her decision to allow discussions to emerge naturally.

Christina could look for the *good reasons* for Roger's rigid insistence on using a talking stick. Why might he need such formality? It might occur to Christina that a talking stick offered structure, and structure implied containment, responsibility, control. In contrast, waiting for conversations to come together might feel to Roger like *ir*responsibility, which, for him, might be akin to freefall or chaos or danger.

Christina could *guess* that structure made Roger feel safe because it implied that someone was in charge. If no one was in charge, Roger might feel vulnerable and afraid. And rather than stay with such terrible feelings, Roger might channel them into anger. Could the anger that Roger felt every day in school be related to a fear of chaos and consequent need for control? Could his impulse to be the teacher in the support group indicate just how uncomfortable he was with the messiness Christina considered normal for groups? Could it be that the level of control he needed to feel safe and deactivated was impossible for him to achieve in his own classroom?

And what about *Roger's preferred relational styles*? What might Christina's emotions tell her about them? Roger's withdrawal and Christina's distinct sense that he was pushing her away implied that Roger might be accustomed to feeling alienated and disconnected from people he needed understanding from. Her feeling of uneasiness could parallel Roger's own sense that his need might be met with disapproval, withdrawal, maybe even anger – the responses he himself exhibited to Christina.

As the group's leader, Christina could have been the target of some deeply ambivalent feelings in Roger. At the same time that he seemed to desire closeness – "You're supposed to understand and value me!" – it also felt as though he sought disconnection – "How dare you try to tell me what to do?" Because he could not actually voice these expectations and disappointments, Christina realized it was possible that he was making her *feel* them instead. And, importantly, he seemed to be teaching her how to treat him – with distance, confusion, and, ultimately, anger.

Even though Christina could not be sure about any of these guesses, she could certainly experiment. The crucial heart of her plan would be to maintain a safe holding environment for Roger where he could learn and grow at his own pace in the presence of compassionate and respectful others. In other words, she could keep the Third open, or go with Roger's resistance, by *becoming the resister* and explicitly examining the issue of control with the teachers in her support group as if the issue were hers alone.

BLACK BELT MOVES

At the next group meeting, Christina could lay out her problem. As the "teacher" of their group, she was unsure how to manage check-in to best accomplish the group's goals. Should she exert top-down control of the teacher support "class" by making teachers use a talking stick? Or should she allow for bottom-up emergence of discussions and enactments? What would the benefits and drawbacks of each approach be? Who felt anxiety where? How could the teachers best deal with that anxiety? How might this discussion relate to the ways the teachers felt about control in their own classrooms?

Despite his apparent resolution to withdraw from active group participation, Roger might have a tough time staying disengaged from this conversation. If Christina was correct in her guess about Roger's anger, he would have some strong feelings about these questions and might contribute some valuable insights. If she was incorrect, she might still gain information she could use to refine her guesses about what Roger needed. Any contributions he made could help to demystify his anger response, both in group and in class. And because Christina and the way she was running the group would be at center stage of the discussion, Roger could do his own emotion work from the wings, where he could protect his privacy and dignity.

Parallel Process

The point of this discussion would not necessarily be to influence Christina's decision about how to organize group discussions. She could continue to allow conversations to come together organically based on her considered professional opinion. Support groups, like classrooms, are not pure democracies.

The point of the discussion would be to reveal participants' responses to chaos and control, the emotions that different ways of governing classroom talk brought up, and the needs the approaches satisfied and neglected. Knowing her teachers' diverse needs — for a sense of control, for a chance to unwind, for aid in getting people's attention or heading into difficult work — would help Christina anticipate and model ways to accommodate them.

And acknowledging their own needs and emotions would help teachers relate to their students' attitudes towards chaos, control, and open-ended discussions. Accepting the dilemma that no teacher decision will win the approval of all students, that teachers will always risk disappointing someone, could help all the group participants live with and adapt to their classroom realities.

In the course of this discussion, Christina would model what it is to be a teacher who sees classrooms psychodynamically. Specifically, she would keep an eye out for additional enactments, for usurious acts, for boundary crossings, for power struggles and other attempts to squash the Third. She would refrain from taking any of the group behaviors personally, least of all Roger's anger. She would act as the teachers' developmental partner. And she would commit to doing emotion work of her own.

In addition, she would draw her teachers' attention to their process — that is, she would educate them about what they were experiencing — while attempting not to hamper that process. She would keep in mind that the discussion of governing group talk, while philosophically and even pragmatically useful, was a front for more personal exploration that she could witness and guide but that, ultimately, had nothing to do with her. It had to do with each teacher and especially with Roger, his history, his psychic structure, and his present ability to grow and learn. The best she could do would be to provide a solid holding environment in which this growth, should Roger wish it, could happen.

Benefits of Supervision

The value of this approach should be obvious. Though there is no guarantee that this one discussion would cause Roger's anger problem to dissolve on the spot, it might set him on a course of self-understanding that could eventually result in favorable changes in his classroom demeanor. His future students could benefit immeasurably from a more patient, detached, and curious Roger.

And Roger would benefit, too. He could release himself from the chronic self-blame that his cycle of anger undoubtedly trapped him in. He could be supported in trying new behaviors. He could revive his love of teaching. Where he might have felt helpless over his automatic responses to students, he could now feel validated in his emotions and empowered to work through them toward personal change. Supervision would be one way to accomplish all this.

The next story gives an example of the type of benefit Roger could have reaped from his participation in group supervision.

REJUVENATION

Mr. Malmrose was not at all looking forward to his fifth period math class. These tenth graders were disengaged and listless, and frankly, they bored him. Because he resented the implication that he was supposed to be the equivalent of a TV entertainer, Mr. Malmrose intentionally delivered his lessons as lectures and had students do worksheets at their desks.

Today, though, Mr. Malmrose happened to walk past a colleague's English class and noticed how much fun everyone in the room seemed to be having. There was laughter and activity but also a very focused energy emanating from the classroom. Mr. Malmrose felt his spirits sag. Why wasn't his fifth period class as lively as this?

His dreary thoughts were interrupted by another colleague who was passing in the hall. "Bob," the colleague called, "can I have those calculators I lent to you a few weeks ago? I need them for tomorrow's class." Mr. Malmrose had forgotten he had even borrowed the calculators and could not remember where they were. His colleague frowned and snapped, "Well, I need them by tomorrow come hell or high water!"

Mr. Malmrose found himself feeling surprisingly low. He felt like a terrible teacher and, thanks to his colleague's rebuke, like an inept child. Shame rose up in him as he rushed back to his empty classroom and closed the door.

Focusing on his feelings, Mr. Malmrose resisted the temptation to blame his colleagues for his misery. The English teacher was genuinely talented and did not deserve any negative judgment. And the other colleague was justified in wanting her calculators back, though her withering tone had been unnecessary.

Where had Mr. Malmrose's sense of self gone? He wondered what the members of his teacher support group would say to him at this moment. "You're allowed to have negative feelings." "There's nothing wrong with you." "What are the good reasons for your emotions? What can you do about them?" "We're here for you."

Just thinking about the group made him feel respected and competent, as if he actually belonged to this crazy club called school. He began to think about other times when he felt competent and proud. Very quickly, images flooded his mind: pictures of him backpacking, kayaking, rock climbing, and biking. Instantly, his body relaxed, and Mr. Malmrose even smiled to himself. "That's who I am," he told himself.

He immediately searched his classroom for the calculators and found them. Then he pulled up some photos on his computer of his most recent nature trip and linked them into a screen-saver slide show. He placed his computer where he could easily see the photos and sat down to redesign his fifth period math class into something he and his students would enjoy.

Mr. Malmrose's Emotion Work

Clearly, Mr. Malmrose had practiced the skills of emotion work. What did he do? And how did his teacher support group help him do it?

Mr. Malmrose was able to *practice self-awareness*; to *describe*; to *find good reasons* for his colleagues' behaviors, in the process setting strong boundaries around his shame so it wouldn't seep out into blame; and, ultimately, to *plan* a means of bolstering himself (the slide show) while he *planned* a lesson that would be fun for him and his students.

Mr. Malmrose's ability to do all this work so efficiently depended at least in part on the practice he got in his teacher support group. He had spent many hours applying the skills of emotion work to his own stories and those of his colleagues in the group. Utilizing the same skills at school, therefore, required very little effort.

Mr. Malmrose's reflections indicate that something else had happened because of his participation in the teacher support group. He had internalized, or *introjected*, his colleagues' support and advice. Having participated in repeated, consistently accurate and caring interactions (corrective emotional experiences) with these colleagues in the weekly group meetings, he was able to support himself in their absence. "What would my colleagues say to me right now?" is a sign that internalization was at work.

FOOD FOR THOUGHT

Internalization, or **introjection** *(see the appendix), is a central force in the learning process. When a student says or thinks, "What would my teacher do?" teachers should rejoice.*

But internalization is just a way station on the road of development. The hope is that students will eventually take ownership of what they have internalized and mold it into their own peculiar knowledge or characteristic or automatic reaction. They must make it their own; the teacher's voice must fade away so the student's voice can become sure and strong.

In other words, Mr. Malmrose had learned. As a result of participating in his supervisory group, he had changed his behaviors and his thinking in the face of self-doubt and shame, two very debilitating emotions. Despite his automatic, self-undermining responses to the various hits he took in the hallway at school, he was able to detach, reflect, and respond responsibly. These new behaviors both released him from his despair and rejuvenated him. Chances are that his fifth period class would notice the difference.

The Power of Supervision
The potential of supervision to support tremendous change in classrooms is great. Teachers who work through enactments, either in a group or singly with a supervisor, can gain invaluable information about themselves, their students, and the ways they relate to each other and to ideas. This information can lead teachers to plug into their students differently and to encourage students to plug into subject matter much more effectively. Supervision allows teachers to get to the heart of teaching by allowing them to focus on the feeling of teaching.

Through supervision teachers can undergo valuable personal transformation. Engaging with trusted others in ways that directly model healthy interaction can provide corrective emotional (and academic) experiences for all participants. Teachers can play, experiment, resist, feel, flare, and fall apart — and learn from their emotions and behaviors. Like their students, teachers can grow: They can develop, as human beings tend to do, in the safe holding environment that good-enough supervision provides.

Supervision also highlights the relational patterns teachers inevitably enact in their classrooms. Like Roger, all teachers carry their prongs and outlets with them; teachers have no choice but to fit with each other in the same ways they fit with their students. And since the teachers in a supervisory setting occupy the role of student, they can experience firsthand the reactions and resistances that their students do to teaching acts. Keeping both the teacher's and the students' perspectives in mind can broaden the scope of a teacher's understanding and effectiveness immeasurably. Supervision is one of the few places where teachers can develop this double focus.

Perhaps most important, and most intangible, is the impact of care. Teachers, who are highly specialized and high-stakes caregivers, must find the energy to care for many things: their students, their students' parents, their colleagues, the curriculum they teach, the ideas and skills the curriculum

306

hopes to enliven, their students' test scores. Many teachers do not have the time to care for themselves. And many teachers are not adequately cared for by others. A surefire way to enable caregivers to find the energy to care for their charges is to give them the care they themselves need. This is one of the central purposes of teacher supervision.

Where can one get supervision?

It is important to note that psychodynamically oriented, nonevaluative, supportive teacher supervision of the sort described here does not currently exist in any formal way. Mentoring does exist, but it can be complicated by the need for eventual evaluation or can be delivered by teachers who are unfamiliar with the discipline of emotion work or the demands of being a developmental partner.

Yet teachers (and administrators) need such support. What steps can they take to get it? Certainly, a few teachers (ideally between four and six) can decide to hire a local therapist, preferably one with experience running groups, to work with them weekly. The downside of this plan is that few therapists are trained as educators, so their knowledge of classroom management and curriculum design would be minimal. But it would be a start.

Another step would be to visit *teachingthroughemotions.com*, a website devoted to emotion work and psychodynamically oriented, nonevaluative, supportive teacher supervision. At that site teachers can post their teaching stories and receive moderated, supportive feedback from other teachers that both reflects and encourages effective emotion work. Teachers can also request consultation as to how to organize a support group at their school and sign up for training that prepares them to become facilitators. Teachers who get involved in this type of supervision will be at the cutting edge of a whole new approach to professional development.

The bottom-line hope is that teachers will begin to request and organize psychodynamically oriented, nonevaluative, supportive supervision in an effort to secure a holding environment that allows for essential self-care and growth that, in turn, promotes care and growth for students.

WRAP-UP

A lot is expected of teachers. They are supposed to be master managers, subject matter experts (sometimes of many different subject matters), punctual record keepers, amiable parent conferencers, obedient team members and school representatives, assiduous organizers, and effective instructional designers.

Now they have to be gurus, too.

Joking aside, the designation of "guru," which means "revered teacher and counselor," isn't such a bad one. And insofar as "guru" implies a highly developed, wise leader whose concern is others' growth and well-being, why wouldn't it be an absolutely appropriate metaphor for great-enough teachers?

Doing emotion work and getting supervision that supports and promotes self-knowledge and personal change, whether it veers into the guru realm or not, is work for teachers who honor themselves and want the best for their students. Difficult as the work can be, it is the most direct and rewarding way to attune relationships, foster desired learning, and possibly even avoid eventual burnout.

CHAPTER ANSWERS

By now, the answers to the questions from the beginning of the chapter should be obvious.

- *How can a teacher develop the skills of emotion work?*
- *Where can teachers find the type of holding environment they need just as urgently as their students do?*

The only way to develop the skills of emotion work — practicing awareness, describing, looking for good reasons, making guesses, self-disclosing, listening, and planning — is to do them. Fortunately, just doing them will make a difference; that is, a teacher does not have to be an expert at emotion work to see results.

In fact, the notion of "expert" makes little sense when it comes to emotion work. The reason is that emotion work never ends. Interactions differ, emotional responses change, situations arise that throw off even the most grounded, secure individuals. Emotion work might get easier, but it never

308

becomes unnecessary or rote. One must be in it for the long haul.

The most reliable way for teachers to get the support they need as they practice and reflect on the findings of their emotion work is to engage in psychodynamically oriented, nonevaluative, supportive supervision. With the aid of supervisors who understand psychodynamics and the exigencies of the classroom, teachers can be "held" as they learn and grow into ever more effective educators, a learning process that, like emotion work, never ends.

KEEP IN MIND

- *Rigorous reflection can be done in the heat of the moment — reflecting-in-action — or after the fact — reflecting-on-action. Both are valuable.*
- *When practicing awareness, teachers must look outward at the classroom context and inward at their feelings and reactions.*
- *Three ways to practice self-awareness are to make the turn, to meditate on emotions, and to journal.*
- *Describing means stripping out from one's observations any bias or judgment and scrutinizing one's assumptions.*
- *Looking for good reasons requires curiosity, flexibility, specialized knowledge, and unconditional positive regard.*
- *Guessing means offering open-ended yet informed hypotheses with an eye toward revision. Guessing works best through statements rather than questions, as statements are more likely to encourage the Third.*
- *Self-disclosing involves making I statements. Because self-disclosing must always serve the students, it is crucial that teachers ensure that the personal information they share with students is appropriate and relevant.*
- *Listening should be done actively to maximize the amount and quality of information a teacher gathers. One mandatory element of active listening is attending wholly to what another person is saying without thinking about one's next comment.*

- *Planning* applies in the social and academic realms. In the social realm planning includes anticipating and preparing for one's own and others' behavioral responses. In the academic realm it involves designing classroom situations that will maximize growth and learning. In practice these two realms often converge.
- Teachers need and deserve **psychodynamically oriented, nonevaluative supervision**, or support in doing rigorous emotion work.
- Supervision can be **individual**, or one-on-one, and it can be in a **group**, which involves several teachers and a trained facilitator.

CONCLUSION

PUTTING IT ALL TOGETHER: SEEING STRUCTURE

THE NEXT DAY IN THE LIFE

Pulling into the school parking lot, Karen Madison felt refreshed and excited about her day. Her supervision the night before had helped her put yesterday into perspective, and she was looking forward to implementing the plans she and her supervisor had come up with.

One of the first people she saw after she entered the school building was the colleague who had given her the menacing look. Having decided with her supervisor not to take the scowl personally, Karen greeted her colleague cheerfully. The colleague smiled back and asked how Karen was doing. In the course of the ensuing conversation, the colleague revealed that he had been worried and preoccupied yesterday by the news that his mother was ill.

It had not been difficult in supervision to guess why the students had packed up before her class had ended the day before. The students were undoubtedly hungry and possibly bored. The big question was why their behavior had so enraged Karen. With her supervisor's help, Karen thought about what her emotional response told her about herself and her students.

Her first realization was that she had felt dismissed and erased by the students' thoughtlessness, feelings that she had struggled with all her life. It really helped her to imagine "unplugging" from her students' normal, self-oriented behavior. What she learned about herself, then, was that she was structured to take students' demeaning actions personally and, importantly, to retaliate in passive-aggressive ways. These were responses she could look for and talk herself out of in the heat of the moment and write down so she could work through them in supervision.

What she learned about her students was that they needed a snack to concentrate. And they needed lessons that were gripping enough to distract them from their natural obsession with lunch. So she had planned a lesson for today that began with a healthy snack, which she provided. She would tell the students that class would begin with snacks from now on and encourage them to bring in their own. And she decided to experiment with a student-centered activity that demanded focus and original thinking.

As for Rochelle, Karen was looking forward to asking her to have lunch in her room today. Karen realized in supervision that she had no idea what was keeping Rochelle from turning in her homework. The only way she could find out was by asking. Because her supervisor pointed out that it might take Rochelle time to open up, Karen was prepared to listen and keep inviting Rochelle back. She didn't need to be told that there could be no Third between her and Rochelle — and hence no useful academic learning for Rochelle — until her student was willing and able to show up.

Despite this good emotion work, Karen was in for yet more emotional experiences in school that day. But she felt prepared for them. And she knew that she could count on supervision for support in both surviving her emotions and using them to continuously hone her teaching.

Emotion work is both a means and an end. It is a means to the end of highly attuned teaching and as such is the basis for student learning. It is also an end in itself, as emotion work as a practice is inseparable from self-improvement. The teacher who commits to emotion work commits to personal change for the better.

The key to emotion work is the notion of psychic structure. Relationships depend on psychic structure, and learning depends on relationships, so ultimately desirable academic learning depends on plugging into people and ideas in productive, meaningful ways. Improvement of oneself as a teacher and as a person — which, in this book, amounts to one and the same thing — also depends on plugging into people compassionately and effectively. Psychic structure is the key, so *seeing structure* is the goal, the end. And it is the means to facilitating transformative learning.

WORKING THE FIT

What does *seeing structure* consist of? For one thing, it involves *working the fit*: looking for the ways people fit together; embracing the fact that people always fit together for good reasons; trying to figure out how the fit works, what the good reasons might be; and, based on all this reflection, trying to fit better, more healthily, more effectively. Seeing structure requires comfort with uncertainty, with speculation, with guessing, as there is no empirical bottom line when it comes to the feeling of teaching. It demands engagement and detachment — that is, an ability to feel in the moment as well as an ability to step back, slow down, and wonder about those feelings both in the moment and afterward.

A very important corollary to the claim that people fit together in patterned ways, a corollary mentioned throughout the book, is that **the fit is coconstructed**. It is mutually accomplished, requiring the participation of all the parties involved in the interaction.

In the world of living beings, no act occurs in isolation. Even the most passive acts — a student's silence when asked a question, for example — play significant roles in relationships and enactments. Seeing structure, then, necessitates seeing the bigger picture, capturing the context of an act, noting the antecedents, or the events that led up to the act. It means taking an unswervingly ecological perspective on human interaction, the view that people are constantly adapting to each other to maintain their own physical and psychic survival.

And when events begin falling into familiar sequences, then patterns have emerged. **Seeing patterns** is one of the great benefits of seeing structure, as patterns with expectable negative outcomes can be interrupted and corrective academic and emotional experiences can be planned.

Because fits are coconstructed, seeing structure means **renouncing the practice of blaming**. In an enactment both (or all) parties are "to blame" — which ultimately means that no one party is "the cause" or "the culprit." Pinning responsibility on one person and tacitly absolving another does not just humiliate or anger the one blamed but fundamentally overlooks the truth about all human interaction.

Seeing structure means accepting this truth:

- that interacting parties collaborate on their behaviors;
- that blaming is irrelevant when understanding is the goal;
- that fine-tuning a relationship requires exploration and experimentation.

The exploration involves doing emotion work to figure out the possible meanings of the emotions, the behaviors, and the mutual fits. The experimentation requires trying new behaviors (based on thoughtful plans) that might invite different, more desirable fits.

Put another way, seeing structure means seeing unconscious collaboration, looking for how people interlock rather than how they act serially upon one other. When phenomena are coconstructed, there is no reliable, pinpointable cause or start. When people fit together, there is no linearity, no single-headed arrow connecting boxes in a flowchart. Rather, there is always mutual influence, always double-headed arrows.

People's feelings, interpretations, and actions are multidimensional, happening simultaneously; their responses double as invitations, and the lines that separate one behavior from another blur. Everyone is always an active participant, picking up on and sending out signals consciously and unconsciously, improvising a relational dance that is constantly emerging, moment to moment to moment. Seeing structure means honoring the cocreated nature of human interaction, looking not for the cause or the person to blame but for the purposes of the fit, the ways the dance works, *for everyone involved.*

When there is no linear cause and effect but rather ongoing mutual influence, there is no unilateral control. Another axiom I have emphasized throughout the book is that **people cannot control each other**. They can control themselves, but they cannot actually control anyone else. What gives people the illusion of control is their success at fitting together with others in productive and desirable ways. These moments, especially when they happen in classrooms, are exceptionally gratifying!

But messy moments, moments of chaos or near chaos, moments when no one seems to be in control, are not necessarily failures. In fact, they can be moments of intense and productive creativity and communication. They can also be alarming and dangerous. At the very least they are full of emotional data that can inform a teacher's future acts.

Whether these seemingly out-of-control moments are exciting or terrifying, they are always coconstructed, arising from the fits teacher and students achieve, not from the unilateral control one person wields over the others. Seeing structure means *not* looking for ways to control but rather seeking ways to *fit* with students and ideas that promote the types of relationships that will foster desired learning. Finding these fits when they are not happening naturally requires, of course, emotion work.

EMBRACING UNPREDICTABILITY

If classroom relationships are always coconstructed, resulting in an ever-active and adaptive network of fits between teacher, students, and ideas, then **there is no such thing as predictability in the classroom**. There is probability, but there is no certainty. This idea is not new to teachers who go into every lesson with a carefully thought-out Plan B. But the bald fact that teachers cannot accurately predict students' reactions, their own reactions, or the academic outcomes of much of what they do every day can be unnerving, especially when teachers are increasingly expected to guarantee predetermined results.

If unpredictability is a fact of classroom life, then what can teachers count on? One thing they can count on is emotion work. They can practice awareness, describe, look for good reasons, make guesses, listen, self-disclose, and plan. That is, they can utilize the emotional and relational data that is always available in their classrooms to anticipate possible scenarios and prepare for them. If, by seeing structure and noticing relational patterns, teachers have put together an accurate understanding of how their students learn and how they resist learning, then teachers can aim instruction at their students' relational preferences, their prongs and outlets.

315

Mr. Apkin's plan to model resilience for his oppositional learner, Sean, is a case in point. Knowing that he couldn't change Sean's automatic argumentative behavior, Mr. Apkin had to think about how to help Sean connect with new ideas and with his classmates so they could all learn from each other. The approaches he could have tried included self-disclosing and listening to Sean (as described in chapter one) and, as discussed in chapter four,

- making conflict statements;
- siding with the resister;
- going with the purpose of Sean's resistance;
- becoming the resister.

All of these approaches took into consideration Sean's psychic structure, his relational preferences. Because they were experiments, Mr. Apkin could not guarantee they would work. But he could be assured that these plans would either yield different behaviors from Sean or produce more information about Sean's resistance — both beneficial outcomes and both dependent on Mr. Apkin's ability to see structure.

The success of emotion work at managing unpredictability rests, ironically, on a *commitment* to unpredictability: the willingness to experiment. When a teacher feels uncertain — when, say, a teaching method that worked beautifully last year is not going so well this year — she can rebel against this uncomfortable feeling by cracking down on her students and insisting they conform to her approach; that is, she can try to control them, or force compliance out of them.

Or she can embrace her uncertainty by coming up with a new plan, an experiment. She can meet unpredictability by embracing it. Seeing structure means just this: recognizing the fact of uncertainty and unpredictability in human relationships and moving freely within that uncertainty by making informed guesses and trying experiments that aim at fostering, not forcing, the types of responses desired.

Paradoxically, embracing uncertainty by doing emotion work can yield *predictable* results: change of some sort.

If one actor in a relational network, especially a crucial actor such as a teacher, makes a behavioral shift, the other actors will generally have to adjust. The change might not be the *desired* or *expected* change; it is not predictable. But it is virtually guaranteed that informed changes in a teacher will influence the classroom system of which she is a part. What can be predicted, then, is not *what* will necessarily happen as a result of an attitudinal or behavioral change by a teacher but *that* something, even something very subtle, will happen.

The stories in this book attempt to illustrate this potential. Because enactments and insults and resistance and boundary crossings all happen for good reasons, they can be addressed and transformed when teachers make guesses and try new fits. How a particular teacher might influence this transformation with particular students is not predictable; how students will respond to particular experiments is not predictable. But one *can* predict that making any move will encourage other moves in the classroom; and one *can* predict that making a move into a better fit will inspire useful learning. The goal is to do the emotion work, try the fit, and watch what happens.

ADOPTING THE STANCE

So far I have described seeing structure in mostly behavioral terms: coconstruction, fitting together, ecological perspective, relational dance, planning for unpredictability. But there is an essential *emotional stance* that seeing structure requires as well. Many words in this book have tried to capture this stance: nonjudgment, detachment, compassion, curiosity, unconditional positive regard. What all these words add up to is a very open-minded and openhearted attitude toward students and toward the developmental role teachers necessarily play for them.

Staying open means resisting the urge to perpetrate and perpetuate enactments, win power struggles, or take oh-so-satisfying revenge. It means lifting oneself out of the fray and exercising the self-restraint necessary to do the right thing, the kind thing, the difficult thing that students have in some way (and sometimes in extremely irritating ways) indicated they need.

Another good word for this openness is "presence," or the ability to stay with people and feelings in a boundaried way, one that allows for attentiveness and empathy but that protects one from overabsorption of toxic emotions. Being present can be difficult, but seeing structure in the classroom will not work without it.

Not-knowing is another essential element in the open-minded, openhearted stance teachers need to take if they are to see structure in their classrooms. The not-knowing stance recognizes that, despite all that teachers know, there is much they do not know. They do not know everything about students' personal histories, about students' internal experiences in the classroom, about the ways students are making sense of what their teachers are saying and doing. If teachers allow themselves to not-know — to put a brake on judging and controlling so as to hear themselves and others clearly, to "let something be revealed" — then they make room for curiosity in themselves and in their students. Genuine curiosity can, in turn, prompt questioning that leads out of not-knowing into ever-increasing, accurate understanding.

In a profession that revolves around *knowing*, taking the not-knowing approach might seem ludicrous or counterproductive. But not-knowing is the attitude that makes emotion work effective; it is the stance that allows a teacher to see others clearly in the service of the Third. A knowing stance predicts what one will see and therefore limits the data that can be gathered and processed. The not-knowing stance welcomes all data, and emotion work organizes it.

BEING A DEVELOPMENTAL PARTNER

Another axiom that I have implied in the book is this: that **what happens in a classroom is *not about the teacher***. Yes, teachers need to feel gratified and fulfilled by what they do. Yes, they need to choose teaching acts and approaches to curriculum that tap into their strengths and that excite and stimulate them. Yes, they need to show up, feel their feelings, engage in relationships, and do emotion work. In short, teachers need to take care of and take responsibility for themselves. And they need both formal and informal places to go where they can be supported by people who can help them bear the emotional burdens of teaching.

But when it comes to enactments, compliments and insults, boundary crossings, and power struggles — when it comes to student learning and the relational struggles that can accompany it — a teacher needs to actively embrace the fact that what happens in the classroom is *about the students*. Seeing structure means, then, being able to discern when something is about oneself and when it is, necessarily, about someone else. Accepting this axiom, because it demands absolute clarity about boundaries and because it makes activation of a strong, supportive network essential, can be quite relieving.

So seeing structure is not just about perceiving and understanding; it is not just about taking thoughtful, informed action and watching (and learning from) what happens; it is not just about doing all this with openness, compassion, and clarity. It is also about holding.

Teachers who are committed to seeing structure must take on the task of **holding their students**. They must model managing their own emotions; they must contain their students' emotions (by setting limits and surviving pushback); they must see and hear their students; and they must tolerate the "mental pain," their own and their students', of learning and growing.

At the same time teachers must be comfortable **letting go**: letting their students be who they are without invading or co-opting or controlling them; seeing and hearing them honestly; respecting and, when necessary, establishing boundaries so all classroom participants can take full responsibility for what is theirs; allowing students to express and develop their own ideas in an environment out of which a third reality can emerge.

Holding (not too tightly) and letting go (not too loosely). Feeling out the difference. Making mistakes and repairing them. Deciding whether and how to be used. Being a great-enough developmental partner. Always, no matter what, thinking about what the students are revealing about themselves and their needs and figuring out how best, within one's own limits, to respond. In order to survive all this, committing to self-care and to supportive, empowering care from others.

COMMITTING TO SELF-CARE

What happens in the classroom is about the students, but teachers are central to those happenings. Given all the emotional and relational data they are exposed to, given the responsibilities of being a great-enough developmental partner, given the academic pressures to cover curricula and cause high test scores, teachers can end their days feeling overwhelmed and depleted. As crucial figures in the classroom system and as human beings in their own right, teachers need the same kind of consideration that they are expected to provide for their students.

That is, **teachers need care**. They need to tend to themselves kindly by eating well, exercising, reading a good novel, playing a sport, finding beauty, laughing with friends — indulging in whatever it is that rejuvenates them. Committing to *self-care* can be difficult for teachers who put caretaking of *others* first, but this difficulty must be overcome if teachers are to be great enough for their students. Exhausted caretakers do not function well. Rejuvenated caretakers are not only happier but much more efficient.

And as has been mentioned repeatedly, **teachers need their own safe holding environment** in which to grow. They need a place where they can be honest and needy, where they can fall apart, where they can relate to their colleagues, where they can support and exhort and celebrate and marvel at the complexity of what they do for a living. They need help and support in making sense of what goes on every day in their classrooms. One place where they can do all this is in psychodynamically oriented, nonevaluative teacher supervision. But more generally, teachers and administrators deserve to get creative about how to make their schools healthy holding environments for all who work in them.

This axiom, that teachers need care, might seem obvious and even trite. But the most self-evident axioms are not always implemented. There are plenty of teachers who, as soon as the school year begins, lose traction in their own lives. "Sure," they might say, "I need to take care of myself. But when? How?" Not knowing the answers to these questions points to a teacher's need to do some emotion work! For sacrificing one's health and happiness does *no one* any good. If teachers won't take care of themselves for their own sakes, then they must do it for their students'.

WRAP-UP

Teachers who are committed to seeing structure open themselves to the emotional and relational worlds they and their students cocreate and coinhabit in the classroom. They agree to embrace the abundant and ever-present sources of information that emotions and relationships provide about how they and their students are doing in the teaching and learning enterprise. They allow themselves to acknowledge and learn from the feeling of teaching.

Of course, teachers are not required to attend to or work with this information. Making it through the curriculum and managing all the other responsibilities of teaching are challenging enough.

But committing to seeing structure can make a vast difference in a teacher's and her students' experience of the classroom. One major difference is that obstacles to learning can be dissolved. But another equally valuable difference is that personal growth can be fostered. And not just students' personal growth.

As has been stated, teachers grow from emotion work, too. The muscles that seeing structure builds — self-awareness, compassion, curiosity, detachment, limit- and boundary-setting, and others — can reshape a teacher's character even as those muscles are flexed in the service of students' emotional and cognitive development. Committing to the process of emotion work, in other words, leads to a constantly evolving, ever-improving self.

And students need teachers who are evolving and ever improving. For when people take on the task of becoming developmental partners for valuable human beings, as teachers implicitly do, their effectiveness depends, ultimately, on who they are, on what kind of person shows up every day to be with the students.

Fortunately, teachers who focus on the feeling of teaching can be this type of developmental partner. Unfortunately, the central roles that feeling plays in teaching are rarely explicitly acknowledged within the profession. But attending to emotions and relationships, honoring the feeling of teaching, can be transformative. This book offers an approach not just to accessing this potential but to cultivating it deliberately and thoughtfully for the sake of one's students and, ultimately, for oneself.

FOR MORE INFORMATION

Go to *teachingthroughemotions.com*, where you can

- contact the author;
- order electronic and paperback copies of *The Feeling of Teaching*;
- post a story of teaching;
- comment on others' stories of teaching;
- sign up for workshops;
- get information about setting up Teacher Support Groups;
- get information about being certified to organize and run Teacher Support Groups

APPENDIX

DEFENSES

Posited by Anna Freud as a function of the ego that battles the nefarious drives of the id, defenses are most simply understood as the means people employ to protect themselves from anxiety and other unbearable feelings (like envy, anger, and hatred). Defenses are unconscious; people utilize them automatically. They provide important clues to the ways people are constructed, to their psychic structures. And defenses, when they are perceived properly, point to opportunities for the emotion work that can melt agitation, offer comfort, and pave the way for learning.

In this section I list a number of defenses and give examples of each from the stories in this book. Note that this list is by no means exhaustive; for a succinct and much longer list (though one that is not geared specifically to teaching and learning), see Goldstein (1995) in the References list below.

PROJECTION

Projection happens when a person unconsciously attributes to another person a disowned feeling, belief, or attitude. Person 1 projects a feeling onto Person 2, then interacts with Person 2 as if that quality belonged to Person 2 rather than to Person 1.

As a defense, projection does two things:

- It protects Person 1 from the anxiety of possessing such an unbearable or unacceptable feeling, belief, or attitude.
- It allows Person 1 to attack the disowned feeling with the vehemence she feels toward it in herself without suffering the consequences directly.

We see projection in several of the stories in this book, most notably in the stories of projective identification. The story about Manny, who threw Unifix cubes in his pre-K classroom, then took forever to get ready for recess, shows

325

how Manny unconsciously projected his anger and frustration onto Ms. Foster, asking her, in effect, to "feel it for me."

In the story about the "oppositional learner," Sean unconsciously projected into Mr. Apkin his fear and sense of threat at being intellectually dominated. The story about Jeannie, who both loved and hated her teacher, gives many examples of how Jeannie projected her fear and anger into Ms. McNamara on a regular basis. In the story of the parent-teacher conference, Mr. White projected his anger toward teachers into Ms. Sodolsky.

In these and other cases of projective identification, Person 1 does the projecting and Person 2, who identifies with Person 1's emotions, does the attacking. "Pure" projection appears in the story about unconscious racism, where Ms. Ellis projected stereotyped expectations onto her Black students; in the story about the teacher committee, where Greer projected his own sense of inadequacy and expectations of rejection onto his withdrawn colleague Samantha; and, in chapter four, when Jason and Raphael projected their homophobia onto the unsuspecting Marco.

INTROJECTION
Introjection is the opposite of projection: It involves taking into oneself another person's qualities. Introjection involves deep identification with those qualities; it is a building block of the personality, of psychic structure. When one introjects negative or positive characteristics, one's behaviors manifest those characteristics. They become part of the personality.

At its best, introjection is a very positive force. It is crucial for the creation of a strong sense of self; that is, people use introjection to internalize "objects" outside of them who are good, who model the characteristics and behaviors that they themselves honor (objects, in other words, that they idealize). Introjection is also at work when people learn, when they take in ideas from the outside and make them their own (Chodorow, 1999). Introjection, then, is central to teaching and learning.

We saw introjection at its best in the final story of chapter five, where Mr. Malmrose reestablished his emotional equilibrium in part by imagining the positive and encouraging comments the colleagues in his teacher support group would have made had they been with him in his moment of distress.

His ability to wonder what his colleagues would say to him was a sign that introjection was at work.

When introjection is defensive, it includes feeling about oneself the way one would feel about the other. In defensive introjection, or introjection that is meant to defend against unbearable feelings, Person 1 sees in herself a quality she hates in Person 2 and, rather than hating Person 2, hates herself. In this way Person 1 actually protects Person 2 from the terrible feelings Person 1 has toward Person 2. At the same time Person 1 punishes herself (and, through projection, others) for the unacceptable feelings.

We can assume that introjection was at work with Sean, the "oppositional learner," and with the bullies in chapter four: Jason (the homophobe) and Zack (the spelling police). These characters and others in this book apparently incorporated other people's hateful and insecure attitudes into their own psychic structures, making those attitudes their own. Note that, while Sean, Jason, and Zack freely projected their negative feelings onto others, they themselves were never far from self-hatred.

A defense that is related to introjection is "turning against the self." This defense is utilized in the moment to alleviate negative feelings; it could be considered "introjection lite."

The story in chapter one that catalogues Jeannie's string of aggravating behaviors shows how Ms. McNamara *avoided* turning against the self. In short, she allowed herself to hate Jeannie. Contrary to popular attitudes toward hatred, this is actually good for both Jeannie and Ms. McNamara. If Ms. McNamara refused to deny or repress her hatred (denial and repression are two very common forms of defense), then she could work with it; that is, she could explore through emotion work her strong negative feelings. Understanding them would help to dissipate them or transform them. Ultimately, this understanding could lead to different behaviors in the classroom that would benefit Jeannie and relieve Ms. McNamara.

If, however, Ms. McNamara had "turned against the self," she would not fully introject Jeannie but would rather hate herself for hating Jeannie. This psychological contortion would happen only because, for Ms. McNamara, it would be less anxiety producing than actively hating Jeannie. And again, it would happen totally unconsciously.

IDENTIFICATION

Related to introjection, identification happens when Person 1 takes on another's attitudes and behaviors as his own. We saw in chapter one Sean's *identification with the aggressor* — his adoption of the dominating, demeaning behaviors with Mr. Apkin (and with classmates) that, one can guess, an early caretaker had used against him. Children who are sexually abusive have generally been abused themselves. They identify with their aggressors. Bullies often identify with an aggressor. Identifying with a frightening person and behaving in the same hurtful ways can alleviate anxiety: It can channel the hatred one feels for the perpetrator onto a victim and can fend off the fear and humiliation of being a victim again oneself.

The move from victim to victimizer is called, in psychoanalytic circles, "turning the passive into active." The idea is that, by becoming the aggressor, an erstwhile victim can reenact his trauma at his own bidding but, at the same time, invite someone new to stop him, to effect a new outcome. It is interesting to note that children do this all the time in their dramatic play (Freud, 1966) and can benefit from the imagined and safely circumscribed power reversal.

We also see identification at work in cases of projective identification. Once again, the story about Manny shows how his pre-K teacher, Ms. Foster, identified with Manny's projected anger, feeling it vicariously but also allowing it to blend with her own anger and frustration. On the one hand, then, she was expressing anger for Manny; on the other hand, she was expressing it for herself, something she would not allow herself to do without the convenient excuse Manny provided. That is, by identifying with Manny's anger, Ms. Foster could blame Manny for a feeling she did not want to own herself, and she could express it with temporary impunity.

Outside of its role as a defense, identification is central to teaching and learning. Children use identification when they internalize their parents' sense of right and wrong or when they develop a love of music as modeled by an admired mentor. Many teachers rely on the possibilities of identification; indeed, identifying with a teacher is one of the benefits of

328

being a student. Identification is a defense only when it acts to protect a person from anxiety and other intolerable feelings, and whether or not it is a maladaptive defense, one that causes additional suffering, depends on the consequences of its having been activated.

SPLITTING

As children develop they introject qualities, both positive and negative, of their caregivers. A child can internalize her mother's generosity (positive) as well as her short temper (negative); the child can both love her mother for being so giving and hate her for being so frighteningly angry. Ideally, children learn to hold the positive and the negative within themselves simultaneously as they learn to know and understand others as whole people rather than as fragments.

In the defense called "splitting," Person 1 has not learned how to view Person 2 as a whole person. Rather, Person 1 categorizes Person 2 as either all good or all bad and shifts confusingly between treating Person 2 well, as if she were a good person, and treating her abominably, as if she were a bad person.

In the story about Jeannie and Ms. McNamara, Jeannie seems to engage in splitting. Sometimes she treats Ms. McNamara as if she were a good person — as when Jeannie objects to having to wait for attention from her teacher and when she hugs Ms. McNamara after art class — and sometimes she treats Ms. McNamara as if she were the enemy — as when Jeannie is disobedient and disrespectful in line and claims that she "hates" her teacher. Part of the frustration Ms. McNamara feels with Jeannie is the impossibility of pinning Jeannie down, of being able to interact with the same person from moment to moment.

To be fair, Jeannie's splitting probably goes hand in hand with her evident insecure attachment style. Her anxieties around connecting with caring adults seem to be so potent that she cannot contain her gratifications and her disappointments simultaneously. She must love one minute and hate the next, as if her teacher were two people. Apparently, Jeannie has not learned that one person can be complicated, both gratifying and frustrating and, ultimately, trustworthy.

Teachers can use the defense of splitting as well. Mr. Birdwhistle in chapter two appears to have a hard time seeing his students as whole people. He divides his classes into "good" and "bad" students and interacts with them in ways that both reinforce his limited definitions and reflect best on him.

DISPLACEMENT

In displacement a person acts out feelings he has for one person or one situation on another person. It works like this: Person 2 offends Person 1. Because enacting the proper response on Person 2 makes Person 1 way too anxious (unconsciously), Person 1 carries the stress of the original interaction until he can act it out on Person 3. Displacement is a very common defense, one parents use when they yell at their children after a stressful day at work (where they are unable to yell at their bosses or coworkers without serious repercussions).

Sean utilized displacement in chapter one when he vented his aggression on Mr. Apkin rather than on his supervisor. Teachers who react overly strongly to students because of personal or professional troubles are using displacement, as are students when they act out in class because, for example, they were helpless in the face of a domestic clash the night before.

DENIAL

Denial happens when a person refuses to acknowledge an aspect of reality that he is, at some level, well aware of — a terminal illness, for example, or a loved one's alcoholism. Despite its overuse in the popular lexicon, denial is not necessarily a bad, or maladaptive, defense. Children often deny their parents' (or teachers') glaring flaws because admitting them would interfere with other important feelings, such as love and healthy idealization. Adults can engage in wholesale denial when they fall in love. In fact, one could argue that falling in love *depends* on denial.

Denial becomes problematic when it impinges negatively on one's ability to function, as with Jeannie's denial, in chapter one, that she was at the front of the line when she was supposed to be at the back of the line. Even if Jeannie wanted very much to ignore reality at that moment and get her way (as is common among children and some adults), she suffered consequences, not least of which was the continuing erosion of her relationship with her teacher.

REGRESSION

Anxiety can make people regress, or revert to behaviors that characterize earlier stages of development that they have already mastered. By regressing, a person might (unconsciously) hope to absolve herself of negative feelings and at the same time inspire caretaking from a more able adult.

Moving to a new home can cause an uncertain and possibly angry toddler who has successfully potty trained to begin wetting his bed again. An unwelcome and unexpected challenge can cause an insecure adult to begin whining and complaining. Regression occurs in chapter one when Manny, who is fully capable of dressing himself for recess, seems to have forgotten how to put his snow pants on. We also see it in the story of the envious professor when Ms. Wilcox behaves like an entitled two-year-old. Under duress people can regress — and their behaviors, because they are so uncharacteristically immature, can be maddening.

OMNIPOTENT CONTROL

If what happens outside of a person provokes too much anxiety, an obvious defense against the anxiety is to try to control the outside world. Of course, exerting control in one's life is not always defensive; it is a necessary aspect of being active, purposeful, and creative. Control, or "omnipotent control and devaluation" (Goldstein, 1995), counts as a defense when the controlling person has grandiose expectations for herself and a low opinion of the person or people she is trying to control.

In chapter one Ms. McNamara was using control as a defense against the anxiety she felt around her obnoxious student Jeannie. Make no mistake: Jeannie was a master at provoking anxiety (probably because she was so familiar with the feeling in herself and her caregivers), and she definitely needed controls, or limits, in her environment. But Ms. McNamara's urge to fix Jeannie, while aimed at assuaging her own anxiety, seems to have served as a gauntlet for Jeannie,

331

prodding her to ever more outrageous expressions of her internal confusion.

Ms. Psacharopoulos, in chapter three, managed her own and her student Gabe's anxiety by taking control of his continent project and doing it for him. Unfortunately, rescuing him through omnipotent control only reinforced, or enabled, his ongoing passivity as a student.

Any time a teacher banishes or silences a student because the teacher cannot handle the student, he is most likely utilizing the defense of omnipotent control. Examples from chapter one are the stories in which Mr. Jackson sent Ingrid out of the room for cheating and in which Ms. Ellis sent her black student, Tajheeka, to in-school suspension. In chapter four Mr. Leonard imposed the impossible rule of immediate silence on his talkative students. In all of these cases, the preferred method of managing anxiety was to control the source of the anxiety completely in hopes that the anxiety, like the students, would disappear.

REACTION FORMATION
In reaction formation an unbearable feeling is avoided through the enactment of an opposite reaction. A classic example is when an older sibling "smothers" her newborn brother with love when, unconsciously and very powerfully, she wants to obliterate him.

In the story about the regressed business program professor in chapter one, Mr. Bloom was enacting reaction formation when he accommodated Ms. Wilcox, who was breaking every professional and programmatic rule to express her outrage at having been passed over for the director position. Rather than crush Ms. Wilcox with his anger, Mr. Bloom suppressed this frightening reaction and treated her in the exact opposite manner, with extreme tolerance and solicitousness. This response, while appeasing his anxiety temporarily, did nothing to contain Ms. Wilcox and, ultimately, led to dire disruption in the business program.

IDEALIZATION
Idealization can be a wonderful element in a child's healthy development. Children can idealize a parent, a teacher, or a

movie star, admiring these people as role models whom they can eventually internalize and transform.

When used as a defense, however, idealization can function a little like reaction formation: By putting Person 2 on a pedestal, Person 1 avoids unbearable feelings of hatred or envy for Person 2. Person 1, in other words, makes Person 2 an object of adoration rather than an object of contempt. In the process Person 1 actually objectifies Person 2; that is, Person 1 makes Person 2 into an object that satisfies Person 1's needs but has little to do with who Person 2 actually is. Not only can this objectifying idealization feel uncomfortable for Person 2, but it is inherently destabilizing. No one is perfect enough to stay on a pedestal forever; Person 2 will inevitably fall. How Person 1 and Person 2 deal with this terrible disappointment is unpredictable but probably unpleasant.

An example of idealization appears in the chapter four story about homophobia. There, Raphael is admired by his classmates as an excellent athlete. We can imagine that, at the same time that Raphael is interested in maintaining his peers' focus on his athletic prowess, as it distracts them from knowing other truths about him, this idealization harms him in that it plays down or overlooks other aspects of his identity. This is true of Mr. Birdwhistle's idealization of Maurice, the flute player, as well. Defensive idealization, in other words, can pigeonhole people in ways that severely limit their capacity for growth.

INTELLECTUALIZATION

When a person intellectualizes, he avoids feeling any emotions and instead thinks or talks about them (or other topics). This defense is actually highly prized in many cultures, including the school culture, where cognition tends to be treated as separate from emotions and where thinking and talking are valued above feeling and intuition.

Being intellectual, of course, does not automatically qualify as a defense, but in schools, especially colleges, the two — being intellectual and intellectualizing as a defense — can be difficult to distinguish. A good example might be the "sage on the stage," or the professor whose sole teaching style is the lecture. Such a professor is undoubtedly highly intellectual, adept at relating to ideas, but may very well be using his intellect to protect him from the unnerving and anxiety-provoking uncertainty of relationships with students, the very relationships that form the basis of student learning. While the professor is probably admired for his intellect, then, his intellectualization actually robs the students of the teaching and learning they deserve.

We saw intellectualization in the story of Sean and Mr. Apkin, both of whom expressed their anxieties in an argument that had little or nothing to do with the emotions that spurred the clash. And we saw it in chapter four, where Victor masked his insecurities by criticizing Shawna's conference presentation. Intellectualization can be a powerful defense, not just because it so ably silences disturbing emotions within oneself but also because it can activate disturbing and distracting emotions in others. Once words and ideas become the focus, one's emotions can be left behind.

GLOSSARY OF TERMS

active listening — avoiding misunderstanding by slowing conversations down and frequently double-checking intentions and meanings

boundary — imaginary line that constitutes the "circle" around every person and is personal, felt, and flexible

compliance — *forced*: when one person or group shuts down the Third at the expense of another person or group
voluntary: when people agree to cooperate because they see its benefits

conflict statement — a statement, not a question, that captures the "yes" and "no" of a conflict neutrally

defense — a psychological shield used to protect one from emotions that are too difficult to feel consciously

detachment — the act of pulling back from one's experience to observe it and think about it

developmental object — someone who is used for another's emotional and cognitive growth

emotion work — the work someone does to see and understand enactments and to plan experiments that will foster desired changes in the classroom; includes practicing awareness, describing, looking for good reasons, making guesses, self-disclosing, listening, and making a plan

emotional object	someone who is used, or acted out on, for emotional relief
enabling	a relational pattern between a highly competent person (the enabler) and an incompetent person in which the enabler takes control, in effect inviting the other to lose control
enactment	how people behave when they are plugged into each other; in this book "enactment" is used to identify disruptive or destructive fits between people
envy	an emotion that seeks to deprive others of what they have, often by tearing them down emotionally
equilibrium	a familiar and comfortable relational state (even if it is unbalanced and dysfunctional)
false self	a façade, or mask, that appeases others while hiding and suppressing one's personal desires and perspectives
going with the resistance	playing along with an uncooperative, conflicted student to keep the Third open *becoming the resister*: taking on the resister's role and modeling alternative ways to act *going with the purpose*: looking beneath the content — what the resister *says* — and responding to the underlying *need*, or why the resister said it

playing the victim role: stepping in to become the object of a student's attacks to protect innocent students and model for the attacker ways to handle unbearable feelings

siding with the resister: agreeing with the resister, joining with him, and allowing him to feel his conflict freely

grandiosity — an inflated, unrealistic sense of one's responsibility and power to change people and things that are actually beyond one's control

positive: the belief that you have more power over circumstances or other people than you actually do (or possibly can)

negative: the belief that others' unhappiness is your fault

"great enough" teacher — a teacher who expects to be used and commits to setting realistic and healthy limits for her students, surviving the students' pushback against these limits, repairing her mistakes, and tolerating her students' frustration with learning and growing, all without retaliating

holding environment — the physical and emotional context within which people are "held" so they can grow and develop safely and healthily

joining — a way of plugging in that requires moving one's perspective around so that one is looking at the world through someone else's eyes; allying

maladaptive behavior	an automatic reaction to stress that tends to work in the short term but can have negative long-term consequences
natural consequence	a result that follows logically from an action
"not good enough"	*too accommodating*: protecting people from the suffering caused by realistic limits *co-opting*: enforcing limits by dominating
not-knowing stance	suspending judgment and deciding to be receptive, to see and hear others and listen to yourself for what might be revealed
parallel process	when one group mirrors the behaviors of another group and gets to analyze the similar dynamics, as when teachers act out in supervision the ways their students act out in class
potential space	conditions characterized by well-bounded, respectful interactions in which people can be creative and innovative
power struggle	a type of enactment in which one person or party attempts to dominate or control another person or party who is unwilling to be dominated
psychic structure	the ways people plug into each other, or fit together, to make relationships work (for better or for worse)

psychodynamic perspective	a stance that looks for prongs and outlets in oneself and in others and seeks to understand the reasons and purposes for the relational fits
reflecting-*in*-action	doing emotion work in the heat of the moment
reflecting-*on*-action	doing emotion work after the fact
reframing	*looking at a situation through numerous lenses in order to see it more fully and clearly*
self-regulation	the ability to exert self-control and soothe oneself in moments of stress
supervision	formal, professional support for teachers' emotion work that is psychodynamically oriented and nonjudgmental and nonevaluative
the Third	the shared "third" reality that can emerge out of interactions that include healthy connections, generous mirroring, and strong boundaries
triangular relationship	a relationship that includes three people in which alliances and power dynamics can shift, making the relationship inherently unstable
unconditional positive regard	an open-minded, nonjudgmental, well-bounded, caring stance or attitude that honors another's right to be herself

REFERENCES

Ainsworth, M. D. S., Blehar, M. C., Waters, E., & Wall, S. (1978). *Patterns of attachment: A psychological study of the Strange Situation.* Hillsdale, NJ: Lawrence Erlbaum Associates.

Alexander, F., French, T. M., et al. (1946). *Psychoanalytic therapy: Principles and application.* New York: Ronald Press.

Bowlby, J. (1969/1999). *Attachment: Attachment and loss* (vol. 1) (2nd ed.). New York: Basic Books.

Chodorow, N. J. (1999). *The power of feelings: Personal meaning in psychoanalysis, gender, and culture.* New Haven, CT: Yale University Press.

Depraz, N., Varela, F., & Vermersch, P. (2003). *On becoming aware.* Philadelphia: John Benjamins Publishing Company.

Elbow, P. (1973). The doubting game and the believing game: An analysis of the intellectual enterprise. In *Writing without teachers* (pp. 148–191). New York: Oxford University Press.

Freud, A. (1966). *The ego and the mechanisms of defense.* Madison, CT: International Universities Press.

Gentile, J. (2001). Close but no cigar: The perversion of agency and the absence of thirdness. *Contemporary Psychoanalysis, 37,* 623–654.

Goldstein, E. G. (1995). *Ego psychology and social work practice.* New York: Free Press.

Kirman, W. J. (1977). *Modern psychoanalysis in the schools.* Dubuque, IA: Kendall/Hunt Publishing.

Lasky, S. (2000). The cultural and emotional politics of teacher-parent interactions. *Teaching and Teacher Education, 16,* 843–860.

Lerner, H. (1989). *The dance of intimacy: A woman's guide to courageous acts of change in key relationships.* New York: Harper & Row.

Morrison, T. (1992). *Playing in the dark: Whiteness and the literary imagination.* New York: Vintage Books.

Obidah, J. E., & Teel, K. M. (2001). *Because of the kids: Facing racial and cultural differences in schools.* New York: Teachers College Press.

Pietromonaco, P. R., & Feldman Barrett, L. (2000). The Internal Working Models concept: What do we really know about the self in relation to others? *Review of General Psychology, 4,* 155–175.

Rogers, C. R. (1961). *On becoming a person: A therapist's view of psychotherapy.* Boston: Houghton Mifflin.

Salzberger-Wittenberg, I., Henry, G., & Osborne, E. (1983). *The emotional experience of learning and teaching.* New York: Routledge & Kegan Paul.

Schön, D. A. (1983). *The reflective practitioner.* New York: Basic Books.

Stark, M. (1994). *Working with resistance.* Northvale, NJ: Jason Aronson Inc.

Stone, D., Patton, B., & Heen, S. (1999). *Difficult conversations: How to discuss what matters most.* New York: Penguin Books.

Tatum, B. D. (1997). *"Why are all the Black kids sitting together in the cafeteria?" and other conversations about race.* New York: Basic Books.

Winnicott, D. W. (1965). *The maturational processes and the facilitating environment: Studies in the theory of emotional development.* New York: International Universities Press.

Winnicott, D. W. (1971). *Playing and reality.* New York: Tavistock Publications.